"The Only Efficient Instrument"

"The Only Efficient Instrument"

AMERICAN WOMEN WRITERS

& THE PERIODICAL, 1837–1916

EDITED BY ALETA FEINSOD CANE

& SUSAN ALVES

University of Iowa Press　Ψ　Iowa City

University of Iowa Press, Iowa City 52242
Printed in the United States of America
http://www.uiowa.edu/~uipress

Stetson® is a registered trademark of the John B. Stetson Company.

The publication of this book was generously supported by the
University of Iowa Foundation.

Printed on acid-free paper

Library of Congress Cataloging-in-Publication Data
"The only efficient instrument": American women writers and the
periodical, 1837–1916 / edited by Aleta Feinsod Cane and Susan Alves.
        p.   cm.
    Includes bibliographical references (p.   ) and index.
    ISBN 0-87745-780-8 (cloth)
    1. American literature—Women authors—History and
criticism.   2. Women and literature—United States—History—
19th century.   3. Women and literature—United States—
History—20th century.   4. American literature—19th century—
History and criticism.   5. American literature—20th century—
History and criticism.   6. Journalism—United States—History.
7. American periodicals—History.   I. Cane, Aleta Feinsod, 1949–.
II. Alves, Susan, 1958–.
PS151.O55   2001
810.9'9287'09034—dc21   2001027987

01 02 03 04 05 C 5 4 3 2 1

For our daughters

Deborah Ida Cane

Rebecca Ann Cane

Irene Rose McLaughlin-Alves

The most important part of our literature, while the work of diffusion is still going on, lies in the journals, which monthly, weekly, daily, send their messages to every corner of this great land, and form, at present, the only efficient instrument for the general education of the people.

—Margaret Fuller, "American Literature"

CONTENTS

ACKNOWLEDGMENTS

We would like to thank David Cane for his tireless technical assistance in the preparation of this manuscript for publication. Without his good help, his suggestions, and sense of humor we could not have completed this project.

We also thank David Cane and Donna McLaughlin for their enormous patience, good counsel, and encouragement throughout this project.

"The Only Efficient Instrument"

Aleta Feinsod Cane & Susan Alves

AMERICAN WOMEN WRITERS AND THE PERIODICAL: CREATING A CONSTITUENCY, OPENING A DIALOGUE

Margaret Fuller apprehended that the periodical press accommodated the vibrant philosophies and politics of this nation in its first century. As an author, journalist, and editor, she realized that women, among others, could make their voices most clearly heard in the dominant culture not just from the lecture podium but from the pages of newspapers and magazines as well. During her career, Fuller expanded her authorial aims from those of developing friendly intellectual conversation with like minds in the *Dial* to advocacy journalism in her columns on the *Risorgimento* (a revolutionary movement to establish a popular government in Italy) in Horace Greeley's *New York Tribune*. The literary work and professional life of Fuller, especially her journalism, offer a keen example of women's contributions to the social, political, and literary discourses of nineteenth- and early twentieth-century America.

Like Fuller, other American women writers and editors from a variety of social backgrounds and ethnicities understood that the periodical was "the only efficient instrument" to make themselves and their ideas known. Their engagement with the periodical press, which the articles in this collection examine, demonstrates American women's vital participation in the intellectual life and political discussions of their times. These writing women employ the periodical, both as newspaper and as magazine, concurrently in three ways: for social and political advocacy, for the critique of gender roles and social expectations, and for refashioning the periodical as a more inclusive genre that both articulates and obscures such distinctions as class, race, and gender. Each of the essays in *"The Only Efficient Instrument": American Women Writers and the Periodical, 1837–1916* represents current research on ideological and methodological strategies exercised by American women writers and editors. Both this introduction and the collection as a whole are organized by these three approaches to periodical writing.

In recent years, scholarly activity has begun to focus on the periodical. While some have taken up the magazine as instrument of social construction, others have focused on the periodical as a genre. Still others have focused on women's and men's reading habits or on women's magazines in particular.[1] Extremely important to the study of the periodical production of specific well-known and little-known authors are *Periodical Literature in Nineteenth-Century America*, edited by Kenneth M. Price and Susan Belasco Smith (1995), and *Outsiders in Nineteenth-Century Press History: Multicultural Perspectives*, edited by Frankie Hutton and Barbara Straus Reed (1995). Price, Smith, and their contributors examine the historical context, the effect of the publishing mode, and other matters as these relate to the writing of such writers as Herman Melville, Charles Chesnutt, and Emily Dickinson. By contrast, the Hutton and Reed collection sheds light on the use of the periodical by writers from diverse ethnic and racial groups in nineteenth-century America, some writing and editing newspapers in their native language and others contributing to mainstream periodicals. The essays in Hutton and Reed raise the significant issue of the periodical as a means to develop and sustain a constituency within the dominant culture. *Periodical Literature in Nineteenth-Century America* and *Outsiders in Nineteenth-Century Press History*, together, make way for *"The Only Efficient Instrument"* because they model a critical study of writers' works within the historical context of the periodical and because they — to different degrees — query the issue of the social and political agenda of not only the writing in the periodical but of the periodical as a genre. Still, neither collection focuses solely on women writers and readers, nor do these fine collections take up the gendered, and politically motivated, constituency-building work of women writers and editors of the American periodical.

"The Only Efficient Instrument" extends and further focuses the critical work of Price and Smith and of Hutton and Reed, demonstrating American women's animated presence in the political and intellectual communities of their day via the periodical press. This introduction locates the work of contributors to *"The Only Efficient Instrument"* within the context of the three ideological and methodological strategies for periodical writing employed by American women writers, thus situating the essays within the function of the genre and considering the contribution of this new critical work to current scholarship. By focusing on women's periodical ventures, the contributors to this critical collection offer new insights into the range of work by American women writers and editors, some well known and others less known in the traditional canon of American literature.

Social and Political Advocacy

The year 1837 was significant in American publishing history for several reasons. It was a year in which Angelina Grimké was censured in the press because she dared to speak, in public, on issues of women's rights.[2] That year saw a great economic panic that closed the doors of several large publishing houses and created a crisis in the industry. The depression in the book industry that followed the panic was caused, in part, by the lack of copyright laws, which allowed the pirating of materials from England so cheaply that American authors could not compete. Many American writers turned to the periodical press, which paid them from four to twelve dollars a page for their work.[3] Louis Godey's *Lady's Book* kept more than one author financially afloat during the late 1830s and into the 1840s, notably Harriet Beecher Stowe, Eliza Leslie, and Catharine Sedgwick. The other significant event of 1837 was the merger of the *Ladies' Magazine* and *Godey's Lady's Book*. When Sarah Josepha Hale became editor of the new *Godey's*, she articulated a wish to encourage American authors, especially women, and to use the journal to speak to issues concerning women.

Although Godey's and Hale's expressed desire was never to mention politics in the pages of their journal, the magazine was instrumental in instructing women in the Victorian politics of gender and in inscribing separate spheres of influence for men and women.[4] Nina Baym asserts that Hale's editorials represent a highly political stance because through them she sought to keep women out of the polls.[5] Hale was a prime proselytizer of the belief that women were more spiritual, more moral, and more religious than men and that, therefore, they should not be sullied by engagement in the male sphere of public life or politics. Rather, Hale argued that women should maintain a separate sphere of domestic tranquillity in which they could soothe their husbands, who had to participate in the brutal world of commerce and moneymaking. It was also in this atmosphere that they were to bring up moral, Christian children, who would then have the proper foundation to withstand the outside world when they had to enter it.

The inscribing of separate spheres for men and women had its parallel in the relationship between Godey and Hale. Godey handled the financial matters of the magazine, and Hale was responsible for the artistic content. She even went so far as to differentiate herself from other male periodical editors by insisting that she was a "Lady Editor" and, furthermore, that when she reviewed books, which she did in every issue, she was merely writing notes or columns but was not critiquing these works. Critics, she felt, were always trying to demonstrate their own cleverness or intellectual superiority, whereas she believed her function as a female reviewer was to point out a work's moral value. While men might "cut up books with the keen dissecting knife of ridicule, or triumph in the superior wit or argument," such behavior did not "accord with the province of woman." Hale's editorials and the nature of the fiction and poetry that she both wrote and accepted for the *Godey's* all inscribe gender-specific social roles. Even though she would advocate for many causes in her long career as editor,[6] women's suffrage was never a goal for Hale. She maintained that men and women were essentially different in psychological and moral makeup and that the two spheres should not overlap. Hale's adherence to True Womanhood, or the Cult of Domesticity, is an important and an extreme example of the role that a woman's magazine played in gender politics. It is, of course, ironic that a successful, visible, self-supporting woman editor should encourage other women not to participate in the public sphere, but Hale adamantly segregated the sexes in her own writings and never wavered from her position.

Other women, such as Fuller, used the antebellum periodical for political purposes beyond issues of gender. Although some scholars have dismissed Fuller's writing for the *Tribune* as apprenticeship work, others argue that her columns represent her desire to "elaborate a radical theory of reading for the culture, one meant to develop a form of political agency that would include a more diverse group of people than those who traditionally hold power." In "Margaret Fuller's *Tribune* Dispatches and the Nineteenth-Century Body Politic," contributor Annamarie Formichella Elsden notes that Fuller, through the lens of revolutionary ferment in Italy, tried to reflect America to itself. Fuller insisted that the American revolutionary soul could be reawakened and that, in its awakening, the nation's soul would realize the efficacy of equal opportunity for women.

The periodical production of Harriet Beecher Stowe provides another example of an antebellum woman writer employing the periodical for political purposes. In response to the Fugitive Slave Act of 1850, Stowe, an editor of *Hearth and Home* from 1868–75, contributed enormously to the abolitionist argument through the serialized publication of *Uncle Tom's Cabin* (1851–52) in Gamaliel Bailey's periodical, the *National Era*. Stowe wrote in the sentimental fashion of the times.[7] Stowe's work had an enormous effect on the nation precisely because she employed these sentimental conventions, which made the horrors of slavery readily understood and sympathetic to its audience.[8]

Although Stowe's political focus was primarily one of abolitionism, a cause that seemed to obliterate lines of gender, as a woman editor, Stowe was highly concerned with the issue of gender. With the well-known self-confidence of her Beecher ancestors and siblings, Stowe envisioned herself as a member of the cultural elite and a writer in the high-culture circle: a writer for the magazines that saw themselves as arbiters of the emerging American aesthetic. Such magazines as *Harper's* and the *Atlantic* projected this hegemonic message that culture was a male domain. Contributor Sarah Robbins asserts in "Gendering Gilded Age Periodical Professionalism: Reading Harriet Beecher Stowe's *Home and Hearth* Prescriptions for Women's Writing," that Stowe (who published not only in the popular journals but in the more esteemed periodicals of the era as well) wrote many column articles that at first seem to set out a way to help other women become magazine contributors but that concluded in attempting to discourage that very production. Thus she set herself apart from the other women who wished to contribute to the periodical press.

Beginning with the essay "Can I Write?" (9 January 1869) and concluding with "How May I Know That I Can Make a Writer?" Stowe demonstrates the inherent gendering of authorship in antebellum America. By focusing her audience of would-be writers' attention on "writing what you know best," Stowe kept women firmly within the home sphere. As a magazine writer and as a collaborator with her sister Catharine Beecher on the housekeeping manual *American Woman's Home* (1869), Stowe wrote extensively on domestic subjects, but as an editor she saw herself as part of the male-dominated high-culture circle and gendered her readers, and those would-be writers, as female. In Stowe's scheme, literary excellence was for the high-culture journals, such as *Harper's, Scribner's* and the *Atlantic*, which were written and edited by men. Stowe, however, did publish and encourage other female writers, such as former Lowell mill girl Lucy Larcom. Stowe also wrote two columns supporting better education for women. She considered the issue of women's suffrage but never fully supported it through her published offerings. A woman who articulated advanced political ideals, Stowe held conservatively to the traditional view of separate spheres for American men and women of her century.[9]

At mid-nineteenth century, many other women writers followed conservative gender constructions in the characters and in the moral tone of their periodical fiction. In addition, Alice Cary, Rose Terry Cooke, and Sarah Orne Jewett attempted to give the American reader a sense of a particular region. Their early regionalism had a didactic grounding, claiming the rural life as more ennobling and wholesome than that of the city. According to "Parental Guidance: Disciplinary Intimacy and the Rise of Women's Regionalism" by Janet Gebhart Auten, these and other authors sought to "persuade readers to submit to the simple lessons found there." Auten contends that women authors' need for the submission of their readers to the didacticism inherent in their works is part of a social continuum. That is, the authors themselves submitted to the demands of their "gentleman publishers" who took on a patriarchal role with their authors.[10] This close personal relationship of author and publisher was encouraged and nurtured by the publishers. "They advocated author-publisher relations that were long term, like marriages, close friendships, or intimate professional associations. Thus they viewed loyalty and trust as central to the author-publisher alliance."[11] And as Auten observes, the publishers required that their women authors observe the culturally dominant proprieties in their relationship with themselves and in their writings. In order to submit their writing for publication, these writers acquiesced to the wishes of their publishers. Critics such as Susan Coultrap-McQuin (1990) have argued that the authors and their publishers adhered to True Womanhood as a reflection of what was happening in America as well as a didactic indicator of what should be happening.

Adherence by both writers and readers to a conservative gender politic ensured that the Cult of Domesticity would have a fairly strong hold upon the women who wrote and read antebellum American periodicals. In "Kate Chopin and the Periodical: Revisiting the Re-Vision," Bonnie James Shaker proposes that even in later years Kate Chopin was far more conservative than she has been portrayed heretofore by literary scholars and that she adhered to careful didactic patterns in the articles she wrote for the *Youth's Companion, Harper's Young People,* and *Wide Awake.* Although Chopin's children's stories do not deal with the erotic subject matter of her adult fiction, Shaker claims that these children's stories are "indistinguishable from her other work in their tone, style, reading level, dialectic diversity, and artistic sophistication." Many of the stories originally published in these youth magazines appear in anthologies of Chopin's work with no editorial notation identifying the original audience for these works. In particular, Chopin enjoyed writing for the *Youth's Companion,* not only for its relatively high payments of contributors but because the magazine was one of the best-circulated journals in America. It was read by entire families and not just by the children. The fact that her stories could be published in venues for young readers importantly indicates Chopin's surprisingly tacit submission to the socially conservative publishers' sense of taste and propriety and suggests that, at the time, Chopin may have had few publishing alternatives.

Gender Roles, Social Expectations, and the Woman Writer

Male publishers and, for the most part, male and female periodical editors were a conservative lot. The male editors of high-culture magazines at the turn of the century were so distressed by rapid social change that they became positively reactionary.[12] However, throughout the period under consideration in *The Only Efficient Instrument*, many women magazine editors held considerably more liberal attitudes than their predominantly female audience.

Of these, Amelia Bloomer, editor of the *Lily* (1849–54), stands as an intriguing example because her editorial work presents such sharp contrast to that of Stowe.[13] Bloomer's journal began as a temperance magazine, but by the 1850s the *Lily* seems to have led both the editor and her readers into a dialogue on many other social issues such as dress reform and women's rights, including such issues as work outside the home, women's property rights, domestic tyranny, and universal suffrage. The *Lily* was significant "in gender politics and media history for the ways it appropriated the popular gender discourse of the day and transformed it, producing new images and stories that were both visible and viable in the public eye."[14] Although often ridiculed in the press, especially for appearing in the costume that derisively bore her name, Bloomer was not deterred from her radical opinions of woman's place, woman's work, and woman's rights. Significantly, political dialogue in the *Lily* demonstrates that the Cult of Domesticity, although culturally dominant, was by no means the only social opinion of the day.

Many parallels exist between the *Lily* and Charlotte Perkins Gilman's journal, the *Forerunner* (1909–16). Both magazines subsisted on small subscription lists. At its height in 1855 the *Lily* had 6,000 paid subscribers,[15] and at its peak the *Forerunner* garnered only 1,500 subscribers. Both magazines relied on sentimental, or "feminine," literary formulae to attract readers to their point of view. An example can be found in a short story in the *Lily*, "What Can Woman Do — Or the Influence of an Example" (September 1850, 65–67). The story is "[h]alf the political parable . . . and half sentimental — domestic story . . . juxtapos[ing] competing discourses to make a transition into new ideas of women's identities and lives."[16]

In "The Heroine of Her Own Story: Subversion of Traditional Periodical Marriage Tropes in the Short Fiction of Charlotte Perkins Gilman's

Forerunner," Aleta Feinsod Cane remarks that Gilman appropriated a similar technique when she expanded the plot outlines of stories of such popular women's magazines as the *Ladies' Home Journal*. Gilman subverted their themes so that the short stories no longer focused on marriage and domestic relations as the culmination of a woman's life. As Gilman wrote in *Our Androcentric Culture* (serialized in the first volume of the *Forerunner* (1909–10), "love and love and love — from 'first sight' to marriage. There it stops — just the fluttering ribbon of announcement, 'and they lived happily ever after.' Is that kind of fiction any sort of picture of a woman's life?" Gilman's didactic stories consider marriage and make the case that every woman must take charge of her own life; she must make her own decisions because these decisions will affect not merely a single life but have implications for the greater human community as well. Gilman understood, as did Bloomer before her, that a better community requires that each woman must be her own advocate. Both the *Lily* and the *Forerunner* championed women willing to change the trajectory of their own lives.

The *Forerunner* was one of many small, significant woman's protest periodicals at the turn of the century. An important contemporaneous magazine was the *Woman's Journal* (1870–1920), a periodical to which Gilman had been a frequent contributor prior to the creation of the *Forerunner*.[17] Founded by Lucy Stone and her husband, Henry Blackwell, the journal declared its aims as "devoted to the interest of Woman, her educational, industrial, legal and political equality and especially to right of suffrage."[18] Working to reinvigorate the suffrage cause among professional women and men by representing the necessity of suffrage, the magazine sought to hearten its adherents in the face of numerous defeats. A clearinghouse for national and international suffrage news, the *Woman's Journal* "aimed to fill its readers with zeal for the cause: and to convert the readers into efficient consecrated workers."[19] In comparison with more radical women's periodicals such as Elizabeth Cady Stanton's *Revolution* (1868–72), the *Woman's Journal* was a consciously conservative paper. Its readers characterized the journal's reformist tone as "encouraging, inspiring, genial and good natured . . . neither defiant nor obsequious."[20] As cultivated readers, subscribers to the *Woman's Journal* viewed the magazine as a mirror of their newly evolved selves, sensible symbols of progressive womanhood.

Another woman's magazine of protest, which from its title might seem a radical journal but which was actually a rather moderate-toned vehicle of opinion aimed at middle-class women readers, was the *Socialist Woman* (renamed the *Progressive Woman* after March 1909). Published in Kansas by the same printer as the fantastically successful populist, muckraking, Socialist weekly newspaper the *Appeal to Reason* (which had a circulation of more than 500,000 by 1904), the *Progressive Woman* enjoyed the economies of scale this arrangement brought. The editor, Josephine Conger-Kaneko, began her career as a columnist for the *Appeal* and so had a strong footing in that publishing organization. Like the *Appeal*, the *Progressive Woman* stressed what it perceived to be simple truths about social justice and the economic system. It was pro-labor and struck a tone that mixed moral indignation with an almost religious zeal for economic justice. Like the *Woman's Journal*, the *Progressive Woman* appealed to middle-class women with at least some education and an interest in current affairs.[21] Much of the eight-page magazine was originally written by Conger-Kaneko, by her publisher husband — the Japanese Socialist Kiichi Kaneko, and by such others as Lida Parce[22] and Lena Morrow Lewis, a national organizer for the Socialist Party.[23]

When the Women's National Committee (WNC) of the Socialist Party adopted the *Progressive Woman* as its official organ at the 1908 Socialist convention, Conger-Kaneko built up the subscription list to about 15,000, and when she published special issues dealing with temperance, prostitution, child labor, or divorce from the Socialist perspective, the circulation usually exceeded 100,000. But with the advent of World War I and the perception that Socialism had peaked as local Progressivism became more powerful, the *Progressive Woman* folded.

Mother Earth (1906–18), founded by anarchist Emma Goldman, also was a consciously radical periodical published contemporaneously with the *Progressive Woman*, the *Woman's Journal*, and the *Forerunner*. Not only did Goldman issue previously published works on topics from sex to political change by well-known activists past and present, but importantly, she provided a forum for literary radicals. Contributor Craig Monk, in "Emma Goldman, *Mother Earth*, and the Little Magazine Impulse in Modern America," discusses this little-known facet of *Mother Earth* and claims that it represents Goldman's major contribution to American literature and letters. More often than not, critics focus on Goldman's place in American social history, particularly her tie to President McKinley's assassin, Leon Czolgosz. Monk rightly holds that Goldman sought not only to articulate a radical social agenda but also "to support innovative literary endeavors." The periodical writing and editorial vision of Goldman differed from that of her peers because of her interest in modern literary aesthetics and her desire to reach a broad audience of male and female readers across class distinctions.

Goldman's anarchist politics nevertheless locates her in the company of Bloomer, Stone, Gilman, and Conger-Kaneko.

The *Lily*, the *Forerunner*, the *Woman's Journal*, and the *Progressive Woman* represent a focused type of protest journal aimed largely at middle-class, self-educated, white women who were concerned with many social causes, while *Mother Earth* maintains a similar focus but expands the scope of readership. As the new century exploded in World War I, Socialism[24] lost its appeal, temperance fell from favor in the pursuit of greater individual freedom, and the passage of the nineteenth amendment to the Constitution (1920) seemed to suck the vital forces from the suffrage movement. Women's protest magazines, as a periodical subgenre, entered into a long period of quiescence.

Protest magazines, however, were certainly not the only periodical vehicles for American women writers. Nineteenth- and early twentieth-century women contributed to high-culture and popular magazines in great numbers. Indeed, so large had their contributions become at mid-nineteenth century that male critics took to derisively describing the period as the "feminine fifties." Although many writers, such as Stowe, Chopin, and Gilman aspired to write for the *Atlantic* or *Harper's*, the magazines of high culture, most often they wrote for the popular magazines that accepted works that could be written formulaically and quickly. Popular magazines also paid the authors more per article or per page, and many women authors very much needed the income from their work. Thus, Rebecca Harding Davis wrote James Fields, editor at the *Atlantic*, imploring him to pay more for her work, but ultimately she had to abandon writing for the *Atlantic* because her writing was the major financial support of her family and she needed the income provided by the better-paying popular magazines. Her story "The Murder in the Glenn Ross," published in *Peterson's Magazine*, brought her three hundred dollars, three times what the story would have paid had it been published in the *Atlantic*.[25] Davis had gained the admiration of the high-culture journals with her first published story, "Life in the Iron Mills," and although she wrote a great number of potboiler mysteries and sentimental stories for *Peterson's* throughout her career, she continued to contribute whenever possible to the more prestigious magazines, producing serialized novels for the *Galaxy*, *Lippincott's*, and *Scribner's*.

In her essay "'An Ardor That Was Human and a Power That Was Art:' Rebecca Harding Davis and the Art of the Periodical," contributor Michele L. Mock argues that Davis was able to use her long association with *Peterson's* to continue writing about human rights and social justice. Davis wrote more than five hundred pieces for various periodicals and in many of them, Mock explains, Davis "conjoined her artistry and activism in a theoretical and pragmatic practice [which] she consistently referred to as her doctrine of the 'Good Samaritan.'" Davis lobbied against the 1852 Pennsylvania state act that allowed a husband effectively to steal his wife's property by having her committed to a mental institution. In the short story "Put Out of the Way," she not only demonstrates the inequities of the legal system as it pertained to women but also the manner in which men, too, were prey to a legal act that permitted incarceration as a mental patient with the signatures of a panel of three doctors, none of whom had to examine the patient. As Mock claims, Davis's serialized fiction often drew the nation's "averted gaze to this crucial issue." Moreover, this woman writer also used short fiction to inspire reform and to create a dialogue on a seemingly well accepted gender construct that allowed women and some vulnerable men to become prisoners of inhumane insane asylums.

Refashioning the Periodical

As many white women writers from the middle class sought to expand the opportunities for American women within the context of the dominant social norms, others — white women of the working classes, Mexican American, Native American, and African American women writers — urged the expansion of American readers' consciousness of countries and cultures beyond and within this nation's borders. These writers employed and adapted the periodical to clarify and to obscure distinctions of class, race, and gender, thus anticipating late twentieth-century uses for the periodical by poor women, women of color, and other women marginalized by the dominant discourses in the United States.

The first generation of industrial workers in Lowell, Massachusetts, in the late 1830s to mid–1840s found themselves in a peculiar social position. Most of the laborers were young women, daughters from New England farm families, daughters of freemen who worked at the will of factory owners and under the gaze of supervisors. They were on the lowest rung in a capitalist hierarchy. Adherents of the Cult of True Womanhood, many of these women workers published stories and poems pseudonymously in the *Lowell Offering* and the *Voice of Industry*. In "Lowell Female Factory Workers, Poetic Voice, and the Periodical," Susan Alves argues that the female editors and writers of these Lowell periodicals inhabited a conflicted space from which they wrote. As True Women, many pseudonymous women writers in the factory-owned *Lowell Offering* eschewed such political topics as abolition and labor reform. Instead, most of their stories and poetry recall bucolic New England and the moral haven of the domestic sphere. Yet, some female factory operatives abandoned pseudonyms, extended the moral agency of True Womanhood into the public domain, and directly addressed such pressing issues as dangerous working conditions and the economic tie binding Lowell workers to slaves in the South. Several female factory writers also abandoned the *Lowell Offering* for the labor union newspaper, the *Voice of Industry*. Alves insists that the former "daughters of freemen" articulate a significant and complex voice not only in American cultural history but in American literature as well, a voice ignored by the editorial framers of culture at the *Atlantic, Harper's,* and the *Century*.

Curiously, editors at "mugwump" magazines such as *Harper's* and the *Century*, who perceived themselves as the arbiters of Anglo-American taste and the protectors of white privilege, published fiction by María Cristina Mena, an upper-class, Mexican-born woman who had lived in the United States from the age of fourteen, and by Zitkala-Sä, a college-educated, mixed-race woman who self-identified as Sioux and who was an Indian rights activist. Contributing writers Amy Doherty, in "Redefining the Borders of Local Color Fiction: María Cristina Mena's Short Stories in the *Century* Magazine," and Charles Hannon, in "Zitkala-Sä, and the Commercial Magazine Apparatus," both rely on a Bahktinian theoretical framework to contextualize and to consider the work of Mena and Zitkala-Sä in the magazines of the American hegemony.

Examining the magazine as a unified cultural entity, Doherty and Hannon study the pictorial imagery that appeared in the same issues of the *Century* and *Harper's* magazines as the short fiction by Mena and Zitkala-Sä. In her essay, Doherty considers the dichotomy between a black-and-white photo-essay entitled "Unfamiliar Mexico" in the September 1915 issue of the *Century* and Mena's stories of Mexican life in the same periodical. Just as nineteenth-century Americans perceived Italy as bucolic, Catholic, fecund, and superstitious before Fuller began writing of the Italian revolution as emotionally charged, urban-centered, intellectual, and important, so too early twentieth-century Americans perceived Mexico as culturally backward and rural. While these photos demonstrate the relatively undeveloped aspect of Mexico, Doherty claims that the *Century* reader is tacitly invited to compare these images to Mena's local color fiction, in which she considers the tension between the domestic and the foreign during a period of increased conflict over national borders. By masking her observations in the form of the white tourist narrator, Mena appropriates the tone and the nativist aspirations of the *Century*, while simultaneously writing stories that demonstrate Mexicans to be cultured, intelligent, artistic, and urbane, thus undercutting the editorial tone of Anglo-American superiority.

Similarly, in his essay, Hannon examines the juxtaposition of illustrations accompanying an article on American manifest destiny by Woodrow Wilson to Zitkala-Sä's short story "The Soft-Hearted-Sioux" in the same Dawes era issue of *Harper's*. While Wilson writes of the glorious westward expansion of a nation, Zitkala-Sä tells of appropriation of Indian lands and the denigration of Native American identities implicit in the Dawes Act. Hannon explains that the drawings participate in the ideological work of the Wilson essays, valorizing the narrative of Anglo-American identity. The drawings subtly belittle Native Americans, while Zitkala-Sä's protagonist demonstrates the complexity of a young man who has "assimilated" to white Christian culture and has removed himself from his father's faith and from his father's people but can function effectively in neither world. Hannon explores Zitkala-Sä's use of *Harper's* assimilationist editorial viewpoint to show the powerful contrast between Zitkala-Sä's fiction and Wilson's narrative. This essay creates an important space for the examination of Native American people and their late nineteenth- and early twentieth-century experience from vastly different perspectives.

Doherty and Hannon demonstrate that María Cristina Mena and Zitkala-Sä, among others, inscribe the culturally hegemonic attitude of white superiority in their fiction while successfully asserting that these widely accepted attitudes and images are not correct. For Mena and for Zitkala-Sä the periodical is a platform from which they urge a change of heart and mind on the part of upper-class American readers on questions of race and national origin. Significantly, Doherty and Hannon break new ground in their research, for recent scholarship has provided little recovery and critical discussion of Mena and Zitkala-Sä.

African American women were not as constrained by the Cult of Domesticity, which inhibited many middle class white women's public participation in the social dialogue of the nineteenth century. Instead, there is a strong oratory tradition among African American women, who used the podium to directly address audiences on such issues as racial equality and uplift, women's suffrage, temperance, and gambling. Frances Ellen Watkins Harper and her contemporary, Pauline Hopkins, were both platform speakers on these and other important social issues of their day.

Harper was an especially gifted and sought-after speaker, making appearances all over the American West. After a speech given in Detroit, a listener exclaimed, "The whites and colored people here are just crazy with excitement about her. She is the greatest female speaker as ever was here."[26] Harper made her living as a lecturer and gave much of her earnings to support the Underground Railroad. Although until fairly recently in this century Harper remained shockingly unknown to many in academic circles, she was considered by many as the most important black woman writer of the last half of the nineteenth century.[27]

Harper's recently discovered earlier novels, *Minnie's Sacrifice, Sowing and Reaping*, and *Trial and Triumph*, serialized in the magazine the *Christian Recorder*, are changing the contemporary critical response to Harper's fiction. Harper wrote these novels specifically for a middle-class, black female audience, although many of her themes, such as making moral decisions and sticking to them, the importance of hard work, and the necessity for temperance certainly address readers of all races. Also, the protagonists of the three newly discovered novels are mulatto, white, and black, respectively. In "'A Deeper Purpose' in the Serialized Novels of Frances Ellen Watkins Harper," contributor Michelle Campbell Toohey offers a metacritical examination of Harper's work in light of the recovery of these three serialized novels and re-evaluates Harper's place in American letters, a place assured her largely through her engagement with the niche periodical. Toohey asserts that Harper uses the periodical to promote "a strong political agenda of vital self-determination for her own race."

Pauline Hopkins was another platform speaker who moved into periodical writing as she argued for social change. The first recorded instance of Hopkins's lengthy contribution to social change and to oratory was a prize-winning speech on temperance that she wrote and gave as a child. In her short and serialized fiction for the *Colored American Magazine*, Hopkins wrote about the middle-class, African American community; she also edited the magazine from 1900–09. Through her editorial work on the *Colored American Magazine*, Hopkins pursued a program of racial uplift by publishing good fiction, reviews of contemporary books, and articles of interest to the middle-class black community of which her readership was comprised. The argument for Hopkins's uplift work can be found in her political alignment with W. E. B. DuBois, who prophetically stated in his 1903 *Souls of Black Folks* that "the problem of the twentieth century is the problem of the color line."[28] Surely, Hopkins was a member of the "talented tenth" of whom DuBois spoke, as was her audience. Hopkins disagreed with Booker T. Washington's 'go along and get along' philosophy. She argued that black people need not limit themselves to lives of manual labor or the second-class citizenship that white society proffered. As a result, Washington's partisans surreptitiously purchased the *Colored American Magazine* and dismissed Hopkins.[29] In this case, the actual periodical served as the canvas upon which were drawn the different paths advocated for the betterment of black citizens by the adherents of Washington and DuBois. And it is through the study of the history of this particular periodical that we can understand the complexity and conflicts within the turn of the century African American community.

American women writers from various social backgrounds, ethnicities, and races understood that the best way to make themselves and their ideas known was through the periodical press. Their engagement with periodical literature, which the articles in this book examine, demonstrates American women's vibrant participation in the intellectual life and the political discussions of their times. Their clear desire to bring about substantial social change and their realization that they could at least create a constituency for, and a dialogue about, such change through the periodical underscore Margaret Fuller's prophetic remark that the periodical was the "only efficient instrument for the general education of the people."

NOTES

1 See Janice Radway, *Reading the Romance* (Chapel Hill: U of North Carolina P, 1984). Although Radway does not specifically focus on the periodical, her discussion of women's reading habits is illuminating. Most noteworthy are a group of critical books on the periodical that were published in the mid–1990s. Among these are: Matthew Schneirov, *The Dream of a New Social Order: Popular Magazines in America, 1893–1914* (New York: Columbia UP, 1994); Helen Damon-Moore, *Magazines for the Millions: Gender and Commerce in the Ladies' Home Journal and the Saturday Evening Post, 1880–1910* (Albany: State U of New York P, 1994); Patricia Okker, *Our Sister Editors: Sarah J. Hale and the Tradition of Nineteenth Century Women Editors* (Athens: U of Georgia P, 1995); Ellen Gruber Garvey, *The Adman in the Parlor: Magazines and the Gendering of Consumer Culture,*

1880's to 1910's (New York: Oxford UP, 1996); Richard Ohmann, *Selling Culture: Magazines, Markets, and Class at the Turn of the Century* (London and New York: Verso, 1996).

2 Karlyn Kohrs Campbell, *Man Cannot Speak for Her: A Critical Study of Early Feminist Rhetoric*, vol. 1. (Westport, CT: Greenwood, 1989) 24.

3 Patricia Okker, *Our Sister Editors*, 92.

4 Grace Greenwood's short editorial career at the *Godey's* is an example. Greenwood published an article in Gamaliel Bailey's abolitionist journal, the *National Era*. Fearing that such a connection would upset their Southern readership, Godey and Hale fired Greenwood from her position as assistant editor at the *Lady's Book*. See Kevin J. Hayes, "Grace Greenwood (Sara Jane Lippincott) (1832–1904)" in *Nineteenth-Century American Women Writers: A Bio-Bibliographical Sourcebook*, ed. Denise Knight (Westport, CT: Greenwood, 1997) 180–83.

5 Nina Baym, *Feminism and American Literary History* (New Brunswick, NJ: Rutgers UP, 1992) 167–82.

6 She raised money to complete the building of the Bunker Hill Monument, started a relief organization for sailors' wives, successfully lobbied to have Mount Vernon made into a historic home for the public, aided Matthew Vassar in starting Vassar College, and successfully lobbied President Lincoln to make Thanksgiving a national holiday, among other projects.

7 For example, incorporating moral truths in a story that appealed to human emotions; intensifying such familiar aspects of mid–nineteenth-century life as the death of a child, the separation of lovers, and the determination to do right by an individual faced with many obstacles; and addressing readers who are constructed as empathetic middle-class individuals who have the moral authority to advocate for the abolition of slavery.

8 Other women writers such as Lydia Maria Child, Lydia Sigourney, and Catharine Maria Sedgwick wrote for women readers in a variety of periodicals, and all wrote in the sentimental mode. In their short fiction, they advocated for such forms of social amelioration as abolition, temperance, and the better treatment of the working poor. See Child's "The Quadroons," Sigourney's "The Intemporate," and Sedgwick's "Fanny McDermott" in *Rediscoveries: American Short Stories by Women, 1832–1916*, ed. Barbara Solomon (New York: Mentor, 1994).

9 See also Joan Hedrick, *Harriet Beecher Stowe: A Life* (New York: Oxford UP, 1994).

10 Susan Coultrap-McQuin, *Doing Literary Business: American Women Writers in the Nineteenth Century* (Chapel Hill: U of North Carolina P, 1990) 28.

11 Coultrap-McQuin 37.

12 Matthew Schneirov, *The Dream of a New Social Order: Popular Magazines in America, 1893–1914* (New York: Columbia UP, 1994).

13 There were several other protest periodicals for women during this period, but for the sake of brevity we have chosen to use the *Lily* as an exemplum. Another equally interesting protest journal for women was the *Una*, which was edited by Caroline Dall.

14 Amy B. Aronson, "America's First Feminist Magazine: Transforming the Popular to the Political" in *Nineteenth-Century Media and the Construction of Identities* (New York: St. Martin's, 2000), 7.

15 Okker, *Our Sister Editors* 56.

16 Aronson 22.

17 One of Gilman's first published poems, "In Duty Bound," was first published in the *Woman's Journal* for 12 Jan. 1884.

18 The *Woman's Journal* masthead, 8 Jan. 1870.

19 Agnes Ryan, "The Torch Bearer: A Look Forward and Back at the *Woman's Journal*, the Organ of the Woman's Movement" (Boston: *Woman's Journal and Suffrage News*, 1916) 1.

20 Letters Column, *Woman's Journal* 9 Apr. 1870, 107.

21 The first issue is representative and contained such articles as "Why Women Should Be Socialists" and "What Socialist Women Are Doing." Later issues included articles such as "Sex Subjugation" in which Conger Kaneko wrote, "by giving woman an equal share in the ownership of the country's industries so that when she goes out of the home to earn something for herself, she will be her own employer. She shall then have the right to dictate the number of hours she shall work, and the amount of wages she shall receive. She shall have a vote and belong to the executive as well as the law-making branch of society." *The Socialist Woman* 1 (Apr. 1909) 3.

22 Parce, a professor at the University of Chicago, contributed a piece titled, "What Is the Woman Question?" In it she wrote that "when man conceived, in his imagination, that woman was utterly different from himself he was able by reason of superior physical condition to establish society on the basis of that theory." *Progressive Woman* 2 (Mar. 1909) 5.

23 Lewis contributed her thoughts on the suffrage issue, arguing "As capitalism has forced women out into the industrial field there has come an ever-increasing need for the ballot in the hands of working women as a weapon to protect their labor and secure their economic freedom." On the same page as the Lewis article there appears a poem that summarizes her ideas humorously and succinctly, thereby creating the sense of a whole focus on suffrage:

> Ma's a graduate of college and she's
> read most everything;
> She can talk in French and German

> She can paint and she can sing . . .
> Oh I can't begin to tell you all the poems
> She can quote;
> She knows more than half the lawyers do
> but Ma can't vote.

The poem was originally published in the *Chicago Herald Record* and reprinted in the *Socialist Woman* 1 (Feb. 1908).

24 American Socialism, made popular in the late nineteenth century by nationalist clubs, formed to create a utopian America based largely on the ideas of Edward Bellamy in his book *Looking Backward 2000 to 1887* (1888), was very different from Marxist Socialism. The Bolshevik Revolution, however, caused a negative connotation to be attached to all forms of Socialism, and the American movement could not dissociate itself from that historical fact.

25 Lisa A. Long, "Rebecca Harding Davis" in *Nineteenth-Century American Women Writers: A Bio-Bibliographical Sourcebook*, ed. Denise Knight (Westport, CT: Greenwood, 1997) 89–98.

26 Margaret Hope Bacon, " 'One Great Bundle of Humanity': Frances Ellen Watkins Harper (1825–1911)," *Pennsylvania Magazine of History and Biography* 113 (Jan. 1989): 21– 43 qtd. in Gretchen Holbrook Gerzina, "Frances E. W. Harper (1825– 1911)" in *Nineteenth-Century American Women Writers*, 213–19.

27 For a while, twentieth-century scholars of African American literature believed that Harper's novel *Iola Leroy* (1892) was the first novel by an African American female. Critics such as Mary Helen Washington suggest that Harper's work was ignored for so long because her theme was always the lives of black women. Paul Lauter, however, states that her work was long neglected because she (like most women writers of her day) did not separate "the social functions of fiction from its artistic form." Lauter further reminds the contemporary reader that the conflation of the political and the literary was very much the standard practice in fiction, especially "among her abolitionist colleagues." *Iola Leroy* received a mixed critical response because it had been seen to essentialize black women characters. More recent critics, such as Hazel Carby, recognize that the figure of the tragic mulatto is a metaphor for the struggle of black people in a hostile milieu. She also argues that, more than just the tale of a tragic mulatto, *Iola Leroy* is "a textbook for the educated black person in the crisis of disenfranchisement, lynching, and the Jim Crow laws." For further detailed discussion, see Lauter, "Is Frances Ellen Watkins Harper Good Enough to Teach?" *Legacy: A Journal of Nineteenth-Century American Women* 5 (spring 1988) 27–32, and Hazel Carby, *Of Lasting Service to the Race: The Work Of Frances Ellen Watkins Harper* (New York: Oxford UP, 1987) 62–94.

28 W. E. B. DuBois, *The Souls of Black Folk* in *The Oxford DuBois Reader*, ed. Eric J. Sundquist (New York: Oxford UP, 1996) 107.

29 Richard Yarborough's introduction to the Schomburg Library of Nineteenth-Century Black Women Writers edition of *Contending Forces: A Romance Illustrative of Negro Life, North and South* by Pauline Hopkins (New York, 1988) provides an excellent discussion of these matters.

SOCIAL &
POLITICAL
ADVOCACY

Annamaria Formichella Elsden

MARGARET FULLER'S TRIBUNE DISPATCHES & THE NINETEENTH-CENTURY BODY POLITIC

In many ways Margaret Fuller was an eccentric among her peers, a puzzle who mystified her contemporaries and who continues to elude her critics. Fuller herself questioned her identity in an 1831 diary entry that recalls a childhood moment of perplexity: "How is it that I seem to be this Margaret Fuller? What does it mean? What shall I do about it?" (Von Mehren 6). Henry James framed her as an enigma when he reportedly inquired, "Would she, with her appetite for ideas and her genius for conversation, have struck us but as a formidable bore, one of the worst kind, a culture-seeker without a sense of proportion, or, on the contrary, have affected us as a really attaching, a possibly picturesque New England Corinne?" (P. Miller xxvii). Contemporary critics such as Ann Douglas emphasize her appearance, calling her "Emerson's difficult and homely friend" (313). Similarly, Joseph Deiss stresses Fuller's "striking" appearance, noting that "she was nearsighted, and had a mannerism of half closing the lids to see more sharply" (14), while Joel Pfister argues that "Fuller's caustic wit and plain physical appearance made her stunning in a different way," contrasting her impressive demeanor with the "'ordinary' feminine manner" of Beatrice in Hawthorne's "Rappaccini's Daughter" (69). And of Fuller's conversations, Perry Miller writes, "Margaret Fuller presided over these bacchanic rites in homemade dresses that her adorers thought to be of Oriental magnificence, and at the climax of each session, when she had reduced the others to awed silence, she would close her eyes in an inspired trance and utter unfathomable words, which they thought emanated from some occult or Delphic wisdom" (xi). Regarding her biography, contemporary readers still wonder, did she and Giovanni Ossoli ever officially marry? Was her refusal to be rescued from the shipwreck off the New York coast a suicidal gesture? And despite Fuller's landmark role in American periodical writing, questions persist regarding her place in our literary canon, as evidenced by the title of the introduction to Joan Von Mehren's recent Fuller biography, "Margaret Fuller: Should She Be Famous?" [1]

While such questions and colorful biographical anecdotes are provocative, they threaten to elide Fuller's historical context and political contributions by representing her primarily as a quirky "personality." [2] Bringing the discussion more firmly back to Fuller's writing is crucial to any understanding of how periodical literature, gender, and nationalism intersect in nineteenth-century America. Fuller's periodical writing connects meaningfully to the political and social climate in the world around her, and dismissals of her as "peculiar" betray the social censure that has frequently attended women who transgressed the nineteenth century's carefully delineated, gendered spheres. The first American woman to work as a foreign news correspondent, Margaret Fuller wrote thirty-seven dispatches between 1846 and 1850 for publication on the *New York Daily Tribune*'s front page under the heading "Things and Thoughts in Europe." The majority of Fuller's dispatches utilize the Italian Risorgimento ("renaissance" or "revival") in which she became actively involved, as a lens through which to assess American democracy. Read with an awareness of context, the dispatches that Horace Greeley contracted Fuller to send home from Europe emerge as a revealing product of and contribution to the nineteenth century's burgeoning nationalistic movements. Not only did newspapers such as the *Tribune* function as a primary means of representing imagined national community, but Fuller's journey to Italy and eventual expatriation also occurred at a historical moment dominated by European struggles for republican government. Like the periodical press within which she worked, Fuller's columns and even her personal life were saturated with issues of national, and international, importance.

Though her concerns were clearly global, Fuller's experiences as a woman crucially inform her political agenda. In her dispatches, America's democratic actualization becomes coterminous with a woman's political right to self-actualization and full citizenship. Fuller helped to promote nineteenth-century American nationalism, but her journalism also critiqued gender constraints on American women of the mid-nineteenth century. This complex and apparently paradoxical agenda is encapsulated in her rhetorical use of body imagery. Fuller writes of the "body" politic in terms that speak for the various bodies that contribute to the nation: individual bodies, of all classes, races, and genders, that comprise the national community. She refers to her country as a "huge, over fed, too hastily grown-up body" in need of "soul," and later asserts, "I do not deeply distrust my country. She is not dead, but in my time she sleepeth, and the spirit of our fathers flames no more, but lies hid beneath the ashes. It will not be so long; bodies cannot live when the soul gets too overgrown with gluttony and falsehood" (166, 230).[3] This mapping of human sentience onto geographic space links body politic to body personal, perpetuating the sentimentality of mainstream American patriotism even as it stands outside the dominant tradition to critique the nation on behalf of its downtrodden members. The alignment of the two discourses, nation and gender, suggests a parallel optimism underlying Fuller's conception of both. Recognizing the potential for struggle to liberate the Italian people, she underscores in her columns that awareness and political action can effect similar freedom for American women and other oppressed groups, and thereby allow the United States to reclaim its glorious founding principles. Certainly the Risorgimento liberated Fuller herself, whose removal from familiar soil and immersion in politics abroad cast her in a powerful role drastically different from the spinsterish eccentricity projected onto her by those at home.

As a journalist paid in advance for news she sent home (reportedly ten dollars per dispatch), Fuller had a distinctive relationship to her audience and her subjects. Greeley's hiring of her was a historic decision, making her "the first female member of the working press" and affirming her right to step into a patriarchal line: "Greeley had hired her to fill the spot vacated by Albert Brisbane (later filled by George Ripley) and he expected her to report on social conditions as well as lend literary prestige to the paper" (Chevigny 288, 290). A political and patriotic publisher, Greeley "hoped to crowd out the sensational rival penny papers by his commitment to morality, social progress, and the arts" (288). Acquiring Fuller's commentary on both political and cultural issues was clearly a significant part of this project. Other nineteenth-century women travelers to Italy, like Catharine Maria Sedgwick and Sophia Peabody Hawthorne, told of their experiences in private journals and letters that became public documents years after their return home. In contrast, Fuller wrote and was read in medias res, her commentary's value determined by how quickly she could "dispatch" it. She wrote words for immediate public consumption, without the protestations about the worth of the "private musings," which "friends were forcing her to publish," often found in conventional travel writing. As a reporter, Fuller spoke with a broader cultural sanction derived in part from her association with the *Tribune* and its well-known editor.[4]

Fuller's dispatches demonstrate her awareness of the newspaper's centrality, its function as the "heart" of the nation. As Margaret Lukens notes, the *Tribune*'s "nickname was 'The Great Moral Organ'" (187), suggesting its vital role in the American nation. Fittingly, Fuller wrote from London, "As for the Times . . . the blood would tingle many a time to the fingers' ends of the body politic before that solemn organ which claims to represent the heart, would dare to beat in unison" (91). The irregular beat she describes indicates her concern that journalistic dysfunction threatened a nation's integrity. The periodical press, a continuous and pervasive infusion into the community, could either sustain or infect the national body. An address to Greeley penned in Edinburgh indicates how powerfully Fuller believed in journalism's obligation to nourish the moral life of its readership: "[T]he publisher cannot, if a mere tradesman, be a man of honor. . . . [H]e who, for his sordid aims, circulates poisonous trash amid a great and growing people, and makes it almost impossible for those whom heaven has appointed as its instructors to do their office, are the worst of traitors . . ." (66). In aligning the publisher's powers with those of statesmen and priests, Fuller indicates the centrality of the periodical press even as she demonstrates that the profit motive threatened to taint its higher aims and poison the civic body. Fuller used her columns as a platform from which to edify the predominantly male publishers of her country who might have allowed greed to distract them from their higher calling. She not only recognized the influential power of the periodical press, but she also wielded it with passion.

Fuller's existence as an American abroad, living a life parallel to those of readers in the States, gave her dispatches their relevance and force. In Benedict Anderson's theory of the building of modern nationalism outlined in *Imagined Communities*, the newspaper is significant because it reflects and enables modern conceptions of time and also because its consumption is communal.[5] What Anderson calls "homogenous empty time," the sense that readers shared the same moment with the columnist, created the conceptual framework within which an audience apprehended Fuller's textual and ideological connection to themselves. The idea of time, in relation to the nation and the journalist, reinforces this bond and becomes a central component of Fuller's columns; the news, a timely commodity, is enveloped in temporal allusions. She boasts of making history by completing "the shortest voyage ever made across the Atlantic — only ten days and sixteen hours from Boston to Liverpool" (39), and each dispatch bears the mark of the transatlantic steamer schedule. One letter, "meant to go by the *Great Britain*" is delayed; later she is "inevitably prevented from finishing one that was begun for the steamer of 4th November" (62, 78). Her columns documented events as they occurred, a concept quite different from the traditional travel narrative or travel-inflected novel, published after the journey when events had often been resolved. The immediacy of the journalistic dispatch kept the domestic reader up-to-date on fast-breaking developments in transportation as well as specific events occurring in Europe, and all the while reminded that the reader shared a moment with an entire community of nationals, even (or especially) a compatriot who resided abroad.

In addition to creating an imagined nationalism that temporally bound the foreign correspondent to the domestic reader, this sense of immediacy, of time bearing down on the frantic journalist and injustice transpiring even as the reader sat down to read the front page at breakfast, empowered Fuller's calls for political reform. In one dispatch, for example, Fuller means to translate the mission statement of a progressive Roman journal, but mailing constraints limit what she can accomplish: "I intended to have translated in full the programme, but time fails, and the law of opportunity does not favor, as my 'opportunity' leaves for London this afternoon" (139). In another dispatch, she closes with the frustrated declaration, "Time fails, as usual. The clock strikes, the postbag opens and leaves only time to make the sign of [a star — the symbol she used to close her columns]" (146). Perceiving how thoroughly time pervades her craft, Fuller explicitly incorporates this fact into the discourse itself, offering her awareness of time as a facet of the columns. The effect is to involve her readers in her own sense of urgency, an effect well suited to her political message — the need for immediate U.S. action to alleviate suffering, both at home and abroad.

Her tactic for catalyzing social activism is to target the individual reader. Fuller utilizes her front-page platform to make large-scale political pronouncements about her nation and its people, harsh assessments designed to promote the reader's self-analysis. When she writes, for example, "The American, first introduced to some good pictures by the truly great geniuses of the religious period in Art, must, if capable at all of mental approximation to the life therein embodied, be too deeply affected, too full of thoughts, to be in haste to say anything" (112), her description invites readers to measure themselves against the standard established for "the American" who is mentally "capable." Similar challenges pervade the dispatches, allowing Fuller to interpolate a diverse population into a cohesive whole with the term "American" and simultaneously to criticize individual members of that population for failing to live up to her high standards. In a representative gesture, Fuller challenges her readers by making categorical assertions about American tourists in Europe. She begins with a pronouncement that again demands self-reflection from her domestic reader: "The American in Europe, if a thinking mind, can only become more American" (161). Left to determine whether he or she is "a thinking mind," the reader then faces Fuller's delineation of the three "species" of American travelers and the task of finding one's place therein. The first type Fuller calls "the servile American — a being utterly shallow, thoughtless, worthless," who "comes abroad to spend his money and indulge his tastes" (162). The second Fuller names "the conceited American," with an excess of patriotism who "does not see, not he, that the history of Humanity for many centuries is likely to have produced results it requires some training, some devotion, to appreciate and profit by" and is thus prone to criticize European culture (162). The final choice is clearly the best, a character Fuller calls "the thinking American," open-minded enough (like Fuller herself) to "recogniz[e] the immense advantage of being born to a new world and on a virgin soil" and also "anxious to gather and carry back with him all that will bear a new climate and new culture" (163).

The *Tribune* readers, who faced these rhetorical challenges in their original context, as one facet of the newspaper's front-page collage, would have been reminded of their imagined national community even as they were encouraged by Fuller to take a critical stance regarding their own obligation to that community. The resulting conflict manifests itself in the dispatches as a combination of yearnings for an ideal America and confessions of faults Fuller cannot deny. In dispatch 18, she opens with the glory of America's destiny, "Thou wert to be the advance-guard of Humanity, the herald of all Progress," but she soon arrives at a series of sobering admissions: "Must I not confess in my country to a boundless lust of gain? Must I not confess to the weakest vanity, which bristles and blusters at each foolish taunt of the foreign press . . . ? Must I not confess that there is as yet no antidote cordially adopted that will defend even that great, rich country against the evils that have grown out of the commercial system in the old world?" (165). Greeley established the *Tribune* in 1841 "as a paper dedicated first to the elevation of the masses — the reading public generated by the new penny papers — and second to the success of the liberal Whigs" (Chevigny 288). Fuller's critique contributed to this project, by addressing a range of subgroups within her audience. She combines a challenge to middle-class liberals (those with access to the "foreign press") with attacks on America's capitalist system that would have appealed to the working class (Greeley's "masses"). In the same dispatch, Fuller fuels her argument by adding commentary on current events in the States: "I listen to the same arguments against the emancipation of Italy, that are used against the emancipation of our blacks; the same arguments in favor of the spoliation [sic] of Poland as for the conquest of

Mexico. I find the cause of tyranny and wrong everywhere the same — and lo! my country the darkest offender" (165). With such accusations, Fuller uses her journalistic platform both to consolidate and to arouse an informed public who would remedy the suffering body politic at home.

Equally worthy of her readers' attention was the revolutionary movement occurring in Italy during Fuller's residence there. As one of America's first foreign correspondents, as a political commentator, as a liaison between American and Italian culture, as a progressive revolutionary who recognized capitalism's moral and social implications, Fuller spoke to and about nineteenth-century cultural movements that were changing the face of the globe. Fuller participated in a unique historic confluence that conjoined the forces of technology, capitalism, and revolutionary activity in Europe. As nationalism came to denote an internal sense of moral commitment and connection, rather than merely a reflection of random, external circumstances, Fuller's columns promoted the ideal that citizens had the right to determine their allegiance based on the values displayed by their country. Indeed, her immersion in radical politics and her awareness of the profound changes redefining nationhood led her to re-evaluate her commitment to the land of her birth: "My friends write to urge my return; they talk of our country as the land of the Future. It is so, but that spirit which made it all it is of value in my eyes, which gave all of hope with which I can sympathize for that Future, is more alive here [in Italy] at present than in America" (230). Her textual expatriation underscored for readers at home the severity of her disillusionment with the United States, the magnetism of the Italian independence movement, and the obligation of individual citizens to make choices that reflected their moral codes.

When Fuller arrived in Italy in 1847, the various Italian city-states (not yet unified into one nation) were engaged in struggles to oust foreign monarchies, limit the Pope's temporal power, and establish a centralized, republican government. The resulting revolutionary activities, collectively known as the Risorgimento lasted throughout Fuller's Italian sojourn and became the central concern of her dispatches and her life.[6] Although ultimately unsuccessful, the Risorgimento paved the way for Italian unification a decade after Fuller's departure, providing the previously fragmented Italian people with national heroes and a common cause. Fuller's dispatches constitute a major textual contribution to this movement. Her columns distributed the demands of the Italian revolutionaries — which included, notably, "freedom of the press" (Hearder 201) — to an international audience and kept Americans apprised of developments in the uprising. In representing the Italian revolution for American consumption, Fuller's dispatches cultivate nationalisms on both sides of the Atlantic. Her reconstitution of American revolutionary history simultaneously revives American patriotism and validates Italy's republican mission.

Part of a mid-nineteenth-century phenomenon in which the nation, as an ideology, became reproducible as a model for emerging nations, Fuller's discourse self-consciously performs the important political and historical work of representing the nation. As Anderson notes, "The close of the era of successful national liberation movements in the Americas coincided rather closely with the onset of the age of nationalism in Europe"; therefore, European movements were "able to work from visible models" (67). Fuller recognized the explosiveness of her political moment and offered the American Revolution as a model for a struggling Italian people: "Still Europe toils and struggles with her idea, and, at this moment, all things bode and declare a new outbreak of the fire, to destroy old palaces of crime!" (164). The nationalistic uprisings that characterized the nineteenth century seemed, to Fuller, the inevitable consequence of centuries of corrupt monarchical oppression, and the "idea" that would rid Europe of this evil was, in fact, the idea of republican nationhood already implemented in America, an idea imported into Europe through print culture and adjusted to fit political conditions there. A woman whose homeland fell short of her humanitarian ideals, Fuller embraced the European uprisings with their demands for universal rights, and her dispatches were dedicated to a twin project of fostering the nascent Italian republic and redeeming her homeland's democratic failings.[7]

Repeatedly Fuller reminds her readers of America's recent revolution and its corresponding debt to the world: "Ah! America, with all thy rich boons, thou hast a heavy account to render for the talent given; see in every way that thou be not found wanting" (160–61). To heighten the emotional stakes, she invokes patriotic signs, symbols of the imagined nationalism that Anderson sees as originating in American revolutionary activity (81). Not eternal but historically produced, such symbols become part of nationalist rhetoric when Fuller writes home, "This cause is OURS, above all others; we ought to show that we feel it to be so. . . . Please think of this, some of my friends, who still care for the Eagle, the 4th July, and the old cries of Hope and Honor" (160–61). Fuller uses strategic appeals to sentimental patriotism to enlist the aid of fellow Americans in the ultimate goal of transporting American ideals and experience to Italy. A secondary result is that her dispatches create a text of nationhood that affirms the American community even as it offers a model for the emerging European republics. In other words, Fuller's attempt to distill the domestic model for foreign consumption actually *creates* the model nation that would serve as precursor. Enabled by the attributes of the periodical press, she inscribed a version of national identity and ideology that would produce patriotism at home.[8]

Despite Fuller's invocations of an idealized American republicanism, she also laments American shortcomings:

> Yet, oh Eagle, whose early flight showed this clear sight of the Sun, how often dost thou near the ground, how show the vulture in these latter days! Thou wert to be the advance-guard of Humanity, the herald of all Progress; how often hast thou betrayed this high commission! Fain would the tongue in clear triumphant accents draw example from thy story. . . . But we must stammer and blush when we speak of many things. (165)

Such blemishes as slavery, the Mexican War, greed, and solipsism are Fuller's evidence that America has failed to fulfill its special destiny. This combination of reminders of America's fortunate history coupled with examples of national failures forwards Fuller's agenda by showing Americans their sins and offering a path to redemption. The suggestion is that America will rise anew by sustaining other countries in their struggles for freedom: "Send, dear America, a talisman to thy ambassadors, precious beyond all that boasted gold of California. . . . Hail to my country! May she live a free, a glorious, a loving life, and not perish . . . from the leprosy of selfishness" (284). Thus Fuller constructs an international connection within which America redeems itself by offering itself as the blueprint for an emerging Italian republic.

By valorizing American destiny, the dispatches contribute to a conceptualization of the nation, despite its historical contingency, as eternal. Anderson argues, "If nation-states are widely conceded to be 'new' and 'historical,' the nations to which they give political expression always loom out of an immemorial past" (11). In other words, "it is the magic of nationalism to turn chance into destiny" (12). Clearly Fuller's columns contribute to the narrative that recasts historical contingency as fate. Reproaching her rich countrymen "who think that a mess of pottage can satisfy the wants of man," that is, who think the poor are content, she writes, "[T]hey have no heart for the idea, for the destiny of our own great nation: how can they feel the spirit that is struggling now in this and others of Europe?" (154). In a later dispatch, she draws a parallel between current political action in Italy and a transhistorical fantasy of American values:

It was the spirit of religion [that infused a Florentine celebration of the National Guard] — such my Country; as welling fresh from some great hearts in thy early hours, won for thee all of value that thou canst call thy own, whose ground-work is the assertion, still sublime though thou hast not been true to it, that all men have equal rights, and that these are *birth-rights*, derived from God alone. (158–59)

If democratic rights, offered as the "ground-work" of "all of value" in America, are "derived from God alone," they not only extend into an immemorial past, but they receive sanction from a transhistorical and superhuman power. These associations transform the nation into a mythical-moral entity rather than a historical eventuality. Further, Fuller's use of an inflated discourse likely to conjure up biblical associations — "all of value that thou canst call thy own" — sought to create a sense of nationalistic worship in her readers.

American destiny translates into international leadership with Fuller's assertion that "the facts of our history, ideal and social, will be grand and of new import," an idea that leads Fuller to speculate that sculpture is the consummate artistic medium for the American. "It is perfectly natural," she argues, "to the American to mold in clay and carve in stone," casting the artist's vocation as both natural and national. As the passage continues, sculpture becomes an expression of civic pride: "He [the American sculptor] will thus record his best experiences, and these records will adorn the noble structures that must naturally arise for the public uses of our society" (267). The repetition of the word "natural" in her argument is significant. Government buildings become "noble structures" that "naturally arise," losing their utilitarianism as they are transformed into organic manifestations of American art and, thus, American greatness. Art, nationalism, and government are combined in Fuller's vision, all representations of the same agenda that arises "naturally" from American soil. In her columns of July 1849, Fuller uses a similar rhetoric to celebrate Roman political strife: "This city [Rome] that has grown, not out of the necessities of commerce nor the luxuries of wealth, but first out of heroism, then out of faith. Swelling domes, roofs softly tinted with yellow moss — what deep meaning, what deep repose, in your faintly seen outline" (285). The city "grows" out of moral ideals, and the nation's buildings symbolize more than mere "commerce." The idea of national destiny is transferred from America to Italy, with Fuller's parallel descriptions of the two republics reinforcing the "rightness" of the Italian revolution for the benefit of an American readership already convinced of its own nation's superiority and leadership role.

In her profound identification with the Italian cause, Fuller betrays a communal perspective that runs counter to those of her American contemporaries. For example, Emerson's proscription of travel in "Self-Reliance": "Let us not rove; let us sit at home with the cause" (180) not only betrays Emerson's naïveté regarding his own nation's formation, but also negates the value of interaction with other cultures.[9] More applicable to Fuller's experience would have been Thoreau's admonition in *Walden*: "Not until we are lost, in other words, not till we have lost the world, do we begin to find ourselves" (217). Yet Thoreau's discovery of self through isolation and withdrawal contrasts with Fuller's self-realization through travel and interaction with other cultures. The transcendentalism inscribed by Emerson and Thoreau, in its insistence on solitude and domestic pride (the sovereignty of the individual man as well as the individual nation), maintains a separatist logic that Fuller sought to transcend. Fuller lost the (familiar) world, and the self projected onto her there, when she traveled to Italy. Her translocation to Italy ignited in her a camaraderie with the Italian people and an emboldened sense of political agency; in addition, the epistolary nature of her dispatches invited a certain intimacy between herself and her readers. Indeed, the essential character of the newspaper column — an evolving pastiche composed of small pieces produced over time, stylistically flexible enough to encompass a range of discourses and voices — uniquely suited Fuller's vision of a literary and political collective.

Her innovative use of the periodical forum, as well as her political engagement, might be demonstrated by her manipulation of the star imprint with which she closed her dispatches. A shifting symbol that reflects Fuller's self-conception, the star becomes increasingly entwined with the content of the dispatches, representing Fuller's growing involvement in Italian politics. In the early dispatches the star is tacked on at the end of the columns, unconnected to the commentary itself. Yet after Fuller's arrival in Italy, a year into her trip, she begins to play with the star's signifying possibilities, implicating her signature in her column's contents. She closes dispatch 15, written from Milan, with the statement "The clock strikes, the postbag opens and leaves only time to make the sign of [star]" (146), thus situating her mark within the text. Five months later, writing from a Rome bombarded by new developments in the fight for independence, Fuller remarks, "Every day the cloud swells, and the next fortnight is likely to bring important material for the record of [star]" (208). The rhetoric implies Fuller's deepening personal involvement in political events, foregrounding their significance in relation to her. After a tour of the hills outside Rome with Giovanni Ossoli, Fuller's star and self are transformed: "Meanwhile the nightingales sing; every tree and plant is in flower, and the sun and moon shine as if Paradise were already reestablished on earth. I go to one of the villas to dream it is so, beneath the pale light of a [star]" (231). The romantic optimism of this dispatch is heightened by the metamorphosis of Fuller's by now familiar byline into a sentimental symbol. In addition, the journalistic convention of self-naming is appropriated and deployed to express the distinctive sensations of an American woman immersed in a foreign culture.

During the height of the revolution, Fuller incorporates Italian speech into her dispatch and essentially writes herself into the narrative of Italian destiny. Calling out her grief to the Virgin Mary over the revolution's violence, Fuller writes, "Ave Maria Santissima! when thou didst gaze on thy babe with such infinite hope, thou didst not dream that so many ages after blood would be shed and curses in his name. Madonna Addolorata! hadst thou not hoped peace and good will would spring from his bloody woes, couldst thou have borne these hours at the foot of the cross." In the final entreaty, Fuller pens the name that applies to herself: "O Stella! woman's heart of love, send yet a ray of pure light on this troubled deep!" (274). Immediately following this exhortation, Fuller's familiar star is printed. The juxtaposition of the star symbol and the Italian word for *star* suggests the closeness Fuller felt to Italian traditions at that moment and even casts her as a savior figure for this troubled people. Perhaps the "star" of her journalism would shine a new light onto the revolution she was witnessing. Significantly, the star disappears entirely from dispatch 34, which reports the defeat of the Roman Republic and is the only dispatch without the symbolic sign-off. The relationship of Fuller and her writing to the Risorgimento, represented by the star, became increasingly intense until the defeat of the movement threatened to erase her discursive self. Indeed she writes in dispatch 35, "To write from Italy is now become a sorrowful business" and then again in dispatch 36, "I have begun to write, yet little do I feel inclined" (312, 317).

In her columns and letters to the *Tribune*, Fuller discovered a politically efficacious way to transcend gender and genre. The columns, in their subject matter and in their extensive distribution to a mixed audience, permitted her to fuse her feelings as a woman and as a writer-patriot. Although the majority of her columns deal with national affairs, she also weaves, into her writing, stories of individual women. Fuller's second dispatch, for example, describes a woman she met during her travels in Scotland. Calling her "a fine specimen of the noble, intelligent Scotchwoman," Fuller goes on to praise the woman as "an only child, a cherished wife, an adored mother, unspoiled by love in any of these relations, because that love was founded on knowledge" (52). The knowledge underlying this Scottish woman's integrity is explicitly political:

> In childhood she had warmly sympathized in the spirit that animated the American revolution, and Washington had been her hero . . . she had known in the course of her long life many eminent men, knew minutely the history of efforts in that direction, and sympathized now in the triumph of the people over the Corn-Laws, as she had in American victories with as much ardor as when a girl. . . . (52–53)

Fuller is clearly smitten with this exemplary woman's ability to combine familial devotion and revolutionary fervor, a mixture that Fuller strove for in her own lifetime and advocated in her writing as a healthier and more respectable option for nineteenth-century women than stereotypical, infantile dependence. In contrast to the sentimental novels that were so popular a form for nineteenth-century American women writers, Fuller makes use of a literary space that permits precisely this fusion — that of the political and emotional self.

Fuller further alludes to her literary values in a passage from a later dispatch written in praise of two European women writers:

> I prize Joanna Baillie and Madame Roland as the best specimens which have been hitherto offered of women of a Spartan, Roman strength and singleness of mind. . . . They are not sentimental; they do not sigh and write of withered flowers of fond affection, and woman's heart born to be misunderstood by the object or objects of her fond, inevitable choice. Love, (the passion,) when do not write of it always; they did not think of it always; they saw other things in this great, rich, suffering world . . . nor was all their speech one continued utterance of mere personal experience. It contained things which are good, intellectually, universally. (89)

In this passage, and in her journalism itself, Fuller lays claim to the entire "great" world as proper subject matter for women who write. Her theory of women's writing self-consciously positions itself in opposition to the conventions of sentimental novels, especially their exclusive focus on home, love, and the wounded woman. In her ideal, the woman writer recognizes that the personal and the political are codependent, that her private experience can encompass a range of issues, and that her literary output should reflect this diversity. An elastic genre that depended upon many individuals' interpretation and transcription of global events, the newspaper underscored an ideology of inclusion and facilitated Fuller's use of personal experience to promulgate a political message.

In contrast to women who "sigh and write of withered flowers of fond affection," Fuller praises women who combine love with knowledge. The Scottish woman gains respect within the home by bringing her concern with public affairs into the domestic sphere: "Dear to memory will be the sight of her in the beautiful seclusion of her home among the mountains, a picturesque, flower wreathed dwelling, where affection, tranquillity and wisdom were the gods of the hearth." Fuller follows this idyllic vision with an impassioned appeal: "Grant us more such women, Time! Grant to men the power to reverence, to seek for such!" (53). The rhetorical devices used in this dispatch illuminate how Fuller manipulates print journalism's power on behalf of women's rights. In this case, the apostrophe to "Time" establishes a lofty and traditional tone reminiscent of classical rhetoric, yet Fuller uses the distanced voice to make demands of her own historical context. The appeal "Grant to men the power to reverence" is a complex gesture that accuses American men, the *Tribune*'s readers, of demonstrating a lack of "power" in their treatment of women. Under the guise of an appeal to the generic concept of "Time," Fuller chastises her *fellow* countrymen. The classical style would have tempered her demands with a tone of formality and diplomacy by making the accusation less direct, though no less weighty. Such hybrid discourse is characteristic of Fuller's journalistic strategies for promoting her feminist message.

When Fuller discovered powerful European women who exceeded their culture's low expectations of them, she incorporated their stories into her column alongside updates on current events and the background on Italy's warring political factions. Fuller describes, for example, "an object which gave [her] pleasure" in Chester, namely an old surveillance tower converted into a museum. What pleases her is that, as the museum relied upon contributions "from all who had derived benefit from Chester," "many women had been busy in filling these magazines for the instruction and the pleasure of their fellow townsmen," with one woman contributing "a fine collection of butterflies, and a ship" (49–50). Putting the women's efforts in context for her *Tribune* readership, she asserts, "I like to see women perceive that there are other ways of doing good beside[s] making clothes for the poor or teaching Sunday school; these are well, if well directed, but there are many other ways, some as sure and surer, and which benefit the giver no less than the receiver" (50). The importance of a woman's private life as a cultural document in a museum is made explicit here, as is the potential link between the present Fuller observes in European countries and the future she envisions for America.

In a later dispatch from London, Fuller initiates what seems a conventional observation about the lack of a "woman's touch" in the London Reform Club: "To me this palace of so many 'single gentlemen rolled into one,' seemed stupidly comfortable in the absence of that elegant arrangement and vivacious atmosphere which only Women can inspire. In the kitchen, indeed, I met them and, on that account, it seemed the pleasantest part of the building — though, even there, they are but the servants of servants" (96). The reflection that women are permitted only in a kitchen where they must serve men inspires the caustic rejoinder "I am not sorry, however, to see men predominant in the cooking department, as I hope to see that and washing transferred to their care in the progress of things, since they are 'the stronger sex'" (96). Fuller's flippant inflection of "stronger" attacks traditional gender divisions, suggesting both that men's physical strength might suit them to manual household labor (rather than intellectual privilege) and also that women historically have been responsible for much of the culture's hardest work.

Yet Fuller's Europe also offers evidence that ancient civilizations conceived of a woman's role differently and thus undermines the essentialism of nineteenth-century gendered spheres. Fuller advises her American readers:

A woman should love Bologna, for there has the spark of intellect in Woman been cherished with reverent care. Not in former ages only, but in this, Bologna raised a woman who was worthy to the dignitaries of its University, and in their Certosa they proudly show the monument to Clotilda Tambroni, late Greek professor there. . . . In Milan, also, I see in the Ambrosian Library the bust of a female Mathematician. These things make me feel that if the state of Woman in Italy is so depressed, yet a good will toward a better is not wholly wanting. These things, and still more the reverence to the Madonna and innumerable female Saints, who if, like St. Teresa, they had intellect as well as piety, became counselors no less than comforters to the spirits of men. (143)

Fuller offers to her contemporary readership not only a history of respect for women but also the hope for similar advancements in her own country.

Fuller's emphasis on St. Teresa's "intellect and piety" echoes her earlier description of the Scottish woman, suggesting that a woman's spiritual and emotional strength depend upon a solid intellectual foundation.

The worship of female saints, which fascinated many nineteenth-century American women writers in Italy, informs a later dispatch in which Fuller confesses, "[St. Cecilia] and St. Agnes are my favorite saints" (241). The stories of Cecelia and Agnes foreground connections between the individual and a higher moral principle, echoing Fuller's discursive links between each citizen and the nation. In Agnes and Cecila, Fuller selected symbols of bodily invincibility who, having pledged themselves to Christ, died defending their spiritual faith. Agnes, "a special patroness of bodily purity," was prosecuted for refusing to marry, then tortured, humiliated, and eventually sent by the governor to a brothel "with liberty to all to abuse her person at pleasure." When young men rushed to take advantage of the thirteen-year-old girl, they "were seized with such awe at the sight of the saint that they durst not approach her," and Agnes remained pure (*Butler's* 133–34). Cecilia also refused marital relations as a means of demonstrating her piety. After converting her husband and brother-in-law to Christianity, she was punished by a prefect who ordered her to be "suffocated to death in the bathroom of her own house" (403). Despite the fact that "the furnace was fed with seven times its normal amount of fuel," Cecilia lived unharmed for a full day. The soldier sent to decapitate her also found his task daunting; having "struck at her neck three times," he left her for dead but she "lingered three days" (403). Like Agnes, Cecilia devoted herself to a faith that gave her bodily invincibility. These women transcended physical limitations through their devotion to a higher ideal, and both determined their fates by refusing coercion. Certainly such heroic foremothers would have encouraged a woman who dedicated herself to journalism's power and sought to transcend the weaknesses her culture ascribed to her. Further, Fuller used her column to valorize publicly women who had been unjustly abused by patriarchal power — certainly the parallels with Fuller's own situation would have been recognized by some of her readers.

Relying upon images of body and disease, Fuller's columns often liken weaknesses within the community to sickness and suggest that national health is maintained either by cure or by prevention. The nation-as-body metaphor was not unusual in American patriotic rhetoric; yet Fuller takes the image of the diseased national body to a provocative extreme by bringing gender into the picture. It is possible to trace the movement from body politic to body personal-feminine over the course of her dispatches. In

May 1847, for example, Fuller penned one of her most aggressive social commentaries in response to evidence of poverty and hunger in France: "The more I see of the terrible ills which infests [sic] the body politic of Europe, the more indignation I feel at the selfishness or stupidity of those in my own country who oppose an examination of these subjects — such as is animated by the hope of prevention" (119). Later, in Italy, Fuller uses similar terminology to remark on the influence of domestic abuse on her sharpening political and social awareness: "[T]he cries of mothers and wives beaten at night by sons and husbands for their diversion after drinking, as I have repeatedly heard them these past months, the excuse for falsehood, 'I *dare not* tell my husband, he would be ready to kill me,' have sharpened my perception as to the ills of Woman's condition and remedies that must be applied" (245–46). The repetition of words associated with sickness and treatment ("prevention" and "remedies") fortify the discursive bond between the individual woman and the state. In contrast to a literary tradition that often feminized the American land to accommodate masculine conquest fantasies, Fuller textualized a feminine body politic to reveal the injuries caused by patriarchal insensitivity to women's needs. In marking domestic violence as a social issue, and in using her status as a reporter to bring the issue to public attention, Fuller was a pioneer. And by presenting injuries to women's bodies as analogous to a sickly political body, Fuller demonstrated the interconnections between woman and nation, between private and public, thereby stressing the state's responsibility to treat the (woman's) body in order to heal itself.

Fuller's dispatches document an urgent call for action that, though interrupted occasionally by her frustration with America's reluctant politicians, ultimately locates hope in radical reform. Clearly concerned with material conditions and capitalism's implication in societal ills, Fuller was an early advocate of Socialism and is credited with helping introduce Marxist thought to the American people. Chevigny reads an 1845 Fuller *Tribune* column as "among the very earliest notices of Marx and Engels in America" (294). As the dispatches attest, Fuller offers an incisive and unflinching assessment of how capitalist class structure depends upon an oppressed working class. From Glasgow, Fuller writes home that "the people are more crowded together and the stamp of squalid, stolid misery and degradation more obvious and appalling" in that city than at any other stop on her European tour (79). She continues, describing "persons, especially women, dressed in dirty, wretched tatters, worse than none, and with an expression of listless, unexpecting woe on their faces, far more tragic than the inscription over the gate of Dante's Inferno" (79). The image of suffering taints the romance of a castle she visits nearby, where centuries ago "lords and ladies gay danced and sang above [while] prisoners pined and wild beasts starved below" (80). The juxtaposition provokes a sober reminder to her readers that while the maintenance of the ancient castle:

> at first blush looks like a very barbarous state of things . . . on reflection, one does not find that we have outgrown it in our present so-called state of refined civilization. . . . Still lords and ladies dance and sing above, un-knowing or uncaring that the laborers who minister to their luxuries starve or are turned into wild beasts — below. Man need not boast his condition till he can weave his costly tapestry without the side that is kept under looking like that, methinks. (80)

Fuller's travels brought her into close contact with the oppression that un-derlies capitalism and contributed to the fervent, radical tone of her dis-patches.

Once again, her medium proves to be well suited to her message. In 1848, the year Marx and Engels published *The Communist Manifesto*, Fuller pub-lished a dispatch detailing for Americans the very issues Marx and Engels were investigating in Europe: "To you, people of America, it may perhaps be given to look on and learn in time for a preventive wisdom. You may learn the real meaning of the words FRATERNITY, EQUALITY. . . . You may in time learn to reverence, learn to guard, the true aristocracy of a nation, the only really noble— the LABORING CLASSES" (211). The periodical press permitted such a radical declaration, providing Fuller with a wide audience and encouraging (indeed, demanding) her immediate, uncensored response to events. Certainly her Socialist rhetoric would have seemed radical to American readers who believed that the class structure rewarded merit, that the upper classes *deserved* their status and its attendant privileges.

Fuller herself had grown up in a community infused with elitism, her fa-ther bestowing upon her a classical education, her brothers attending Har-vard, her early conversational circles comprised of wealthy and educated cosmopolitans from the Boston area; but the encounter with Europe and Italy, poverty and revolution, led her to form new and radical allegiances, ac-companied by rebellious declarations. She transcended the national affilia-tion imposed upon her at birth, expressing throughout the dispatches a closer affinity to Italian culture than to her own. The birth of her son (to an Italian father) seems to have broadened and complicated her sense of national belonging. Fuller collapses her political and maternal connections to Italy tellingly in a letter written to Caroline Sturgis Tappan in December 1849. Describing an afternoon outing with a friend, Fuller writes, "We sat down on a stone seat in the sunny walk to see the people walk by. The Grand Duke and his children, the elegant Austrian officers who will be driven out of Italy when Angelino is a man . . ." (Chevigny 492). The chronology, linking Fuller's son's maturity to the overthrow of the occupying forces, suggests causality; a mother's heightened investment in the establishment of republican government casts Angelino as the hero of the revolution.

With new allegiances came Fuller's endorsement of Socialism, as she grew to believe that only radical reform could ease the world's suffering: "Here lie my hopes now. I believed before I came to Europe in what is called Socialism, as the inevitable sequence to the tendencies and wants of the era, but I did not think these vast changes in modes of government, education and daily life, would be effected as rapidly as I now think they will, because they must. The world can no longer stand without them" (320). "Hope" is an important term in this prognosis. Despite the defeat of the Italian revolutionaries, and what she saw as America's failures, Fuller's dispatches remain cautiously optimistic. Comparing the Italian zeal for reform with American domestic policy, she asks the barbed question "And my country, what does she? You have chosen a new President [Zachary Taylor] from a Slave State, representative of the Mexican War" (245). She continues with a prescription for American redemption and sends a hopeful message on behalf of her own sex: "Pray send here a good Ambassador — one that has experience of foreign life, that he may act with good judgment; and, if possible, a man that has knowledge and views which extend beyond the cause of party politics in the United States. . . . Another century, and I might ask to be made Ambassador myself . . . but woman's day has not come yet" (245). In its suggestion that Fuller herself possessed the requisite characteristics to serve as a diplomat, and its evocation of an approaching "woman's day," the dispatch offers a feminist hope to American readers.

Although her nation often disappointed its citizens' dreams, Fuller did not ultimately relinquish her faith in American destiny or her reliance on the concept of nation itself. In light of her literary accomplishments and social activism, it is ironic that Perry Miller felt compelled to assert that Fuller "may easily be dismissed as an eccentric, as no true voice of American civilization" (xii). Clearly her discourse, situated at a historical moment of crisis abroad and problematic expansion at home, critiques America's greed even as it participates in constructing that nation as a manifestation of the ideal republic. A "true voice" speaking to the contradictions inherent in her nation's ideology, she was a radical *and* a patriot, working within the emerging nineteenth-century periodical press and in response to the major nationalistic upheavals around her. Margaret Fuller's columns and commentary blurred the line between public and private affairs as she attempted to supersede, on a personal and political level, the limitations of her time.

NOTES

1 In the foreword to the revised edition of *The Woman and the Myth: Margaret Fuller's Life and Writings*, Bell Gale Chevigny provides a comprehensive and invaluable survey of recent Fuller criticism and other relevant secondary sources.

2 For a useful discussion of how and why the "Fuller myth" was constructed and is perpetuated, see Marie Urbanski's "Margaret Fuller's *Woman in the Nineteenth Century*: The Feminist Manifesto" in *Nineteenth-Century Women Writers of the English-Speaking World*, ed. Rhoda Nathan.

3 Throughout this article, citations from Fuller's dispatches are taken from Larry J. Reynolds's and Susan Belasco Smith's *"These Sad But Glorious Days": Dispatches from Europe, 1846–1850*, the most complete collection of Fuller's journalism. Other collections, like *The Essential Margaret Fuller* and Perry Miller's *Margaret Fuller: An American Romantic*, excerpt only selections from the dispatches. The original publication of the collected dispatches, *At Home and Abroad* (1856), is no longer in print.

4 The newspaper is not a private document attributable to one author but rather the result of a network of forces. Fuller's involvement in such a network both contributed to her literary reputation and testified to the stature she had attained as a writer.

5 Anderson connects the communal consumption of the newspaper with the creation of imagined community:

> Each communicant is well aware that the ceremony he performs [that of reading the daily paper] is being replicated simultaneously by thousands (or millions) of others of whose existence he is confident, yet of whose identity he has not the slightest notion. Furthermore, this ceremony is incessantly repeated at daily or half-daily intervals throughout the calendar. What more vivid figure for the secular, historically clocked, imagined community can be envisioned? (35)

Printed and consumed on a national scale, the newspaper becomes the common link for a republican nation that accepts any given issue as a coherent whole despite the fortuitous common denominator (time) that determines its contours. Likewise, citizens accept the nation as an organic whole, its inhabitants bound together in some essential and meaningful way, despite their merely coincidental co-habitation and ignorance of each other's lives.

In addition, Anderson distinguishes between a medieval belief in time infused with religious predestination, "a simultaneity of past and future in an instantaneous present" in which "Christ's second coming could occur at any moment," and, on the other hand, a modern apprehension of time that has lost its religious inflection (23–24). Whereas "the mediaeval Christian mind had no conception of history as an endless chain of cause and effect or of radical separations between past and present," in the modern era "what has come to take the place of the mediaeval conception of simultaneity-along-time is . . . an idea of 'homogenous empty time,' in which simultaneity is, as it were, transverse, cross-time, marked not by prefiguring and fulfilment [sic], but by temporal coincidence, and measured by clock and calendar" (23–24). This understanding of time as a simultaneity connecting the various members of an imagined community is both a result and a precondition of the modern newspaper.

6 Not only did Fuller work as director of the Fate Bene Fratelli hospital for the wounded in Rome, but she also became intimately involved in friendships with two key revolutionaries, Giuseppe Mazzini and Adam Mickiewicz, and romantically involved with a rebel fighter, Giovanni Ossoli.

7 Demonstrating the extent of the populist sentiment in Europe, Polish revolutionary Adam Mickiewicz, Fuller's close friend, made the following demand of his country: "To the companion of life, Woman, brotherhood, citizenship, entire equality of rights" (222). It is not surprising that Fuller included this "declaration of faith" in one of her dispatches nor that Mickiewicz and his humanitarianism appealed so greatly to an American woman whose own "democratic" nation made no such provisions for women or nonwhite Americans.

8 It is interesting to consider how *Godey's Lady's Book* and sentimental literature enabled different kinds of imagined group consciousness. Of *Godey's*, Isabelle Lehuu writes, "[W]omen's pictorial representations shared in the construction of sentimentality and domestic femininity" (90), and Lauren Berlant argues that "sentimental ideology served as a structure of consent in which domestically atomized women found in the consumption of popular texts the experience of intimate collective identity" (270). Such forms of "women's" writing contributed primarily to an imagined community based on the home and traditional values, while the newspaper constructed the public community, the "nation" in its most conventional and masculinized sense. Much critical work remains to be done on the intersection of these two imagined (gendered) communities, specifically on women's "collective identity" as a central component of nation formation and conception.

9 Both key figures in the rise of transcendentalism, Emerson and Fuller are often

compared by critics, with Emerson's individualist philosophy often placed in opposition to Fuller's wider, communal perspective. Dorothy Berkson writes, for example, "[Fuller's] vision, though not so fully and often articulated as Emerson's is, I would argue, a larger and more complex vision than his in that it recognizes and attempts to accommodate human weakness, the existence of evil, and the potential for failure and despair" (26).

Sarah Robbins

GENDERING GILDED AGE PERIODICAL PROFESSIONALISM: READING HARRIET BEECHER STOWE'S HEARTH AND HOME PRESCRIPTIONS FOR WOMEN'S WRITING

In the top left corner of its front page, the 1860s–1870s periodical *Hearth and Home* regularly rendered its own title in image form, reflecting and reinforcing the popular culture's view of white, middle-class American domestic life in the decade after the Civil War. The array of objects in this recurring illustration carried easily recognizable messages about nineteenth-century family literacy practices for the publication's anticipated readers.[1] Perhaps predictably, a hearth with a comfortable fire dominated the midsection of the picture and, though the particular objects on the mantelpiece were obscured by the periodical's nameplate, other visual cues suggested this home was a properly educated and refined one. Beside a stuffed chair facing the fireplace, for instance, stood a reading table and its lamp, and the other side of the illustration included another side table with a carefully draped cloth and a dainty vase of flowers, signaling a close relationship between the homemaker's attention to aesthetically pleasing decor and the family-based development of the mind in a middle-class domestic setting. The centerpiece of the image foregrounded a third small table holding several books, with one thick volume perched on top at an angle that seemed to invite an opening of this text or of the periodical itself.

Anyone who opens the tabloid-size pages of *Hearth and Home* at the dawn of the twenty-first century is probably doing so, as I have been recently, because Harriet Beecher Stowe served as its coeditor during its early life. In the wake of moves to reposition *Uncle Tom's Cabin* in the field of American literary studies, whether as a prime example of an alternative feminine aesthetic or as an embodiment of women's significant cultural work, we are beginning to take a closer look at other writing Stowe produced in her long career as a professional author. Re-evaluations of novels like *Dred* and

The Minister's Wooing have been one result of this scholarly recovery process. Eager as we are to celebrate Stowe the author, however, we may be a bit disappointed, at least at first, when we turn to her weekly columns for *Hearth and Home*. To put the case too bluntly perhaps, Stowe the 1860s periodical writer was no Fanny Fern.[2]

Today I find myself scanning a good bit of the writing Stowe did for *Hearth and Home* with impatience, irritated to see the same writer who had galvanized the world against the major sociopolitical issue of her day redirected toward filling column inches with passages like this one about "beauty as applied to the living-rooms of houses": "And now our friends having got this far, are requested to select some one tint or color which shall be the prevailing one in the furniture of the room. Shall it be green? Shall it be blue? Shall it be crimson? To carry on our illustration, we will choose green, and we now proceed . . . to create furniture for our room" ("Cheapness of Beauty" 200). Unlike the satirical stance of Stowe's recently reappreciated *Atlantic* essays on carpet selection, this column was unstintingly straightforward, offering practical help for women readers eager to create a tastefully decorated parlor — for example, those who wanted to purchase a "very pretty curtin muslin" and who needed to know how many yards of fabric to buy for a typical window. ("Six," Stowe advised.)

Stowe's labor on such prose may seem to be lacking in subtlety and polish, and thus in aesthetic interest as well. On the one hand, "How to Treat Babies" (6 Feb. 1869) may have been genuinely reassuring for readers whose colicky infants really could drive them to near distraction: after all, if such moments made the world-famous author of *Uncle Tom's Cabin* feel "like crying [her]self," what could be expected of anyone else? On the other hand, even if I try to follow Patricia Okker's advice to appreciate such social value as Stowe's "sisterly editorial voice" in these texts,[3] I still find myself reluctant to see something like "Growing Things" (6 Mar. 1869) as substantial cultural work. Even if I re-view it within a feminist-materialist framework, sensitively aware of the complex role gardening could play in the lives of women of earlier eras,[4] "Growing Things" basically offers little more than quick summaries of two books about garden techniques that Stowe recommends to her readership. Clear calls to social action, like "The Woman Question," are relatively scarce in Stowe's *Hearth and Home* columns. Certainly, in that one piece she righteously exhorts her audience to read "John Stuart Mill's account of what the legal position of woman is under English common law" and to reflect that, in the postbellum United States, a married female "can make no contract and hold no property," that she is essentially in a position "precisely similar to that of the negro slave" (520). But in the rest of that year's worth of sketches, the politicized author of *Uncle Tom's Cabin* is far harder to find. So, what are we to make of this seeming shift to conservatism?[5] And how do we reconcile our continuing moves to position Stowe among the "best" makers of American literature with the notably uneven quality of her writing for *Hearth and Home*?[6]

Answering these questions requires situating Stowe's work for the periodical within the marketplace context for such publications in her own day, as well as distinguishing between the advice she gave others when acting as a work-a-day editor and the artistic aspirations that she seems to have cherished for herself as an American author whose best work could be expected to meet more permanent aesthetic criteria. Beginning to address such questions also involves taking a look at Stowe's life as a practicing professional against a larger backdrop of gendered literature-making in the post–Civil War United States. Therefore, it includes situating the particular venue of *Hearth and Home* within a network of publications competing for white, middle-class national readership in that marketplace while trying to recapture a sense of who those readers were and how Stowe imagined herself as meeting their needs in her columns. In addition, it includes cultivating an awareness of how our own reading practices, as well as our beliefs about "literary" value, shape our interpretations of nineteenth-century texts; of the authors' specific processes for writing and circulating them; and of the original readers' interactions with those printed products.

One especially fruitful site for such an analysis is the series of essays Stowe wrote *about* women's professional writing during her year as editor. Originally appearing in January 1869, these sketches now provide a kind of window into the range of forces operating in the periodical marketplace during the late 1860s, and they convey a sense of Stowe's own efforts to negotiate a gendered professional position — for herself and other aspiring women writers — within that shifting set of values and practices.[7] Beginning with "Can I Write?" (9 Jan.) and progressing in order through "How Shall I Learn to Write?" (16 Jan.), "Faults of Inexperienced Writers" (23 Jan.), and "How May I Know That I Can Make a Writer?" (30 Jan.), the essays reflect tensions then inherent in the evolving, frequently contested views of what professional American literature making should and could entail. By exploring Stowe's efforts to acknowledge but also to manage these tensions in her series on authorship for *Hearth and Home*, we can better understand both her particular professional writing career and the periodical context in which it continued to develop.

That Stowe chose to write on this topic in this particular periodical may have served to heighten some of the tensions inherent in her own position as a major American literary figure, since the character of the publication matched some aspects of her gendered professionalism but challenged others. *Hearth and Home*, established in 1868 as a weekly publication with Donald G. Mitchell and Stowe as coeditors, entered a national literary scene that had moved since mid-century from a long tradition of genteel amateurism to an expanded print culture selling literature as a commodity necessarily reflecting mass market values and interests. That its owners and founders were the advertising firm of Pettengill, Bates and Company suggests the extent to which this venture was seen from the outset as a business operating within the burgeoning U.S. literary marketplace. According to Frank Mott, the niche the publication sought to fill was not unique: while committed to publishing works of domestic literature, *Hearth and Home* also offered a wide range of nonfiction self-help fare about the hearthside, the garden, and the farm (99). In that vein, although *Hearth and Home* lasted only seven years, its association with other 1860s–1870s New York–based periodicals centered in American home life (such as *Wood's Household Magazine, Domestic Monthly*, and *Our Neighborhood*) underscores ways in which literature writing in the United States was increasingly being seen as a moneymaker. But this same linked construction of imagined readership and periodical content also points to another trend in Gilded Age publishing: the growing divide between an urban, "high culture," masculine model for literature making and an increasingly distanced alternative tradition, grounded in the values and practices of a more rural or domestic, middlebrow — and feminized — space for textual consumption *and* production.

Stowe served as coeditor of *Hearth and Home* for only a year. Yet, although her editorial tenure was relatively brief, her taking on the job in the first place reminds us that, for Stowe at this point in her life, her writing was as much a generator of domestic income as anything else. As Joan Hedrick has pointed out, Calvin Stowe had retired from his professorial position in 1863, leaving his wife as the primary breadwinner for a large and demanding family that included adult children who had proven themselves incapable (or at least unwilling) to support themselves (310). In the interval between the end of the Civil War and the start-up of *Hearth and Home*, the Stowe family's expenses had been on the rise (given the added expense of their new Hartford home) so that Harriet's efforts to increase the amount of money she made with her pen became even more pointed (as reflected, for instance, in her correspondence with publishers like James Fields). Thus, Stowe's taking on the duty of a weekly publication needs to be seen in part as an example of her growing sense of herself as a professional (read "for pay") author.[8]

This emphasis on earning money through writing helped gender Stowe's work for *Hearth and Home* by connecting it with a network of other women, periodicals, authors, and editors whose labor had already begun to distinguish male from female literary professionalism during the antebellum era. Specifically, Sara Parton (Fanny Fern) had gained as much attention for the amount of money *New York Ledger* editor-publisher Robert Bonner was willing to pay for her columns as for the quality of her prose.[9] Similarly, as Okker has noted in her recent study of Sarah Josepha Hale, that redoubtable "editress" consistently conceived of professionalism in women's writing as writing for pay as opposed to producing "unpublishable, amateur writings" (99). From Okker's perspective, one result of this stress on becoming financially successful as a mark of professionalism was to distance Hale's view of serious writing from the continued calls for "artistry" over income in the rhetoric (if not the life practices) of male cultural arbiters like Hawthorne. In other words, whereas Hale herself would have argued that top women writers who earned good salaries were not merely "pander[ing] to their audiences" but instead showing that "they had talent *and* worked hard" (100), another kind of contrast associated men's presumably more elitist authorship with "an eighteenth-century model of the leisured gentleman author" and women's with "scribbling" perceived as less worthy (100). Later in the century and on into the twentieth, such African American women writer-editors as Josephine Ruffin and Ida B. Wells-Barnett would also devote notable energy to the moneymaking side of their work as writers, especially since publications like the *Women's Era* were dependent on such female business acumen to survive and thereby to carry out their race-oriented uplift missions.[10] American women writers, in other words, have often written within a gendered tradition of entrepreneurship. Viewed in this context, Stowe's labor for *Hearth and Home* was part of an ongoing process associating *women's* writing more with moneymaking than with art-for-art's-sake.

Stowe's tenure at *Hearth and Home* should also be set against the pragmatic political background of her growing interest in women's social issues, to the extent that she even flirted with the idea of joining, in some influential capacity, the political movement led by Susan B. Anthony and Elizabeth Cady Stanton (Hedrick 358). Within this context of Stowe's increasing fascination with women's rights, a consideration of her work at *Hearth and Home* would also take into account Hedrick's observation that Stowe "for the first time [had] a shaping power over columns other than her own, a power she used . . . to promote women writers such as Lucy Larcom," as well as issues like woman suffrage.[11] Seen in this light, Stowe's occasional forays into women's rights issues in *Hearth and Home* take on more weight. One of those issues, for example, was a question that had held her attention from as early as her coteaching days at the Hartford Seminary in the 1820s — the proper education of young middle-class ladies, both in school and at home. Scattered through her *Hearth and Home* sketches were recurring complaints about the still-constraining limits of female education, and two columns in June 1869 specifically addressed the topic of what young girls should study at home.[12] Like her assumptions that professional female authorship involved serious work for pay, Stowe's support of women's learning in *Hearth and Home* affiliated her work with a gendered tradition of restrained yet persistent editorial advocacy nurtured by Hale's *Ladies' Magazine* and *Godey's*.[13] Along these lines, we might note, too, that Stowe left the publication after just one year, not because of philosophical or artistic differences but because she was eager to throw her energies into her book-length, proto-feminist defense of Lady Byron (Hedrick 366).

Considering that Stowe was evidently preparing to enter into a battle that would lead a number of her contemporaries to classify her writing as distinctly and dangerously unfeminine,[14] Stowe's recommendations to other would-be authors in the series of columns printed during the four weeks of January 1869 may seem surprising. The bulk of her advice urged aspiring women writers to start off modestly, in terms of both content and monetary aspirations, and then move gradually, through study and practice, to a strategically maintained professionalism. One way of interpreting this apparently conservative stance is to see it less as restraining than as mentoring — that is, to note that the trajectory Stowe described for other aspiring writers was something of a record of her own development as an author. The advice Stowe offered to novices in her *Hearth and Home* series came straight out of her own experience during her attendance at Litchfield School, her membership in Cincinnati's Semicolon Club, and her earlier magazine writing for women's venues such as *Godey's*. Stowe's essays, in other words, encouraged would-be writers to follow in her footsteps, imitating both the specific stages she had progressed through and her basic acceptance of the gendered expectations for feminized authorship. For example, John Brace, her favorite composition teacher during her own schooling, was the source of one tenet she stressed here: "FIRST THINK OF WHAT YOU WANT TO SAY, AND THEN SAY IT" ("Can I Write?" 40). Stowe explained: "It is not enough to have a general desire to write; the author must have a very particular and definite conception of something that she wants to say. We would say to such a person: 'Is there any subject on which you feel so deeply and vividly, that it seems to you that you have something to say on that subject?' If it be so, then try to put that something into the very clearest, plainest, and simplest words that you can" (40). According to a reminiscence by Stowe and a later retelling of the same tale by her sister Isabella Hooker, John Brace had given just such guidance to young Harriet when she was a student in his writing course at Miss Pierce's famous Litchfield School many years earlier, and it remained a cornerstone of Stowe's composing process for the rest of her life. Though Harriet first encountered Brace at Litchfield, they both were also associated later with the Hartford Female Seminary, and Stowe drew upon his teaching strategies when she instructed young ladies while working there with her sister Catharine Beecher.[15] Stressing his ability to build on shared conversations about topics of interest, Stowe often praised Brace's particular talent in "teaching composition" and associated her early development as a writer with his approaches (Hartford 28). Specifically, in recalling Brace's model for teaching writing, she described two of her own successful papers, written at ages nine and twelve respectively, as apt examples of *his* pedagogical skill. The first, though devoted to the ambitious topic "The Difference between the Natural and the Moral Sublime," Stowe insisted was not too difficult to write since "the discussions which he held with the class not only made me understand the subject as thoroughly as I do now, but so excited me that I felt sure I had [the] main requirement" for success at writing (Hartford 28).

By advising would-be authors to write of something they knew and cared about, Stowe may appear to us today to be offering little more than a cliché. But her elaborations on this point in the introductory sketch for the 1869 series clarify that part of her goal was to help her audience of potential *female* writers value the rather limited domestic subjects most available to them. In that vein, the shift from "men and women" writers to "a woman" in a later passage of "Can I Write?" is worth noting:[16]

Now, a great many men and women, when beginning to write, attempt too much; they take some great general subject, and flood it with platitudes and commonplaces. There is a whole class of ideas and words that go floating around the newspaper world, that belong no more to one person than another, and that by this time one person can say about as well as another. . . . But now, to come down to a practical point. If there is a woman who could take this subject, "how to quiet a fretful baby," and write a good, sensible, shrewd article on it, though she were not literary at all, and though there might not be a fine figure in it, yet if there were a good share of practical sense and evident experience, we think her article would make a hit. (40)

Stowe went on to catalogue other "specimens of a certain class of topics," all of which she described as "a homely and practical kind," "relating to the whole field of matter covered by the HEARTH AND HOME paper" — that is, "subjects . . . where a person who would follow our rule of thinking what *she* wanted to say, and then saying it, might get opportunity" (emphasis added). These suggested topics included "How to keep boys at home evenings," "How best to unite warmth and ventilation in a house," and "How to make Sundays both pleasant and useful to children" (40).

On first reading, this series of topics may seem to embody just the kind of overdetermined gender-based distinctions that feminists have resisted in our own lives and in portrayals of nineteenth-century "spheres" that oversimplify the separations between male and female cultures in that era. A closer look at Stowe's advice here, however, especially in the context of her ongoing efforts to stake out effective positions for her writing in the years after *Uncle Tom's Cabin*, indicates that at least one aim for this essay was savvy and pragmatic: to help would-be authors for *Hearth and Home* understand and adapt to the increasingly gendered position such periodicals might need to stake out in a marketplace moving unremittingly toward an urban and male-dominated view of "the literary."[17] One positive point that Stowe offered, accordingly, was that, despite the increasing influence of forces like the male-run, highbrow *Atlantic*, there might still be available niches for small-circulation papers devoted to woman-oriented audiences, much as today's television broadcasting and cablecasting includes specialty "narrowcasting" slots such as the History Channel and the Home Shopping Network. With this point in mind, her reference to "a certain class of topics" and her listing of specific examples represent a defensive yet potentially useful demarcation of relevant women's work in writing, work that need "not [be] literary at all" in order to be professional; work that, if not likely to be printed in a place like the *Atlantic*, could still find an audience.

In the second series entry on 16 January, Stowe would explain: "Now, the kind of writing for which there is a call in our paper, HEARTH AND HOME, is writing about domestic and rural subjects, and subjects of a practical nature, such as lie more fully within the sphere of woman's knowledge and observation than in that of ordinary men" (56). Besides arguing that such writing could find a place in her own particular periodical, Stowe also insisted that it could have a value in its own right. After all, she wrote:

"[I]t is a fact that the experiences of woman in real life, in all that comes to her in her domestic capacity as mistress of a family, sister, daughter, wife, and mother, do furnish a class of subjects wherein a woman, trained to think wisely and justly, may find a great deal to say that is worth saying. She may have subject matter of peculiar weight and importance — subject matter which woman, and only woman, could possibly be able to present."

Valued as something "which woman, and only woman, could possibly be able to present," Stowe's list of topics in the first sketch for the series is elevated beyond the mundane level of the literal ("How to keep boys at home," "How best to unite warmth and ventilation in a house") to a special compact between writer and reader, one bound to the unique experiences of womankind.[18] In this sense, Stowe's recommendation to avoid "some great general subject" ("Can I Write?" 40) becomes not an injunction assuming others' inability to take on just the kind of grandiose topic she herself had tackled for John Brace (in "The Difference between the Natural and the Moral Sublime") but rather a celebration of women's own space of experience and communication. That this space deals with the everyday is one of its strengths, not a fault, according to Stowe: "There is a great deal of writing," she asserted, "very charming, very acceptable, and much in demand, which consists simply in painting by means of words the simple and homely scenes of every-day life" ("How Shall" 56).

Stowe's formula positioned women's writing and the particular periodical she was editing within a gendered tradition of genteel entrepreneurship — one affiliated with venues like Hale's *Ladies' Magazine*, from its inception earlier in the nineteenth century, and also anticipating eventual descendents such as *Better Homes and Garden* and the *Ladies' Home Journal*. By implication, achieving the first two traits she cited — being "charming" and "very acceptable" — could ensure successful attainment of the third — having a product that was "much in demand." Indeed, writing for magazines and newspapers was a way that middle-class women could make money without surrendering their genteelness, since composing a "charming" piece (e.g., depicting decorous and uplifting feminized behavior in parlor, school, or village) with an "acceptable" topic (e.g., temperance, courtship, child rearing) would not violate expectations for female social action.

Within just such a set of expectations, Stowe's early-career pieces for James Hall's *Western Monthly Magazine, Godey's Lady's Book,* the *Evangelist, Christian Keepsake,* and other periodicals had often taken the form of brief descriptive sketches and "charming" short narratives of everyday life. For instance, "Feeling," which was later reprinted in the *May Flower,* offered detailed descriptions of the students in a country schoolroom, where one seemingly unproductive boy was singled out by the narrator because, although not a great scholar, he exhibited "the very temperament which often makes the noblest virtue"— compassion, or intense feeling (141).[19] At the end of the sketch, the reader discovers that the young boy eventually became a vibrant orator, beloved friend, and caring citizen-neighbor — precisely because he had "quick perceptions, the tenderness, the gentleness of an angel" (143). Similarly, Stowe's sketches of "Old Father Morris" and the "Alice H." of "Frankness" are not frequently read today, but they at least avoided the errors Stowe critiqued in the "Faults of Inexperienced Writers" column for her *Hearth and Home* series. Both pieces used focused themes and straightforwardly colloquial language instead of the overly "fine writing" or "hifalutin' style" Stowe would decry in her "Faults" essay: they aimed instead for "the simple language of ordinary conversation" and the unpretentious content she would extol in the *Hearth and Home* prescriptions (72).

Stowe's advice to aspiring lady authors, then, was that they follow a path she had taken by positioning their professional goals within the circulation venue most readily available for them — the periodical marketplace — even though the price of that access would be accepting gendered constraints on their writing. If Stowe seemed, in 1869, to be urging would-be women writers away from the very path she had chosen with *Uncle Tom's Cabin*— taking on the most crucial social issue of the day and then writing page after page until she had created an impassioned, novel-length work — she would probably point out that her first best-seller was not her first piece of professional writing; that she began it, in fact, planning to produce just a short series of sketches; and that she churned out the original version facing all the exigencies of periodical serialization.[20] And she could also have emphasized that, before expecting to succeed as a well-paid professional, she had herself carried out exactly the kind of patient training program she outlined for her *Hearth and Home* readers. Her original writings for the Semicolon Club and for the "little" magazines of the antebellum era perfectly fit the rules for novices she proposed in "Can I Write?": "Young writers must begin by giving away their writing while they are learning to write. In fact, some [like Stowe herself] who were [eventually] reaping large incomes from writing began by sending articles to magazines, with no other expectation of remuneration than the insertion of them" (40–41). Overall, even as she asserted the need for patient "practice in writing," for the acceptance of gendered norms, and for a commitment "to give their minds seriously to the work of forming themselves into good writers," Stowe offered her column readers some hope of success, if they followed her advice.

One caveat already present in the series' early stages, however, received more and more emphasis as Stowe's exploration of professional writing continued throughout the month of January. From the outset, if not at first too insistently, Stowe cautioned that she was basing her directions on the assumption that her would-be protégés would be capable of producing "really good writing," which she declared would "always bear its price in the market" (41). Interestingly, as the series on professional writing progressed, Stowe placed more and more stress on this issue of quality. Her later installments exhibited repeated, increasing slippage between celebrations of the special, productive, and relatively open place for women's writing in a burgeoning marketplace and her continued revisitings of an idealized model for serious writing more devoted to aesthetic, "genius"-associated values than to an impressive paycheck. Perhaps such tensions in Stowe's portrayal of authorship were inevitable, given the fluctuating state of literary professionalism in 1860s American culture. But they are fascinating, nevertheless, since they suggest she may have been struggling to define a position for herself in the already emerging pantheon of "great" American writers, and to do so in a way that would prevent her being excluded because of her gender. This goal would naturally be at odds with efforts to open up professional writing to any woman willing to work hard and play by the rules. That is, if Stowe wanted to carve out a unique place for herself as a great writer according to the developing framework of the high-culture model for American literature, she could hardly argue at the same time that the profession was fully accessible to anyone willing to learn the craft by way of steady practice.

This dilemma of mixed goals helps explain what would otherwise seem an unfathomable inconsistency in tone and content when Stowe addressed or depicted aspiring women authors in the series on professional writing. In the January 1869 articles on women's writing, she may have occasionally taken on the voice of a lecturing schoolmarm, but she still conveyed a faith in the potential worth of her readers' writings, assuming they were willing to follow the dictates she recommended at the end of her first article. In such passages, Stowe positioned herself as the novice's experienced mentor but also as her companion in suffering the restraints of their shared gender. Thus, in "How Shall I Learn to Write?" she contrasted the extended opportunities for education enjoyed by men with the constraints suffered by women, and her satirical attack on those limits situated her firmly on the women's side. Similarly, she frequently shifted throughout the series from third-person description of novice writers to the more collegial use of second person. In "Faults of Young Writers," for example, she first imagined "a writer," then slid into the friendly "you": "Now, as a general rule, a writer should take this caution: keep yourself from those authors who impress you too powerfully. If there is a general style that is running loose through all the literature of your country, and is coloring all the magazines and stories, try as much as possible to lift yourself out of it, by choosing for yourself, resolutely, quite another circle of reading" (72). In addition, Stowe occasionally addressed her anticipated reader for the series quite affectionately, as in a passage from "How May I Know That I Can Make a Writer?" when she directly called the novice writer "my dear friend" (88).

However, for every time she reached out to embrace and encourage aspiring women writers throughout her January series, Stowe also made moves to distance herself from them. One sign of this tendency was her repeated citing of male rather than female writers as positive models. For instance, in "How Shall I Learn to Write?" after inviting her female readers to take on the "subject matter which woman, and only woman, could possibly hope to present" and suggesting that, to do so, her readers need only "*get the gift of expression*" (emphasis added), Stowe went on to explain that such a "gift," though a "fine art," could be "studied" and "practised" — thereby indicating that her readers could work their way to professionalism (56). But just a few paragraphs later, when she began offering models for her readers — presumably female — to emulate, all three of those provided were male: Washington Irving, Honoré de Balzac, and Nathaniel Hawthorne, whom Stowe designated "the greatest American writer" (56).[21]

An outline of Stowe's entire "How Shall I Learn to Write?" sketch highlights her tendency to shift back and forth between empowering and constraining her women readers who wished to become writers.[22] She observes that "the best writing is done by men," then attributes American women's general authorial shortcomings to their deficient educations. She moves to proposing that some subjects for writing are the particular property of women, who could learn to depict those topics by practicing carefully; then limits her examples of "the most celebrated and most admired writing" available for imitation to male-written texts. She creates an analogy for such study of models that cast the aspiring writer as another male ("a gymnast [who] becomes graceful by constant use of his muscles"), then offers specific examples of pages in Hawthorne's *American Note-Books* that combine both masculine and feminine experiences (e.g., "digging potatoes" and working as "a little seamstress"). In short, Stowe's position on the possibility that (other) women might become successful professional writers — much less highly regarded ones — is unclear even in an essay where she purportedly seeks to help female readers achieve just such a goal.

Another relevant point should be raised about Stowe's depiction of would-be women authors and her attitude toward them. Many of her less encouraging comments exemplify the perspective of someone already vested with professional authority determining to share it with others only *after* they have earned it — a common stance in other traditionally male professions, such as medicine and the law. Admittedly, such conceptions of professionalism as having carefully regulated membership do not always exclude in the end. In other words, just because Stowe depicts writing as difficult doesn't mean in itself that she expresses doubt that other women could ever succeed at it. We should surely note, however, that her repeated emphasis on the *degree* of difficulty involved in achieving success is often cast in distancing terms. The opening paragraph of "Can I Write?" is consistent with that kind of monitoring and even with a rather exclusionary perspective toward other would-be woman professionals. Invoking an editorial "we" and moving toward a distinction between already-professional authors like herself and mere aspiring ones, Stowe notes that "[w]riting is becoming a source of income to many women in these days, and we get many letters, the general drift and purport of which is to ask the question ["Can I Write?"] we have put at the head of this article." Stowe then confides that she "often" finds these letters "touching, eloquent and interesting — of a kind which make us wish with all our hearts that the authors of them could, as they desire to do, make writing a source of profit." Even as she portrays herself as feeling sympathy for these correspondents, however, Stowe declares their submissions to be "not of a kind which would justify our giving encouragement to the writers." Why not? "In short," her editorial voice intones, "the style of a graceful, easy, feminine letter-writer is something so different from what is necessary in newspaper or magazine articles, that one can seldom form a judgment from a lady's letter as to what she could do" (40). By claiming that she finds these letters from women readers to be "touching, eloquent and interesting" but that she also feels herself unable to "form a judgment from a lady's letter as to what she could do," Stowe distances herself — the published author-editor and thus the arbiter of professional writing — from the milieu of *unprofessional* literacy, which she casts in feminine terms and for which (mere) letter writing could not suffice to make meaning for in a public, professional sphere. Though she eventually moves on within the body of the article to provide numerous helpful suggestions both global and specific, Stowe takes an initial stance toward her female correspondents that still contains them in a culture of letters distinct from her own, especially given that, even in her most supportive passages, she continues to hold back from full affirmation of their wishes or their abilities. The rhetorical devices she calls upon to maintain this distance include repeated invocation of a rather royal editorial "we" (implying her close association with the male community of already professional authors like Hawthorne and Irving); frequent use of subjunctive verb forms and qualifying connectors when describing aspiring women writers' work (e.g., "If it be so . . ."); repetition of negatives in connection with their writing (e.g., "It is not enough," "have not succeeded"); and the choice to frame three of the four titles for the series in very tentative question forms, from the point of view of the would-be writer ("Can I Write?" "How Shall I Learn to Write?" and "How May I Know That I Can Make a Writer?")

If Stowe's attitude toward her female readers-who-would-be-writers seems ambivalent through most of the series, her negative stance toward them is most pronounced in the 30 January installment, where she offers her striking final thoughts on the topic of female literary professionalism. Stowe opens "How May I Know That I Can Make a Writer?" with an attacklike description of "an unfortunate class of persons troublesome [both] to themselves and others from the fact that they suppose themselves to have a call and a talent for doing certain things, when, in fact, these are the very things for which they have neither call nor talent" (88). After asserting that spending as many hours as the hardworking Paganini trying to make music would never make a tone-deaf amateur into a true musician, she complains that such "persons forget one thing: it is not merely practice that makes perfect, but *practice resulting from a natural aptitude* in a certain direction. . . ." While her reference to the well-known male artist Paganini as an unreachable model is telling in and of itself, perhaps even more notable in this opening salvo against the inept amateur is Stowe's insistent pulling back from her earlier emphasis on hard work as the main ingredient for success as a writer. We should juxtapose this column's dismissive lead paragraphs against the comforting suggestion in "Can I Write?" that aspiring authors might start learning the craft "the way that artists begin to draw," "not . . . [by trying] the cartoon of an historical picture," but with more modest practice activities such as sketching "an eye, a hand, a foot," and then moving on to more challenging pieces (40). Similarly striking is the contrast between her insistence in the last installment that having "a restless desire to be a painter or sculptor" would not ensure success even for someone who practiced incessantly and her encouraging earlier suggestion "to our young students" that they study and then work to emulate "some special pages of Hawthorne's *American Note-Books*" ("How Shall" 56).

By the final installment of her series, Stowe appears to have shifted her position on the qualifications for serious authorship from a flexible (or unstable) view allowing for hardworking lady writers to achieve professional status, at least within some venues and for some audiences, to a more elitist stance affiliating her own work and current status with masculine-gendered standards of excellence. Interestingly, she depicted this firming up of her position not as a shift but rather as a clarification:

> We have endeavored, in our last papers, to induce persons who have a natural talent for writing to cultivate themselves by sedulous and careful practise, and have set before them the example of one of our greatest American artists, whose industry in self-cultivation was equalled only by his genius. But if Hawthorne had not had a natural genius for writing, do you suppose keeping a journal and writing down minutely the particulars of every squirrel and walnut-shrub, and bird and leaf and flower and man and woman he saw, would have enabled him to compose the *Scarlet Letter*? . . .
>
> Our remarks as to culture, then, were directed to those who have confessedly some natural gift — or what is called, for want of a better word, *genius — for writing*; and our object was to show them how this gift or *genius*, supposing it to exist, was good for very little without laborious and careful study and culture. (88, emphasis added)

Along with these rather obviously labored moves to portray herself as consistent, another intriguing aspect of Stowe's assertion of elitism was her effort to justify her exclusionary stance by referring to the correspondence that she had been receiving in response to the series' earlier installments: "Since writing these articles, we have received other letters, saying over again what we so often hear — that their authors wish to become writers for the papers, because writing for the papers is an easy way of earning money." Stowe's response to these wishes to use writing for "easy . . . money" was markedly sarcastic:

> So it is, dear lady, if Providence has given you a talent for saying things — if you have a natural gift of expression; but some of your letters do not indicate this. They do not show, so far as we can see, either that you have anything to say which you think it might be useful to have said, or that you have any particular facility in the matter of expressing yourself at all, but only that you would like to make money by writing. (88)

In this record of a dialogic encounter with her "dear lady" reader, Stowe most clearly unveils a stronger affiliation with masculine conceptions of "the success of genius" than in her earlier pieces. Here her address to this would-be "lady" author eschews the maternally mentoring tone of her earlier sketches in the series and replaces it with a deprecating lecture, dismissing both the letter writer and her goal, which Stowe *now* judges inadequate — "to make money by writing." In the final piece for this series of essays, Stowe rejects the model of open access to professional women's authorship that her earlier sketches had affirmed, however tentatively. Furthermore, by indirectly asserting her own position among those possessing "a talent for saying things" or "a natural gift," Stowe erases the social support systems that had nurtured her own writing to link her personal story of professionalization with a model of individual genius, whereby "[a] young man (or woman), unknown, without patronage or means of putting himself forward" draws upon special talents (like those of "Dickens, Thackeray, all the best writers") to excel. At another extreme, she declares, the hapless pretenders who simply wish they could be writers had better give up the goal: "There are a great many persons setting their hopes on writing as a profession to whom a friend could do no greater kindness than to convince them . . . that it would not be worth their while to try. Better plant a peach-orchard, and flood the world with rosy peaches . . . than to write second-rate poems and trashy stories" (88). Such doomed aspirants to the role of professional author, Stowe indicates, should step aside for the few who, even if they started out as a "nameless power," would eventually "burst forth," like the great Hawthorne, to full-fledged success.

Stowe returns to a more rousingly populist tone for her essay's last paragraph, predicting that "[i]f the public want to hear you, if they call for you, if what you say begins to pass from hand to hand, and heart to heart, then go at it with courage" (88). However, since this scenario is limited to those who could be true "artists," the end note of the series is still one of clear constraint and elitism, positioning Stowe the writer-editor, at this point in her own career, on the side of high culture, espousing an increasingly elitist, male-dominated vision of what professional authorship in the United States should be. Leaving a part of her own legacy behind, then, in her *Hearth and Home* series, Stowe articulates and promulgates a model of professional literature making that would exclude others trying to follow the road she had originally taken herself. Thus, whatever the aesthetic shortcomings we might identify today in this particular series of essays and in the whole body of her work for the periodical, we can see that some of her labor there helped undermine the very traditions of domestic, popular authorship that had supported her own progress into gendered professionalism.

NOTES

1 See Heininger's *At Home with a Book* discussions of reading habits and the furnishings associated with them in nineteenth-century culture. I wish to thank Diana Royce, then librarian at the Stowe/Day Library in Hartford, CT, for suggesting that I review Stowe's writing on authorship in *Hearth and Home* and for finding copies of the periodical for me. Support for my research was provided by the regents of the University System of Georgia, with Stowe's essays being recovered in part for a team-taught course on American women's work during the nineteenth century.

2 Fern (1811–87), whose real name was Sara Payson Willis Eldredge Farrington Parton, is today remembered for her novel *Ruth Hall* (1855) but was best known in her day as a vibrant journalist. She was the first woman in America to write a signed column in a newspaper. Her witty and engaging work for Robert Bonner's *New York Ledger* (which ran from 1856 to 1872) helped increase the newspaper's circulation from 100,000 to 400,000 by 1860.

3 Okker characterizes this stance as one of "relative informality and an assumed equal and personal relationship between editor and readers," making use of such friendly addresses as "old friends" for readers. Along those lines, in the "How to Treat Babies" sketch cited earlier, Stowe began by declaring that a "friend has sent us an article on a subject suggested by us" (6 Feb. 1869: 104). Similarly, "What Shall the Girls Read?" opens by referencing a letter from "a young friend in the Female Seminary at Steubenville" and then moves to a response, with the salutation "My Dear Rose" (19 June 1869: 408).

4 See Alice Walker's moving essay, "In Search of Our Mothers' Gardens."

5 Certainly Stowe was not an extreme radical. She identified herself as nonaboli-

tionist while living in Cincinnati. Even *Uncle Tom's Cabin* (despite its initial publication site in the *National Era*) drew as carefully on the conservative rhetoric of republican motherhood as it did on the more liberal stance of white women's abolitionist writing. See my "Gendering the History of the Antislavery Narrative." See also Hedrick's "Woman's Rights" chapter, where she says that, despite being drawn to the women's movement, Stowe could not imagine her name "on the masthead of a journal called the *Revolution*" (361).

6 Of course, many male canonical writers of the nineteenth century produced work judged, in our own time, as uneven or even pedestrian. Melville's *Pierre*, Hawthorne's *Marble Faun*, as well as several of Twain's works, have incurred critical attack at times.

7 Examining Stowe's series on writing thus seems quite consistent with Susan Albertine's recent observations in the introduction to *A Living in Words*. Albertine cautions against setting "a fixed reading of women's participation in print culture," and stresses that "there is no one female response to the print business, any more than there is a set patriarchal reaction to women who venture into traditionally male preserves" (xvi).

8 One helpful context for interpreting Stowe's work for this and other periodicals, as well as her advice to aspiring authors, is offered by Christopher P. Wilson's chapter "'Magazining' for the Masses," where he points out that "[s]ince midcentury, the magazine had occupied a middle landscape between the frenetic world of newspaper work and the status of book writing," and that magazines had "an intermediary position" in publishing, often providing "a vocational springboard" (41). See also Wilson's discussions of "the commercial motive" driving work by editors and writers for magazines (46 ff.).

9 See Warren's treatment of the productive, mutually respectful relationship between Bonner and Fern. Warren includes details about Bonner's announcing in print that he was paying Fern the until-then unheard-of sum of one hundred dollars per column and his later bragging in another issue of the *Ledger* that his investment had already been paid back "three times over" due to increased circulation (56).

10 See Streitmatter's essay on Josephine St. Pierre Ruffin in *A Living in Words*. As Streitmatter points out, "Ruffin devoted most of her energies to the business side of publishing," including trying out a number of strategies for increasing circulation of her newspaper, the *Woman's Era*. "She did not intend to make a financial profit from her newspaper, but she expected it to pay for itself" (53, 54–58).

11 See Hedrick, 361. John R. Adams described Stowe's duties at *Hearth and Home* as "slighter than her title of associate editor suggested," that is, "limited to supplying a weekly column, with [coeditor] Mitchell shouldering the main labors" (80).

Both Hedrick and Okker, however, depict Stowe as more actively involved in the range of editorial duties, and whether or not she served as prime shaper of the periodical's overall content, her writing *about* professional writing in *Hearth and Home* highlights women's complex position in the literary marketplace at that historical moment.

12 See "What Shall Girls Read?" and "Reading for Girls, Again." An example of Stowe's negative attitude toward young ladies' formal education appeared in "How Shall I Learn to Write?" (16 Jan. 1869), where she observed: "The education of the woman stops short at the point where the boy's education really begins. At the age that the boy enters college for an arduous and mature course, the girl comes home and addresses herself to going into company; and the five or six years following, that her brother spends in severe intellectual drill, she fritters away in what is called society" (1). This complaint was echoed in the opening to "What Shall Girls Read?" where Stowe printed a letter from a "Rose P.," who wondered about what she and her classmates could do for a "course of reading for girls after they leave school" (1). After attacking the limited learning available to seminary graduates at that time, Stowe outlined such a course.

13 Stowe's position on the need for improving women's education was consistent with her sister Catharine's and with Sarah Josepha Hale's, as expressed in the *Ladies' Magazine* and, later, *Godey's Lady's Book*. Hale initiated her campaign for improved female education very early on and sustained it throughout her long editorship. A few examples from the many pro-education pieces early in her tenure include "Female Education," "How Ought Woman to Be Educated," and the "Female Seminaries" series appearing in 1833.

14 This would not be the first time Stowe was accused of unfeminine writing, of course. Some of the most vitriolic critiques of *Uncle Tom's Cabin* attacked her on this very point. Stowe's awareness that revealing details of Lord Byron's illicit relations could well produce a similar complaint against her may help explain why she wanted to devote focused time to writing her defense of his wife (see Hedrick, 356–57).

15 In 1892, at a reunion of the Seminary, Brace was remembered in a major address. (Both Catharine and Harriet had worked there in the 1820s, and John Brace had later served as principal in the early 1830s). The speaker praising Brace's contributions to female pedagogy was Isabella Beecher Hooker, another of Harriet's sisters, and the majority of Hooker's talk was actually a reading of Stowe's words about her former teacher, as written for the familially composed biography of Lyman Beecher years earlier. References to pages from this talk are cited within the body of the essay as "Hartford." Quotations from Hooker's speech about Brace represent *her* quoting of Stowe.

16 Stowe's support of gendered topics and locations for writing, then, appears here to be quite different from one Joyce Warren has recently identified with Sara Parton (Fanny Fern). Warren argues that Fern "preferred a paper that was intended for both sexes, she said, because it put her 'on the same level as the men in the house.' *The Ledger* was such a paper" (59), with Fern enjoying an unusual free rein since her male editor never altered her writing (64).

17 See, in this regard, Hedrick's insightful discussion of "The *Atlantic* and the Ship of State" in her biography of Stowe, especially her description of the magazine's perceived mission (288), her explanation that "women were not full-fledged members of the *Atlantic* club" (289), and her treatment of the infamous dinner purportedly arranged "for" Stowe but actually carried out in ways that reinforced the increasingly masculinized slant of both the periodical and its view of literature's place in national culture (290–91).

18 Stowe erases (or at least obscures) social class differences here, just as she does racial ones elsewhere in her writing for *Hearth and Home*. In one of her pieces on girls' proper reading choices, for instance, she observes:

> [I]f a girl, when she leaves school, will be resolute and determined, especially for the first few weeks, she may form such a habit of regular reading as will be of the greatest possible use to her. . . . I recommend that you take some one particular country; and since we are of Anglo Saxon origin, it had better be England. But as we are also partly French in our origin, and as English history for a great many hundred years consists almost entirely in the quarrels between the French and the English, you will do well to take the French history along with it. ("What Shall the Girls Read," 408)

In this case, Stowe imagined all young ladies having the seminary experience her purported correspondent "Rose" did, as well as the chances for continued home study not as available to working class girls. Similarly, her references to the "Anglo Saxon" and "French" background that "we" share with her reflect not only a view of who her audience is — white European-American females — but also her tendency to equate that audience with all (who really matter) in womankind.

19 The *May Flower* anthology was originally published in 1842 by *Harper's*. According to the introduction written for an 1896 reissuing of some of its contents in *Stories, Sketches and Studies*, Stowe's early magazine writing marks her as already "an active litterateur" by the early 1840s but one for whom financial rewards were still "meagre" (vii). Thus, the 1842 *May Flower* anthology had only "a modest reception, and a short life" until her blockbuster novel prompted an 1855 republication by Phillips and Sampson (vii).

20 See Hedrick's comment that Stowe originally predicted to editor Gamaliel Bailey

that her submission would "run 'through three or fours numbers,'" and would take the form of "a series of sketches" (208).

21 See Brodhead, chapter 3, "Manufacturing You into a Personage." Stowe's discussions of Hawthorne in her series on authorship provide one example of what Brodhead describes as "writers' cultural identities [being] created and sustained by an interlocking network of literary agencies in the nineteenth century, agencies that were themselves being fashioned at the same time as those authors' writings" (58).

22 The combination of her restraining and authorizing advice echoes what Nicole Hoffman has described as Hale's stance toward women readers. Hoffman observes: "Paradoxically, the ideas her publications promulgated were both constraining and enabling to that readership" (51).

PARENTAL GUIDANCE:
DISCIPLINARY INTIMACY &
THE RISE OF WOMEN'S
REGIONALISM

Women writers made a place for themselves in antebellum periodicals by conforming: they both complied with the judgments of editors and publishers and appealed to the tastes and interests of readers. In the case of writers whom we now label "regionalists,"[1] however, this deference was tempered by a desire to school their audience of predominantly urban easterners to appreciate the rural, regional way of life. Therefore, antebellum regional sketches were shaped by the seemingly conflicting needs of submission to the prescriptions and preferences of editors and publishers and of assertion of authority in order to put readers into place and persuade them to submit to the simple lessons to be found there. These regional writers shared the periodical editors' belief in the corrective discipline of reading rightly, avoiding the evil influences of superficial fiction, and connecting with a cleansing, rustic reality. In response, they created a new genre based on the complex interaction of purpose and publication. Three of the regionalist authors, Alice Cary, Harriet Beecher Stowe, and Rose Terry Cooke, illustrate the negotiation of the competing demands of editorial submission and authorial control: dutiful compliance and parental guidance.

Women regionalists established a relationship with their readers that mirrored in many ways their editors' relationship with writers. As the publishers of the *National Magazine* announced in their first issue (1852), writing for periodicals had "become the chief power of the pen" in antebellum America. And access to this power was granted to writers who submitted to an editorial rule that, as Richard Brodhead puts it, was similar to the "disciplinary intimacy" exerted by middle-class Victorian parents as a means of control through precept and example rather than intimidation. In the familial framework of periodical publishing, editors and publishers cast themselves as custodians of the public good, parental figures who aimed to instruct and nurture not only their readers but also the writers who submitted manuscripts for their consideration. But regional writers exerted a similar shaping influence through narrative intimacy with their readers. As women found a congenial "home" in periodicals such as *Godey's Lady's Book*, the *National Magazine*, and the *Atlantic Monthly*, they drew on the personal, domestic, informative qualities of the periodicals themselves to help create an appropriate relationship with readers, a kind of parental role that combined intimacy and instruction. Just as editors offered access to the power of the pen while they exerted control over the way writers deployed it, regional writers offered readers apparent access to a locale even as they powerfully put readers in place. In a market where editors and publishers looked for literature "such as shall combine the lighter graces of imagination with solid instruction" ("Editorial Notes" 96), women regional writers used the apparently airy form of the literary sketch to instruct readers about rural life.

Editorial exhortations created a receptive climate for a popular periodical literature that focused on sturdy inhabitants of villages and farms and located "instruction" in rural simplicity. An 1849 editorial in the *Ladies' Repository* ("A Monthly Periodical Devoted to Literature and Religion") cautions against the tendency of readers to "seize upon a superficial work, written in a popular style, in preference to one that is solid and plain" because such works appeal to an appetite for "undue excitement" (Edwards 115). In an 1852 editorial the publishers of the *National Magazine* claimed a disciplinary "duty of the conductors of periodical publications" to keep control of "the already superabundant fugitive literature of the times" because "it is liable to be superficial, and needs the corrective influence of more substantial reading" ("Periodical Literature" 1). They saw their "duty" as setting standards for both readers and writers to value "literary excellence" not as "a product merely of the intellect, but of the heart of man; it has even more to do with his sensibilities than with his speculations" (2).

In her preface to the first published collection of her sketches, *Clovernook Papers* (1852), Cary presented her regional sketches as just such a literature of "sensibility," aimed at readers whom she pictured as "inhabitants of cities where . . . there is surely little of sympathy for the poor and humble" and intended to help readers recognize in rural people a "capacity for those finer feelings which are too often deemed the blossoms of a high and fashionable culture" (*Clovernook* 8). Like most other regionalists, Cary had a personal connection to her subject, having spent her childhood in the kind of Ohio farm community she usually wrote about. Her early poetry and sketches appeared frequently in the Cincinnati *Ladies' Repository*, where an editor once commended her rural upbringing and, therefore, her natural sympathies.

Cary's "Old Christopher," which appeared in the *National Magazine* in 1855, offers a childhood memory of a misunderstood community character who confides his sad history to a sober and sympathetic narrator. Yet while it touches on the tragic circumstances of lost love and ungrateful offspring who wounded and isolated the old man, the story is not a romantic tale of his dramatic past — the melodrama occurs offstage — nor a conventional story of virtue rewarded but a kind of parable about the importance of human connection. It focuses on the narrator's response to her encounter, "for the wrongs he suffered from his children and the world first kindled my pity, then grew to interest, and interest to faith and trust. And who is so blind in mind and heart that they are unconscious of trust reposed in them — of love entertained for them?" (171). Here the narrator presents a pattern for reading regional sketches: an initial sympathy with human suffering should lead to connection and then understanding. This plan of instruction informs much of Cary's work and gives it a compassionate, sentimental dimension while meshing neatly with the publishers' interest in schooling "sensibilities."

The instructional and uplifting mission of periodical literature — and the superior ability of women writers to carry it out — was a perennial theme of the influential editor Sarah Josepha Hale. In her "Editors' Table" columns for *Godey's Lady's Book*, the preeminent women's periodical of its day, Hale voiced a Victorian belief in the power of periodical fiction as a moral force and her own conviction that women were the natural purveyors of that power. In her column of February 1857, for example, Hale asserts that "a good woman naturally tends to moral utility more than a good man. This is one of the distinguishing traits of the feminine mind. The early guidance and moral training of children devolve on the mother; her office is to mould the heart. Therefore women have an instructive readiness to paint a moral 'when they adorn a tale.'"

But as recent studies by Patricia Okker, James Machor, Nina Baym, and Susan Coultrap-McQuin have shown, getting published also meant submitting to a male-dominated editorial culture. Editors privileged a controlled narrative voice and a proper hierarchical relation to readers, maintaining what the *National Magazine's* publishers called "a literature vigorous, strenuous, manly" ("Periodical Literature" 3). In order to translate such standards for themselves, women writers needed an "ability to represent reality and to please" at the same time (Okker, *Our* 160). Women regionalists developed a literature that was persuasive yet pleasing by using their personal connection to a place to establish authority. Cary argues in her preface to the first collection of Clovernook sketches that "[t]he masters of literature who at any time have attempted the exhibition of rural life, have with few exceptions, known scarcely anything of it from participation, and however brilliant may have been their pictures, therefore, they have seldom been true" (*Clovernook* 8). Cary implies that her collection of sketches from experience surpasses the alien artistry of the "masters" of the literary mainstream who lack real experience of rural culture. But while poverty could be genteel, professional writing for money was not. Cary also needed to conform to the editorial ideology of a women's sphere separate from the masculine world of commerce and competition, so in her preface she warns that she has "no invention and I am altogether too poor an artist to dream of any success which may not be won by the simplest fidelity" (8). Shrewdly, Cary makes "fidelity" a feature that distinguishes her art from that of the "masters" and deploys a public and editorial taste that identified truthfulness as a superior quality of fiction and made the absence of artistry denote the presence of sincerity.

Claiming for her Clovernook sketches a "natural and probable air which should induce their reception as honest relations" (8), Cary invokes the prevailing "nineteenth-century rhetorical ethos," as described by historian Janet Gabler-Hover, in which good rhetoric was "culturally codified to be synonymous with trustful relations and with truth" (Gabler-Hover 6). Her "fidelity" fit well with an editorial view that railed against the public taste for romance fiction, stirred by Sir Walter Scott and other such storytellers whose tales were serialized on both sides of the Atlantic, with its unrealistic "hair-breadth escapes, sudden reverses of fortune, heart-rending separations, and miraculous meetings" (Edwards 115). The regional writer's focus on rural reality stood in sharp contrast to novels that seemed to "have flung a charm about the cottage, and a rapture into the humbler walks of life, which never was realized by the poor man, toiling for the support of his family" (116).

The narrator of Stowe's *Pearl of Orr's Island* echoes the editorial sentiment that "[i]t is novels that give false views of life" (309), and Stowe fought this falseness during the periodical publication of the novel, published serially in the *New York Independent* in 1861. Her narrator wryly remarks in the first installment, "I cannot think of anything more unlikely and uninteresting to make a story of" than the old sea captain Zephaniah Pennel and his wife Mary, "a pair of worthy, God-fearing people, walking in all the commandments and ordinances of the Lord blameless; but that is no great recommendation to a world gaping for sensation and calling for something stimulating"(9). Periodical pieces by Cary, by Stowe, and by Cooke all show writers working in opposition to the romanticization of region represented by Cooper's *Leatherstocking Tales* and its many imitations, with their unrealistically "glowing description of humble life," as the 1849 editorial in the *Ladies' Repository* complained (Edwards 116).

Cary begins her story "About My Visit to Uncle William's," published in the *Ladies' Repository* in 1853, with the claim that "the story is less interesting than a simple narration of facts. They are no wonderful experiences that I am going to relate; nevertheless, fragments of actual biography as they are, they seem to me better than fiction" (400). Of course, this "simple narration of facts" is itself a fiction that constructs the narrative as other than fictitious. But Cary has aptly adapted her creation to the view that facts are "better than fiction." Many antebellum regional writers struggled with the dual demands of truth and fiction — and with the sometimes contradictory expectations of the editors and publishers they wrote for. While writing truthfully for and about "common folk" could be elevating both for readers and for magazine circulation, editors also looked for that edifying instruction they associated with "women's work."

During her long career as an editor, first of the *Ladies' Magazine* (1828–36) and then of *Godey's Lady's Book* (1837–77), Hale took on the role of motherly moral guardian. She wrote in her "Editors' Table" column of April 1850, "[E]verybody reads novels; but it is reserved for the magazines and reviews to sift these crude works, select those appropriate for their own readers, and . . . to furnish a family book superior to any other popular work." If periodicals were like family albums, the authors who contributed to those albums not only submitted to the benevolent rule of parental editors but also joined in the general effort to both engage and instruct their "family" of readers. Writing about region, women like Cary established an intimate voice and a realistic way to share their conviction that commonplace people and events were worthy subjects, and they were rewarded by publishers and editors as truthful and dutiful daughters.

Rose Terry Cooke and other women regionalists portrayed the simple life in terms that their sister readers would understand. Unlike male regional humorists such as William Gilmore Simms, Cooke confines the rural otherness of her characters to traces of country colloquialism in dialogue and presents her regional pictures from a female point of view.[2] In "Ann Potter's Lesson" (*Atlantic* 1858), for example, a female first-person narrator explains, "Father died when we were both small, and didn't leave us much means beside the farm. . . . It's hard work enough for a man to get clothes and victuals off a farm in West Connecticut; it's up-hill work always; . . . but a woman ain't of no use, except to tell folks what to do" (419). Cooke's narrator goes on to describe her mother's struggle to survive, her effort "to raise potatoes and beans and onions enough to last us the year round, and to take in sewin' so's to get what few groceries we was goin' to want" (419), in a rustic but respectable dialect. Her story avoids the rapturous view of rural life while walking primly on the path of middle-class morality, containing its interest in the way subjects sound within the confines and conventions of "civilized" society. And in the end, a tornado teaches Ann Potter her "lesson" as Cooke's tale conveys it to her readers: "I'd had a good home, and a kind husband, and all I could ask; but I hadn't had a contented mind; I'd quarreled with Providence, 'cause I hadn't got everything — and now I hadn't got nothing" (427). Moving from an unflinching picture of rural poverty, Cooke's story comes around to counsel acceptance of the ordinary, the virtue of contentment within the confines of home.

The cultural context into which these women inscribed their regional sketches in the 1840s and 1850s was already alive with women writers, many of whom had, as Jane Tompkins says, "designs upon their audiences, in the sense of wanting to make people think and act in a particular way" (*Sensational Designs* xi). The regional writer, however, constructed a narrator who seems to act *with* rather than *on* her audience. The narrator of Stowe's *Orr's Island*, for example, breaks into the narrative at several points, positioning readers at her elbow by asserting, "[G]ood reader, you and I, following invisibly on tiptoe, will make our observations" (240). While cozy relationships between narrators and readers were common in Victorian fiction, the regional narrator assumes a particular, familial intimacy in order to instruct readers by pulling them into place with her.

Stowe's "The Canal Boat," published in an 1841 issue of *Godey's*, illustrates the way in which early regional sketches, addressing readers as intimates, instructed by sharing an experience. Stowe uses a language of bodily *presence*, which leads readers along firmly to the desired conclusion:

Did you ever try it, reader? If not, take an imaginary trip with us, just for experiment. "There's the boat!" exclaims a passenger in the omnibus, as we are rolling down from the Pittsburgh Mansion House to the canal. . . . "What! That little thing?" exclaims an inexperienced traveler; "dear me! We cant half of us get into it!" . . . "You'll see," say the initiated; and, as soon as you get out, you *do* see, and hear too, what seems like a general breaking loose from the Tower of Babel, amid a perfect hailstorm of trunks, boxes, valises, carpet-bags, and every describable and indescribable form of what a Westerner calls "plunder." (203)

Stowe puts readers into place with the disarming "you" — controlling her reader by assigning her a role as "imaginary" companion and then predicting that "as soon as you get out, you *do* see." Moreover, her direct address puts the reading "you" *in place* of a narrating "I." Acting as authoritative guide, she organizes her readers' response to a region and imposes her own vision much as the editors and publishers of periodicals paternally pointed their readers and contributors in the "right" direction. The regional narrator imposes her construction of accepted truth on her reader by asserting what "we" do and defining what "you" do, exerting her parental presence even while allowing a reading "you" to experience a place as if firsthand.

The narrator of Cooke's "Miss Lucinda" (*Atlantic* 1861) wryly scolds her audience into sympathy with an aging Miss Lucinda in love: "Don't laugh at her, Miss Tender-eyes. You will feel just so yourself some day, when Alexander Augustus says, 'Will you be mine, loveliest of your sex?' Only you won't feel it half so strongly, for you are young, and love is nature to youth; but it is a heavenly surprise to age" (158). The implied audience for Cooke's lecture here is not a general congregation but the impressionable and inexperienced audience that *Godey's* Hale addressed in her column of March 1850: Hale urged "on our young lady readers the importance of entering on some grave and profitable studies . . . at the beginning of this long, cold month." Engravings in the periodicals where regional fiction was often published depict this genteel audience of female readers gathered together in familial intimacy, an interpretive community of like-minded, well-educated, white, middle-class sisters. This is an audience receptive to both intimacy and instruction, the reader as perpetual "Miss Tender-eyes." The regional writers sought to draw readers into a region and, with strategies of sentimentality, make them feel "at home." They invited readers toward sympathy, simulating the influence of place and presence on readers' sensibilities.

Another of Cooke's *Atlantic* pieces, "Dely's Cow" (1865), locates readers "on the Derby turnpike, just before you enter Hanerford," and adds, "[E]verybody that ever travelled that road will remember Joseph German's bakery." Cooke ingeniously constructs the reader as a companion who already knows the locale, situating us as neighbors who "will remember" the "red brick house, with dusty windows toward the street, and just inside the door a little shop, where Mr. German retailed the scalloped cookies, fluted gingerbread, long loaves of bread, and scantily-filled pies in which he dealt, . . . where in summer you caught glimpses of flour barrels all a-row, and men who might have come out of those barrels, so strewed with flour were all their clothes . . ."(665). Cooke's confident, confiding tone and direct address suggest a shared sense of place. Her inclusive "everybody" gathers readers in a shared memory, a tale-telling about a familiar landscape ("just before you enter Hanerford"), a place readers already know. Pretending "you" the reader is present, Cooke seems to empower readers to become part of the place, yet she controls the terms by which the reader participates: to share the experience, readers must participate in "remembering" a place where they have never been, yet "where in summer you caught glimpses of flour barrels."

This narrative guidance, with its combination of authority and intimacy, had implications for the form as well as the content of these periodical pieces. As they guided readers with an intimate authority to observe the rhythms of ordinary lives, these writers created companionable but un-eventful reading. Judith Fetterley describes Cary's writing as "fiction, moving slowly from detail to detail and freed from the forward driving impulse of anything the world might recognize as plot, [that] recreates for her readers the context within which the events she records have gained their significance" ("Entitled" 105). It is only a reader who has been intimately apostrophized by the editorially omniscient voice of the author who can appreciate the emotional power of so slight a sketch.

In her August 1861 *Atlantic* story, "Miss Lucinda," Cooke comments on the tension between the popular appetite for romance and adventure stories and her barely plotted regional sketches, offering a mock apology "for a story that is nowise tragic, nor fitted to the fashion of these times" and gives "no sentimental history of fashion and wealth; but only a little story about a woman who could not be a heroine" (141). Cooke's "little story" has little plot: a middle-aged woman, who "quietly settled in her little house, [where] her garden and her pets gave her such full occupation that she sometimes blamed herself for not feeling more lonely and unhappy" (144), falls in love with a man who comes to help her with her runaway pig. The charm and humor of the tale — and a feeling for the title character — emerge from Cooke's carefully chronicled history of her heroine's circumstances and her detailed descriptions of Miss Lucinda Manner's world, such as this tour of her china cupboard:

A half-gone set of egg-shell china stood in the parlor-closet, — cups and teapot rimmed with brown and gold in a square pattern, and a shield without blazon on the side; the quaint tea-caddy with its stopper stood over against the pursy little cream-pot; and the three-legged sugar-bowl held amid its lumps of sparkling sugar the oddest sugar-tongs, also a family relic; beside this, six small spoons, three large ones, and a little silver porringer comprised all the plate belonging to Miss Manners, so that no fear of burglars haunted her, and, but for her pets, she would have led a life of profound and monotonous tranquillity. (144)

The realist's eye for detail invests Cooke's humorous picture of prim Miss Lucinda with sympathy and humanity. Relying on her reader's own experience of domestic life, she renders the reality of a circumscribed life and modest social status through the kind of everyday objects with which her audience is familiar.

This detailing of the context of middle-class material culture creates a definitive texture in women's regional sketches that sets them apart from stories set in the vague, stereotypical "vine-clad cottage, embosomed among wide-spreading oaks; and surrounded by romantic scenery" (Edwards 116) with their dramatic but improbable plots. After 1840 the literary marketplace was, as Brodhead pictures it, centered around the middle-class home. Appropriating the intricate intimacy of domestic sketches, women regionalists created character-driven vignettes that fit comfortably into both the agenda of popular periodicals and the living rooms of their readers. As Isabelle Lehuu has pointed out, a women's magazine such as "*Godey*'s pictured a world of objects to be possessed and appropriated, and in so doing defined itself as another object in middle-class interiors" (79). In the context of middle-class materiality created by engravings showing details of dress and articles about homemaking, a space was open for fiction of the tangible that paid attention to the significance of objects.

Like the stories that accompany them, articles and engravings in periodicals also invoked the ideal of the pastoral landscape in connection to the regional and rural. Pastoral landscapes, with their vision of the harmonious blend of humans and nature, offered an attractive sense of order and tranquillity to a mid-century culture that was struggling with change and separation, not only of North and South but also between male and female, city and country, mainstream and backwater. Regionalism reflects the readers' and writers' fascination with difference, one rural area's difference from other regions and its difference from the dominant urban culture. But while male local color writers, from Augustus Baldwin Longstreet to Mark Twain and Bret Harte, focus on those differences — the humorous contrast between rural folk and the normative northern urban culture — the women regional writers draw attention to the familiar patterns of everyday life and ordinary human emotions, the internal dimension to region that reflected a sense of American place.

The regionalists' sometimes stark scenes of hardscrabble farm life even won their fiction a place in such national publications as the *Atlantic*, which sought to draw readers away from the fantastic romance tales of faraway places toward the solid ground of their American home. Regional writing gained popularity in the second quarter of the century as interest in a national literature reached an almost feverish intensity.[3] The publishers of the *National Magazine*, for example, saw the development of a literature that reflected "the national characteristics of common sense, practical aims and direct utility," claimed "we have the germ of a vigorous and noble literature in the soil," and therefore prescribed "the first condition of a national literature is, that it be a type of the national character, and national character depends largely upon the physical circumstances of a people" ("Periodical Literature" 3). The physical circumstances of people living on the land, the defining subject of women's regional writing, provided readers with a tantalizing and reassuring glimpse of "the national character" as inherent in the simple, rural farmer. An 1858 issue of the *Atlantic* pronounced, "Partial culture runs to the ornate; extreme culture to simplicity" ("Suggestions" 818).

Cooke's "Sally Parson's Duty," published in the *Atlantic*'s first issue in 1857, recalls readers to simple virtues represented by rural New England farmers. Set in Revolutionary times, the simple story concerns a farmer's daughter who has "such a sunny, healthy, common-sense character, one is almost afraid to tell of it, it is so out of date now" (24). Sally's duty, like that of Cooke herself, is to instruct a reluctant young man to join the fight against the British "tyrints" and do his own patriotic duty. With slavery an issue of central concern in the *Atlantic*, and angry divisions apparent in her society, Cooke makes New England characters who "did things because they were right and wrong . . . [because] they were good and pure" (32) a type for readers to emulate.

These regional writers found a form — the literary sketch — and an intimate yet authoritative style that worked to insinuate their narrators into the community of periodical readers sharing stories in the privacy of their homes. As Baym demonstrates in her study of antebellum American reviewers, an author's place was to serve the story and the readers, not to draw attention to herself; and a nineteenth-century reader expected the voice of fiction to sound like her own and to blend unostentatiously with the other voices of her world. There was a widely held view that "by effacing himself in the service of his art, the writer in fact achieves the mastery that he does not attain when he deliberately displays himself" (Baym, *Novels* 133). Periodicals were an important site of the struggle of women writers between display and deference, between assertion of authorial presence and submission to editorial expectations.

Cary, Stowe, Cooke, and other women writers saw their submissions accepted by editors who expected regional sketches to furnish inspiration for a renewal of the national spirit. With a paradoxical kind of submission that maintains control, they developed an intimate relationship with readers that mirrored the parental guidance afforded writers by periodical editors. At the same time, they conformed to the magazines' own efforts to attract readers and encourage consumers, to reflect readers' tastes and influence their behavior. Adapting such disciplinary intimacy to their rhetorical purpose, women regional writers could empower readers with an intimate understanding of a region and its residents. While they conformed to the dictates of editors and the interests of their audience, their distinctive expository prose invites and instructs readers willing to submit themselves to the lessons of reading region.

NOTES

I wish to thank my colleagues at American University for their perceptive comments on successive versions of this article, which started life as a presentation at the 1996 Nineteenth-Century American Women Writers Conference in Hartford, Connecticut.

1   I will be assuming a distinction here between women's regional writing and the "local color" movement with which they are sometimes identified. It is important to note that antebellum women regionalists initiated a tradition quite different from that of male regional humorists who were working at the same time. Neither were these women's periodical pieces solely sentimental fiction, village sketches, travel guides, or memoirs but a blend of techniques taken from popular genres and put to the service of a particular vision.

2   For example, in collections of comic sketches published in 1845 by Simms (*The Wigwam and the Cabin*), William T. Porter (*The Big Bear of Arkansas*), and Johnson Jones Hooper (*Some Adventures of Captain Simon Suggs*), male writers pictured rural people in terms of dialect and difference, emphasizing the humorous contrast between town and country reality, middle-class visitors and lower-class

"locals." Starting in the 1830s with Albert Pike's *Prose Sketches and Poems, Written in the Western Country* (1834) and Augustus Baldwin Longstreet's *Georgia Scenes* (1835), this so-called "local color" writing showed a folksy, funny, sometimes nostalgic, and always colloquial regional world.

3   This nationalistic element in regional writing has sparked thoughtful discussions from Judith Fetterley, Marjorie Pryse, Sandra Zagarell, and others. See, for instance, Fetterley's "'Not in the Least American': Nineteenth-Century Literary Regionalism" in *College English* 56 (1994): 877–95.

Bonnie James Shaker

ʻKATE CHOPIN &
THE PERIODICAL:
REVISITING THE
RE-VISION

Kate Chopin is best known to us today as the daring author of *The Awakening*, that scandalous novel of 1899 that candidly represented a white, bourgeois woman's desire for autonomy and sexual fulfillment outside the sanctified bonds of Victorian marriage. The importance of *The Awakening* as a subversive feminist text has come to define Chopin's place within the American literary canon; and the many narrative accounts of this single, shocking novel's far-reaching effect — the furor it caused within polite society and among genteel editors, its banning from the St. Louis Public and Mercantile Libraries, Chopin's expulsion from the St. Louis Artist's Guild and the Wednesday Club, and her resultant despair that curtailed any further literary production — all have justified Chopin's inclusion in the canon.

These early narrative accounts of *The Awakening's* literary importance, its critical reception, and its impact on Chopin's life have served the author well in the effort to afford her recognition and respect within the academy. Nearly all of them, however, have been revised. More recent scholarship reveals that Chopin was just as often exculpated by contemporaneous reviewers for *The Awakening's* bold themes as she was excoriated. Emily Toth has convincingly demonstrated that *The Awakening* was never a banned book, nor was Chopin ever ostracized from her hometown's Artist's Guild or Wednesday Club, and Heather Kirk Thomas has cogently argued that when Chopin's literary production did begin to decline, she was suffering from ill physical health, not mental depression.[1]

Thus, the mythologies emerging from the revisionist effort in the latter half of the twentieth century to include Chopin as a canonical writer are themselves undergoing scrutiny, especially as the critical project in literary studies inches away from canon formation and moves toward considering writers in their historically specific contexts. In light of this theoretical shift,

Chopin is an interesting subject not only for a re-visioning of gender issues, but for a re-evaluation of formerly held notions of her relation to periodical publication. This relationship requires scrutiny in terms of her position as a contributor and as a wage earner. In just this last decade, scholars such as Helen Taylor, Michele Birnbaum, and Sandra Gunning have taken issue with Chopin's reputation as a feminist writer whose unconventional stance on gender extends to her racial politics. Their position — that while Chopin may have been nonconformist on issues of gender, she maintained a thoroughly orthodox position on race — is best articulated by Gunning when she writes that Chopin's "value is precisely the troublesomeness of her antipatriarchal stance that emerges, paradoxically, through her embrace of white privilege."[2]

Invaluable as Birnbaum, Taylor, and Gunning's scholarship have been to a reading of Chopin's racial politics, Gunning's statement is itself supposititious in that it suggests that an "antipatriarchal stance" is characteristic of Chopin's writing and that her conservative racial articulations necessarily emerge through her feminism. Chopin's late twentieth-century canonical status as a feminist rebel and reformer, however, conflicts with the fact that one of the most supportive publishers throughout Chopin's lifetime was the *Youth's Companion*, a thoroughly orthodox publication that had much in common with such other of the Gilded Age's conservative genteel periodicals as the *Atlantic, Harper's,* or the *Century*. Not only are Chopin's stories that embrace orthodox femininity concentrated in number in the *Companion*, but her reinscription of such traditional female roles in fact advances ideas of white supremacy.[3]

One of the most important aspects of Chopin's writing to be obscured by late twentieth-century accounts of her life and work is that Chopin was primarily known to and valued by her contemporary reading audience as an author of short fiction. Marketing her work first through periodicals and then in collected volumes of short fiction, Chopin gained her national reputation as a short story writer and was remembered in critical histories for some thirty years after her death for her accomplishments in the genre.[4]

Chopin was a short story writer by both necessity and choice. She wrote in a day when, as her predecessor Margaret Fuller observed, periodicals were the "only efficient instrument," not only through which readers could receive materials but also through which authors could disseminate it. As a medium, the periodical was particularly hospitable to women, in part because the short story form that the periodical featured was becoming feminized as a literary genre. Attitudes that Susan Koppelman expresses about the short story today, that it suffers from "a loss of status, currently being viewed by many in the literary world as an apprenticeship genre, preparation for fiction writers on their way to tackling the greater task of writing novels" (799), were under construction at the very moment Chopin was writing. Chopin's contemporary, William Dean Howells, one of the period's most influential magazine editors and a main proponent of realism, was, in fact, actively feminizing short story writing as he worked concomitantly to masculinize novel writing.[5] His construction of the short story as a gendered genre coincided with "the growth of the magazine industry['s] . . . inexhaustible market for stories oriented toward specific audiences" (Koppelman 802). Opportunities for women's writing increased as venues for gendered writing — ladies' fashion magazines, family papers, and juvenile periodicals — emerged. Such market conditions lead Koppelman to conclude that "the fact that so many [women writers] settled on the short story as the literary form in which to develop their greatest skills had as much to do with the popularity of the genre and their consequent greater financial opportunities as it did with creative inclination" (799).

In the 1890s, when Chopin was writing and marketing her fiction, the term "woman writer" was, for all intents and purposes, an oxymoron. Susan Coultrap-McQuin, Anne Goodwyn Jones, Any Kaplan, Mary Kelly, and Mary Ryan are just some of the scholars whose pioneering efforts have detailed how mid-to-late nineteenth-century ideals of white bourgeois femininity, such as privacy, domesticity, reproductivity, docility, dependence, and self-effacement, conflict necessarily with the public, commercial, productive, active, independent, and self-promotive demands of writing and publishing fiction.[6]

Periodical writing, however, conveniently provided female authors with a façade behind which to camouflage any concerns that their writing might compromise their womanhood. Because writing periodical fiction allowed women to perform their work within the confines of the domestic locus, it appears that such work did not conflict with a woman's primary duties as wife and mother. Since such traditional roles were assumed to be a woman's first priority, periodical writing could be promoted as a hobby along the lines of cross-stitch, an amusement that was effortlessly performed during leisured hours amid much activity and interruption by family members.[7] And such a "leisured activity" further allowed women to deny that any personal ambition motivated their doing it; some women even argued that they wrote in the name of some higher, public good. As Jane Benardete and Phyllis Moe have observed:

In an era when going "out" to work represented a loss of status for women, writing was an acceptable occupation that allowed women to work in the home, while putting their education to use and turning their largely domestic experience to profit. In the post–Civil War decades the burgeoning list of periodicals for women and young folk offered such women a suitable market and the more talented among them found that writing was more rewarding in every way than telling stories to children, which, either as wives or spinsters, might have been their fate. (9)

One standard strategy women used to break into periodical writing was to begin with juvenile periodicals, the least-threatening and least-questioned venue of publishing for women because child care was the Victorian woman's quintessential concern. Particularly new and unknown women writers initially published in highly acclaimed and widely circulating children's periodicals to catch the attention of prominent adult magazine editors and eventually break into other fiction markets.[8] These women "capitalized upon woman's traditional relation to children and the home. They were, in fact, ingenious entrepreneurs" (Benardete and Moe 9).

Chopin was one such woman writer. Whether she was doing so consciously, or whether she was simply following an established career path for women, Chopin relied on juvenile periodicals as her stepping-stone to broader literary acclaim. In the thirteen years that Chopin was marketing her manuscripts, from 1889 to 1902, sixteen of the seventy-seven short stories she published were first printed in juvenile periodicals. Between 1891 and 1902 Chopin successfully placed one story in *Wide Awake*, four in *Harper's Young People*, and eleven, including her last, in the *Youth's Companion*.[9] She earned $787 from these magazines, a sum that makes up more than one-third of her lifetime's literary income of $2300.[10]

But both the ideological and market conditions of Chopin's day required business savvy for success, especially if a woman writer did not have a male editor friend to escort her into the field, which Chopin did not. In her article "Kate Chopin and Editors, 'A Singular Class of Men,' " Phyllis Vanlandingham denies Chopin such shrewdness when she addresses the 1897 essay Chopin published in the *St. Louis Criterion*, where Chopin expresses her frustration with male editors. Chopin wrote:

[E]ditors are really a singular class of men; they have such strange and incomprehensible ways with them.

I once submitted a story to a prominent New York editor, who returned it promptly with the observation that "the public is getting very tired of that sort of thing." I felt very sorry for the public, but I wasn't willing to take one man's word for it, so I clapped the offensive document into an envelope and sent it away again — this time to a well-known Boston editor.

"I am delighted with the story," read the letter of acceptance, which came a few weeks later, "and so, I am sure, will be our readers."

When an editor says a thing like that it is at his own peril. I at once sent him another tale, thinking thereby to increase his delight and add to it ten-fold.

"Can you call this a story, dear madam?" he asked when he sent it back. "Really, there seems to me to be no story at all; what is it all about?" I could see his pale smile.

It was getting interesting, like playing at battledore and shuttlecock. Off went the would-be story by the next mail to the New York editor — the one who so considerately gauged the ennui of the public.

"It is a clever and excellent piece of work," he wrote me; "the story is well told." I wonder if the editor, the writer and the public are ever at one. (Seyersted 717–18)

Vanlandingham's article celebrates what she assumes to be the "fact" that Chopin and her editors were seldom "at one," claiming that such symbiosis would have foreclosed the possibility of Chopin writing such a daring text as *The Awakening*. Vanlandingham thus concludes readers should "be thankful that [Chopin], unlike Grace King and many of her contemporaries, continued to find editors 'strange and incomprehensible'" (166)

Such an argument necessarily centers around the following broad — and dubious — assumptions: that periodical publishing practices did not influence Chopin's literary production: and that in fact she was completely oblivious to, uninformed about, or unconcerned with a periodical's target audience. Vanlandingham reaches such conclusions as: "[W]ith few exceptions, [Chopin] wrote to please herself and then tried to find publishers for her work" (159); "some of Chopin's problems with editors stemmed from her failure to consider the audience a magazine or journal was designed to reach" (162); and "she simply sent her work wherever she wanted to see it published, without worrying about the periodical's audience, editorial policies, or esthetic principles" (163)

However, Chopin's Account/Memo books — in which she meticulously logged by hand the submission, rejection, and/or acceptance dates of most of her stories, along with their remuneration — indicate the contrary. To make her point, Vanlandingham uses the example of the story "Lilacs," which Chopin finally sold to the *New Orleans Times-Democrat* after unsuccessful attempts to place it elsewhere, and then later to *Vogue*, in what must have been a resubmission.[11] Admittedly, Chopin's business sense in marketing "Lilacs" is difficult to defend. Vanlandingham accurately cites Chopin's illogic in sending that manuscript both to the "highly ethical *Century* . . . and to the decadent, antiestablishment *Yellow Book*" (162), a premiere genteel periodical on the one hand, and an avant-garde art press on the other.

But Vanlandingham's reconstructed history tells only part of the story. Chopin understood where her stories would be well received and thus fashioned her identity politics into fictional formats that were acceptable to a broad range of publications. Her logbooks document that the *Century* was the first and the *Yellow Book* the last of eight consecutive submissions Chopin made by sending out her manuscript to groups of ideologically compatible publications. Choosing the most prestigious — and most conventional — genteel periodicals first, then moving on to non-literary ladies' magazines where she had had some success, before finally approaching the (long-shot) innovative art presses, Chopin sent her manuscript to the *Century, Atlantic, Scribner's,* and *Harper's*; then to *Vogue* and *Cosmopolitan*, and finally, to the *Chap-Book* and *Yellow Book*, before placing it with the *New Orleans Times-Democrat*.[12]

Thus, Chopin's logbooks demonstrate that there was some form of logical consistency to her marketing strategy, regardless of how misguided that plan of action was. For "Lilacs," as it turns out, was hardly suitable for any periodical of the Gilded Age, not because Chopin wrote a story about illicit sexual activity and female sexual longing, as she did in such published stories as "La Belle Zoraïde" and "At the 'Cadian Ball," but because she represented such longing as same-sex desire between women.

Although Emily Toth describes the plot of "Lilacs" as being about "the widowed Adrienne Farival who retreats to the Sacred Heart convent every spring — never telling the sisters who love her that for the rest of the year, she is a decadent woman of the world, [a Parisian] actress who takes lovers" (Chopin 238); and Vanlandingham simply describes it as being "about a woman who has several affairs" (162), neither critic addresses the explicitly homosocial environment of the convent or the homoerotic attachment between the former convent schoolgirl-turned-actress Adrienne Farival and one of the Sacred Heart nuns, Sister Agathe.[13] While the homosocial world of female "love and ritual" was still accepted and practiced in the late Victorian era when Chopin was writing, the homosexual attraction between Adrienne and Agathe in "Lilacs" clearly deviated from this norm and would have been read as an aberration of female friendship that had crossed the line, so to speak, into the realm of the perverted.[14]

Furthermore, Vanlandingham reads in Chopin's note that accompanied the manuscript of "Lilacs" to the *Chap-Book* a "naïveté" that goes hand in hand with her alleged disregard for a periodical's audience. Vanlandingham notes that when Chopin sent "Lilacs," along with "Three Portraits" and two poems to the *Chap-Book,* she expressed in the most indiscreet terms her eagerness to be published therein. Chopin wrote, "I would greatly like to see one of [my writings] — some of them — something — anything over my name in the *Chap-Book*" (162). While one cannot dispute Chopin's desire evident in the letter, her so-called "naïveté" can more accurately be described as the weary experience of rejection, especially when the *Chap-Book* letter is juxtaposed against the sentiments expressed in her essay "A Singular Class of Men." Looking back, then, to that same essay, we can read in her sarcasm not a genuine bewilderment of acceptable standards for fiction writing but a frustration with the politics that regulated her authorial success: the arbitrariness of individual judgment and the fact that her access to publication was so thoroughly controlled by editors, who, for the most part, were male.

Given her cultural milieu, then, it is not surprising that Chopin found the most accepting forum for her bold themes of female autonomy and sexual desire in a magazine edited by another woman. Josephine Redding, the editor in chief of the ladies' fashion magazine *Vogue,* printed nineteen of Chopin's manuscripts, the largest number of short stories published by any single periodical in Chopin's lifetime. *Vogue* and Chopin were indeed "at one" in their nineteenth-century feminist politics for white, middle-class women. In 1894 the magazine made this editorial statement regarding fictional portrayals of female love and romance: "The pink and white — débutante afternoon tea — atmosphere in which convention says we must present love, means intellectual asphyxiation for us."[15] Clearly, *Vogue* was mocking a dominant discourse that suppressed female sexuality by depicting it in a purified, "débutante afternoon tea" atmosphere. And *Vogue,* like Chopin, was interested in representing women as sexual beings.

By the time *Vogue* made such a public statement, Chopin had already learned that it was the showcase in which she could count on placing her "experimental" feminist fiction. Between 1892 and 1895, *Vogue* was either

Chopin's first- or second-choice periodical for publishing much of her fiction, an indication that the author was both tracking and targeting the markets where she would be most successful. In those three years Chopin sent first to *Vogue* (whose editor accepted the following manuscripts upon first submission) "Désirée's Baby," "Caline," "Two Summers and Two Souls," "Ripe Figs," "A Lady of Bayou St. John," "La Belle Zoraïde," "A Respectable Woman," and "The Kiss"; and upon having a first-choice periodical reject a manuscript, she sent out to *Vogue* as her second-choice publisher "A Visit to Avoyelles," "The Unexpected," "The Letters," and "Dr. Chevalier's Lie," all of which the periodical also published.[16]

But there were reasons why Chopin was sending only her most experimental fiction to *Vogue*, why she didn't want to stake her literary reputation on her success with this one magazine, and why, once established as a writer, she later attempted to broaden her market by sending her work to other, more prestigious presses before resorting to *Vogue* as her "ace in the hole." Unlike more prestigious "literary" periodicals, *Vogue* — a ladies' fashion magazine — was not known for its fiction. Outside of New York circles, it attracted a relatively small readership, so it was not a direct route to literary acclaim; and as an added disincentive, it paid relatively little for fiction.[17]

Thus, in addition to *Vogue*, Chopin cultivated an amicable relationship with a second periodical that would provide her with a national showcase for her work from the beginning of her career to the very end of her life. That periodical was the *Youth's Companion*.[18] Between 1891 and 1902 the *Companion* bought twenty of Chopin's short stories, published eleven of them, and paid her anywhere from $15 to $65 for each manuscript, a tidy sum compared to *Vogue's* pay range of between $3 and $25 per story.[19] "For Marse Chouchoute," Chopin's first *Companion* piece, appeared only eighteen months after she debuted "Wiser Than a God" in the *Philadelphia Musical Journal*. And after *The Awakening* was published in 1899, the *Companion* was one of two periodicals to remain a loyal vehicle for Chopin's work. While *Vogue* published its last Chopin tale, "The White Eagle," on 12 July 1900, the *Companion* accepted Chopin's final two stories to appear in print during her lifetime: "The Wood-Choppers," 29 May 1902 and "Polly," 3 July 1902.

By the 1890s, when Chopin was writing and marketing her work, the *Companion* was not only the longest-running periodical in America, it was among the most widely circulating.[20] Begun by Nathaniel Willis and Asa Rand in 1827 as a Sunday School weekly reader, the four-page weekly folio was a children's "companion" to one of the most important religious newspaper of the age, the *Boston Recorder*. Not surprisingly, the material in the early *Companion* reflected its somber Puritan roots and the heavily didactic tradition of eighteenth-century children's literature.

In 1857 Willis and Rand sold the *Companion* to the partnership of John W. Olmstead and Daniel Sharp Ford, the latter of whom took sole ownership of the *Companion* in 1867. Ford increased the *Companion's* then 48,000 circulation figure to more than 500,000 by the mid-1890s, accomplishing this monumental feat through many methods. In addition to instituting new marketing strategies, two other changes Ford made in the *Companion's* content were just as important, if not critical avenues, to the magazine's phenomenal success. First, he began to value a model of children's literature that more closely imitated adult fiction. And by means of this move, Ford facilitated his second tactic: he broadened the magazine's audience base to include the composite age groups and sexes of the entire Victorian family.

As the editor of a magazine as popular as the *Companion*, Ford was not only following trends by favoring such fiction, but through his ability to accept and reject submissions, also exerting enormous power in shaping the period's literary production. R. Gordon Kelly's valuable work on the *Companion's* history documents that Ford influenced the very production of material potential contributions wrote for the *Companion* by sending them a leaflet detailing what he would and would not publish. Quoting from such a leaflet mailed out in the 1890s, Kelly writes that Ford "called for stories that had 'well-devised [plots] and at least one strong incident' but were untainted by sensationalism, melodrama, or improper language. . . . 'The moral tone of the stories must be irreproachable,' Ford admonished in a leaflet sent to possible contributors. . . . An ethical purpose was always desirable, but the moral was to be revealed 'by the story itself, not by any comment of the writer'" (12–13).

In addition to composing the leaflet, Ford and his staff of largely anonymous editors influenced a priori the production of literature for their particular publication. A conscious and highly codified editorial policy shaped the final versions of pieces merely proposed to the magazine, and this gate-keeping process of acceptance and rejection determined what type of material potential contributors would come to associate with its title.[21]

One other significant aspect of editorial policy that guided the *Companion* was its perceived position as a morally upright publication whose aim was partly to interest juveniles and partly to acquire the approval of those same juveniles' parents. As a result, editor Ford began to favor a genre of fiction that itself contained such a mixed-audience appeal. Ford's endorsement of such fiction emerged along with the rising tide of juvenile-fiction writers who were borrowing from and modeling their work after popular adult texts. From Martha Finley's *Elsie Dinsmore* (1867), a "girls' novel" imitation of the overwhelming popular adult domestic novel *The Wide Wide World* (1850) by Susan Warner, to Louisa May Alcott's cross-generational novel *Little Women* (1868), clear distinctions between children's and adults' texts were breaking down in the latter half of the century.[22] Following suit, then, the fiction Ford favored for the *Companion* appealed not exclusively to juvenile readers but to a dual audience of young adults and adults. Even younger readers were accommodated with verse, riddles, and short, short stories on a separate "Children's Page."[23]

The *Youth's Companion's* marked success can be attributed in large part to this broad, mixed-audience appeal. It attempted to accommodate the interests of all members of the family by publishing such renowned authors and poets as Harriet Beecher Stowe, Elizabeth Stuart Phelps, Mary E. Wilkins Freeman, Sarah Orne Jewett, Alfred Lord Tennyson, Henry Wadsworth Longfellow, and Walt Whitman. Similarly, articles on such timely topics as science, health, the environment, education, politics, and current events, though written at a young adult reading level, were nonetheless authored by leaders in these fields, among them Theodore Roosevelt, Grover Cleveland, Booker T. Washington, Henry M. Stanley, Lillian Nordica, and P. T. Barnum.[24] And advertisements for medicinal remedies, household and garden instruments, and adult male and female hygiene products clearly were directed at parents rather than their children.

Thus, regardless of its front-page profile as a youth's companion, the periodical was, in fact, marketed to a mixed audience of children, young adults, and adults, a deliberate targeting strategy that gave it as much in common with the so-called adult, "genteel" periodicals of the Gilded Age, such as the *Century, Scribner's, Harper's*, and the *Atlantic*, as with magazines more exclusively targeted at young readers, such as *Our Young Folk* and *St. Nicholas*.

The *Companion's* self-identification began to reflect its multi-age marketing strategy more prominently as the years progressed. While throughout its history the magazine maintained a front-page profile as a "youth's" companion, the words "a family paper" began appearing regularly on a back page editorial statement in 1865, as a subtitle on page six of each issue in the mid-1890s, and as part of the masthead in 1903. Thus, editor Ford continued to increase the *Companion's* circulation not only by attracting new generations of subscribers but by retaining previous ones who, though having outgrown an exclusively juvenile product, nonetheless appreciated a paper "for all the family."

Chopin's fiction published in the *Companion* embodied this mixed-audience appeal. It belonged primarily to the genre of the "family story," a short story version of the popular adult female domestic novel, which, like the novel, represented characters of various ages and both sexes in a domestic setting.[25] Occasionally, too, her fiction targeted the middle ground of that age span, what we recognize today as the "young adult," by addressing concerns specific to adolescent girls and boys on the brink of adulthood. Because her fiction's sophisticated reading level required at least a teenage, if not adult, reader, Chopin's *Youth's Companion* texts were never exclusively children's stories but rather cross-audience pieces equally suitable for older children and adults.

Thus, the cross-audience quality of the family story genre allowed Chopin to submit her manuscripts to other "adult" periodicals in addition to the *Companion*. Contrary to assertions such as Vanlandingham's, Chopin was a seasoned veteran of the periodical marketplace who honed her writing skills to take maximum advantage of the commercial opportunities available for her fiction. By dramatizing her concerns within familial settings and various age readers, Chopin blanketed the publication markets of both adult and juvenile magazines, thus creating better odds for placing her fiction. Although as a less well known female writer Chopin was more easily authorized to write for—and had reasons for desiring that her work be published in—the *Youth's Companion*, she created fiction that was eminently suitable for a variety of genteel, family, and juvenile publications alike. The suggestion that Chopin manipulated fictional formats in order to maximize her marketing potential underscores just to what degree Chopin's choice to author a particular type of text may have been born of considerations other than literary.

NOTES

1 See Emily Toth, appendix 3, "The Alleged Banning of *The Awakening*," *Kate Chopin* (Austin: U of Texas P, 1990) 422–25; and Heather Kirk Thomas, "'What Are the Prospects for the Book?': Rewriting a Woman's Life," *Kate Chopin Reconsidered: Beyond the Bayou*, eds. Lynda S. Boren and Sara deSaussure Davis (Baton Rouge: Louisiana State UP, 1992) 36–60.

2 Sandra Gunning, *Race, Rape, and Lynching: The Red Record of American Literature, 1890–1912* (New York and Oxford: Oxford UP, 1996) 142–43. See also Michele Birnbaum, "'Alien Hands': Kate Chopin and the Colonization Race," *American Literature* 66.2 (1994): 301–23; and Helen Taylor, *Gender, Race, and Region in the*

Writings of Grace King, Ruth McEnery Stuart, and Kate Chopin (Baton Rouge: Louisiana State UP, 1989).

3 As I argue elsewhere, I see a political agenda beyond Chopin's feminism operating in her local color fiction. That agenda I articulate as "the discursive act of coloring locals," or the narrative construction of racial differences for Louisiana peoples of African American, Native American, and French American ancestry. Chopin's attempt to "color" her beloved Louisiana Creoles and Cadians "white" at a time when their racial status was uncertain and the necessity of that agenda to occasionally deploy orthodox representations of femininity in its service speak to the importance of her *Youth's Companion* stories and their role in facilitating our understanding of the body of her work. See "'Lookin' Jis' like W'ite Folks': Coloring Locals in Kate Chopin's 'A Rude Awakening,'" *Louisiana Literature* 14.2 (Fall 1997): 116–25 and "Coloring Locals: Identity Politics in Kate Chopin's Youth's Companion Stories, 1891–1902," diss., Case Western Reserve U, 1998.

4 See *Library of Southern Literature*, eds. Edwin Anderson Alderman and Joel Chandler Harris, vol. 2 (Atlanta: Martin, 1909) 863–66; Fred Lewis Pattee, *A History of American Literature Since 1870* (New York: Century, 1915); *Dictionare of American Biography*, eds. Allen Johnson and Dumas Malone, vol. 4 (New York, Scribner's, 1930) 90–91; and Arthur Hobson Quinn, *American Fiction: An Historical and Critical Survey* (New York: Appleton-Century, 1936) 354–57.

5 See Amy Kaplan, *The Social Construction of American Realism* (Chicago: U of Chicago P, 1988) 15–43.

6 Susan Coultrap-McQuin, *Doing Literary Business: American Women Writers in the Nineteenth Century* (Chapel Hill, U of North Carolina P, 1990); Anne Goodwyn Jones, *Tomorrow Is Another Day: The Woman Writer in the South, 1859–1936* (Baton Rouge: Louisiana State UP, 1981); Amy Kaplan, "Edith Wharton's Profession of Authorship," *Social Construction*, 1988 65–87; Mary Kelley, *Private Woman, Public Stage: Literary Domesticity in Nineteenth-Century America* (Oxford: Oxford UP, 1984); Mary P. Ryan, *Empire of the Mother: American Writing About Domesticity, 1830–1860* (New York Institute for Research in History and Haworth P, 1982).

7 Such fictions actually have been handed down to us about Kate Chopin. Anne Goodwyn Jones, for instance, has claimed that Chopin "wrote quickly, once her idea had formed, in a room swarming with children, their friends, and their activities" (139). It is interesting to note that by the time Chopin began writing in 1888, her "children," the youngest of whom was nine, were old enough to respect their mother's privacy when she desired it.

8 See Koppelman, 801.

9 *Wide Awake* published "The Lilies"; *Harper's Young People* published "A Very Fine Fiddle," "Boulôt & Boulotte," "The Bênitouis' Slave," and "A Turkey Hunt"; and

the *Youth's Companion* published "For Marse Chouchoute," "A Wizard from Gettysburg," "A Rude Awakening," "Beyond the Bayou," "Loka," "Mamouche," "A Matter of Prejudice," "Polydore," "Aunt Lympy's Interference," "The Wood-Choppers," and "Polly."

10 These figures include ten stories that the juvenile periodicals paid for but didn't print. *Harper's Young People* bought but never published "Old Aunt Peggy," as did the *Companion* with "A Red Velvet Coat," "After the Winter," "Madame Martel's Christmas Eve," "Ti Frère," "A Little Country Girl," "Alexandre's Wonderful Experience," "A Little Country Girl," "Alexander's Wonderful Experience," "A December Day in Dixie," "The Gentleman from New Orleans," and "Millie's First Party." Although four of these stories were purchased by the *Companion* between 1899 and 1900, the first year *The Awakening* was out, I would argue that the fact that they weren't published stems less from concerns over *The Awakening* than from the fact that the *Companion's* long-time editor, Daniel Sharp Ford, died on 24 December 1899 and the magazine was undergoing a change of management. And some publications pay upon acceptance of an article — with no promise of a publication date — while others pay only upon publication. Figures are calculated from Chopin's Account/Memo Books, 1888–95 and 1888–1902, Kate Chopin Papers, Missouri Historical Society, St. Louis. See also Toth's account of such events in *Kate Chopin*, 372–73.

11 In her biography on Chopin, Toth writes that "Lilacs" "eventually appeared in *Vogue*" (296), though she does not document when, either in the body of her text or in her "Appendix II: Kate Chopin's Writings," 413–21. Chopin's Account/ Memo books only document that *Vogue* rejected "Lilacs" upon its first submission.

12 Chopin's Account/Memo Books.

13 Thomas Bonner has noted that "Adrienne and Agathe's relationship has romantic overtones." See Bonner's entry "Agathe, Sister" in *The Kate Chopin Companion: With Chopin's Translations from French Fiction* (Westport, CT: Greenwood, 1988) 4.

14 See Carroll Smith-Rosenberg, "The Female World of Love and Ritual: Relations Between Women in Nineteenth-Century America," *Disorderly Conduct: Visions of Gender in Victorian America* (New York and Oxford: Oxford UP, 1985)53–76.

15 Qtd. in Toth, *Kate Chopin* 280.

16 Chopin's Account/Memo Books.

17 In her Account/Memo Books, Chopin documents that *Vogue* paid $204.80 for eighteen of the nineteen stories it accepted and published. Chopin does not record the amount *Vogue* paid for "Two Summers and Two Souls," which it published on 7 August 1895.

18 The following information on the *Youth's Companion* is taken from Richard Cutts,

"Introduction," *Index to the Youth's Companion 1871–1929* (Metuchen, NJ: Scarecrow, 1972) in the Rare Books and Manuscripts Room, Boston Public Library; R. Gordon Kelly, *Mother Was A Lady: Self and Society in Selected American Children's Periodicals, 1865–1890* (Westport, CT, and London, UK: Greenwood, 1974) and *Children's Periodicals of the United States* (Westport, CT: Greenwood, 1984); and Frank Luther Mott, *A History of American Magazines*, vol. 2 1850–65; vol. 3 1865–85 and vol. 4 1885–1905 (Cambridge: Harvard UP, 1957) 262–74.

19 While some of the pay discrepancy can be explained by story length, even the pay-per-word seems to vary throughout Chopin's career, perhaps owing to the author's notoriety at a given time, along with other market concerns, such as the magazines' circulations in a particular year. Figures are taken from Chopin's Account/Memo books.

20 Although Cutts writes that the *Companion* had "the largest audience of readers in the world" in the 1890s (xiv), Mott's figures are more reliable. With the exception of mail-order papers, the *Companion* outpaced other American magazines in 1885 with a circulation of 385,000; it fell behind *Ladies' Home Journal* and *Comfort* in 1890 with a circulation of 500,000; and it was fourth in line in 1895 with 600,000 subscribers. See Mott, vol. 3, 6 and vol. 4, 16–17.

21 For an extensive and interesting discussion detailing Ford's editorial policies see the Letters of William Henry Rideing to William Morris Colles 1894–1918, MS.Amm1144, Rare Books and Manuscripts Room, Boston Public Library, Boston, Massachusetts.

22 My account of the emergence of children's literature as a genre is taken from the following: Anne Scott MacLeod, "Children's Literature in America from the Puritan Beginnings to 1870," 102–29; Julia Briggs and Dennis Butts, "The Emergence of Form (1850–90)," 130–66; and "Children's Literature in America (1870–1945)," 225–51, all in *Children's Literature: An Illustrated History*, ed. Peter Hunt (Oxford: Oxford UP, 1995).

23 See also Susan R. Gannon, "'The Best Magazine for Children of All Ages': Cross-Editing St. Nicholas Magazine (1873–1905)," *Children's Literature* 25 (1997): 153–80.

24 In vol. 2, Mott writes that "many an adult liked the simpler manner which these great writers adopted for the benefit of the *Companion* readers," 270.

25 See MacLeod, "Children's Literature," 126–28; and Mott, vol. 2, 268, for discussions of the family story genre.

GENDER ROLES, SOCIAL EXPECTATIONS, & THE WOMAN WRITER

Aleta Feinsod Cane

THE HEROINE OF HER OWN STORY: SUBVERSION OF TRADITIONAL PERIODICAL MARRIAGE TROPES IN THE SHORT FICTION OF CHARLOTTE PERKINS GILMAN'S FORERUNNER

The short fiction written and published by Charlotte Perkins Gilman in her magazine, the *Forerunner* (1909–16), concerns ordinary women who deflect the traditional trajectories of their lives to create better situations for themselves and, in so doing, improve the lives of those around them. A sample comparison of the fictional representations of marriage made in the *Ladies' Home Journal*, the dominant and characteristic woman's magazine of the period, with those in the *Forerunner* will help to clarify the goal for Gilman's project for humankind: with her own journal, Gilman sought to change the perception of woman from object to subject and from passivity to agency; to demonstrate that there could be more than a single model of marriage; and finally, to assert that women have many choices both within and outside of marriage that they must exercise in order to reinvigorate humanity. In sum, Gilman understood that in order to achieve full humanity and build a better community, each woman must make her own decisions and become the heroine of her own story.

During the first two decades of the twentieth century, the *Ladies' Home Journal* projected and reflected a white, middle-class norm for women's conduct that was home based and fully focused on marriage, the conduct of married life, and the resolution of familial issues. Gilman's *Forerunner*, on the other hand, existed to counteract popular images of women and such personal limitations on their everyday lives that the mass media promulgated. Yet by appropriating the literary conventions of popular fiction that dominated magazines such as the *Journal*, Gilman found her own way to subvert the traditional marriage plot and to foreground realistic and available alternatives for the conduct of women's lives. As Carroll Smith-Rosenberg asks,

"[I]f the marginal or powerless wish to challenge the dominant discourse, must they frame their challenge in the language of the dominant mode?" (246). For Gilman, the answer was a powerful yes. She skillfully manipulated the dominant mode so that her program for female empowerment became both evolutionary and eminently possible for the middle-class women who were her readers.

Rather than re-creating the typical, white, middle-class scenario of patriarchal power and dominance that portrays women's lives as tragic and that negates women's agency by replicating a traditional male view of an unchanging and unchangeable society, Gilman offered her readers small, evolutionary changes. Thus, she sought and discovered, within the existing social structure, ways to insinuate her own perceptions and analyses to demonstrate alternatives, usually individualized solutions to common problems: small rearrangements made palpable and possible in almost familiar stories that serve as examples of changes that would work. For example, for the unschooled woman looking for meaningful work, Gilman recommends such jobs as boarding-house keeper, personal shopper, or running an employment agency for servants. In addition to offering solutions to common problems yet in keeping with her grander utopian themes, Gilman's short fiction also espoused a thoroughly utopian perspective. Progress toward utopia remains a prospect, but Gilman holds each reader responsible to herself in the present. As Carol Farley Kessler observes, "[Gilman's stories] permit no complacency regarding human existence and urge upon us experimentation. Gilman hypothetically urges . . . possibilities that may, in fact, constitute realizable utopias" (115). The very possible solutions that Gilman offers as examples demonstrate to her readers that such small changes can make a happier present.

According to Gilman, individuals who follow her suggestions will have the short-term benefit of a happier life without disrupting the extant social order. Relying, as always, on an evolutionary model, Gilman understood that, when numbers of people undertake what appear as small individual changes, greater societal shifts inevitably occur. Herein lies Gilman's most striking social application of the evolutionary principle. As she insists in *Women and Economics* (1898): "The change considered . . . is not one merely to be prophesied and recommended: it is already taking place under the forces of social evolution; and only needs to be made clear to our conscious thought, that we may withdraw the futile but irritating resistance of our misguided will" (122). Clearly, Gilman took a conservative, slow-going approach to social change for two main reasons: First, she adhered to the notion that social change was based on the scientific evidence of evolution and she understood the evolutionary process to be gradual; second, as an observer of the suffrage campaigns undertaken within her lifetime, she had learned that the less radical approaches were the ones that won adherents, while more revolutionary schemes frightened and alienated many middle-class women. The *Forerunner's* approach was modeled more on that of the conservative *Women's Journal* of Lucy Stone than on that of the militant and strident *Revolution* of Elizabeth Cady Stanton. Since the *Women's Journal* succeeded for fifty years as the most widely read and influential suffrage publication in America, while the *Revolution* had a miniscule circulation and a very brief run, Gilman apparently made the proper choice for the *Forerunner*. More generally, her commitment to gradual, evolutionary change informs all of Gilman's proposals for social progress.

The *Forerunner* and the *Ladies' Home Journal* shared many of the same readers. Gilman herself wrote a few articles for the *Journal*. And since the *Journal* was nationally circulated and ubiquitous, and because its influence was so widespread, it became a normative text, useful today as a contrast to the relentlessly iconoclastic fiction of Gilman's *Forerunner*. At the peak of its circulation, the *Forerunner* claimed 1,500 subscribers. It was dedicated to the continuing theme of progressive social and human development, which Gilman believed was hindered by androcentric thought. With a circulation of more than one million by 1900, the *Ladies' Home Journal* claimed to be the most widely read magazine in America (Damon-Moore 27). More importantly,

> the *Journal* was a pioneer in reflecting upon gender roles, creating a forum that continues to this day to foster the popular representation of and discussion of gender issues. In fact, the assumed propensity of women to seek to understand their lives, especially in relation to men, actually informed almost every feature of the early *Journal*— its general advice articles, short stories, editorial comments and homilies, letters from readers, and even advertising. (37)

Under its second editor, Edward Bok, the *Journal* seemed far less progressive than it had been under his predecessor, Louisa Knapp. With Bok at its helm, the *Journal* both created and reflected that normative view of womanhood and woman's sphere that Charlotte Perkins Gilman found distressing, limiting, and life denying. Bok advocated women's higher education, for example, but only so far as it pertained to making better housewives. In an article for the May 1900 edition entitled "3000 Sensible Girls," Bok wrote: "When over 3000 girls voluntarily come to their senses, and deliberately elect to know something of browning as well as Browning, it is a very fair indication that all American girls are not quite so silly and heedless of the true elements which constitute a woman's life as some would have us believe." Bok spoke against woman's suffrage and often scolded clubs and club members for taking too much time away from home, husband, and children. As editor, he solicited guest columns from conservative clergymen whose ideas about marriage and home were as conservative as his own. One such article was written in the *Journal* for January 1902 by J. Cardinal Gibbons of New York. The writer inveighs against suffrage, club activities, and work outside the home. He reminds the readers: "American women, your husbands are the sovereigns of America and if you be the sovereigns of your husbands, then indeed you would rule the nation. That should be enough for you" (6). This traditionally androcentric ideology of the *Journal's* editorial policy is mirrored in its short fiction.

At its inception, the marriage plot provided, by far, the most pervasive theme in the short fiction of the *Journal*. It still does. But, in the *Forerunner*, Gilman rarely deals with courtship, focusing instead upon the problematic situations in marriage that she assures her readers are usually reparable. In fiction, Gilman's solutions always work, allowing the writer to depict the improved lives and new hopes of the protagonists, whose lives are similar to those of her reading audience. As Shelley Fisher Fishkin notes: "Gilman refused to rely on logic alone to make her case. . . . Fiction gave Gilman the chance to delineate alternative ways of organizing the world. . . . It was in her fiction that Gilman could explore dimensions of human experience that elude logic and reason — such as fears, dreams, insecurities—and could marshal those dimensions in the service of social change" (236). Gilman's short fiction, then, must also be read as a condensation of her larger utopian projects.

The stories published between 1900 and 1910 in the *Ladies' Home Journal* stand out in sharp contrast to the suggested mode of conduct taught by Gilman's fiction. These stories represent the cultural milieu that Gilman sought, ultimately, to challenge in life. In the *Journal*, women play traditional self-sacrificing roles, marrying and learning to accommodate their husbands. Women who do not conform to those norms must suffer and then repent. Good women submerge their identities and sacrifice their best interests for those of others. Women learn to accept the natural superiority of men, as in Hamlin Garland's serialized story, "The Light of the Star," in the 1904 *Journal*. Here, a successful actress nurtures the career of an unsuccessful young playwright. After his early failure, she continues to encourage him, and she marries him after he achieves the success that she has quietly fostered, never letting on that she had made his career.

Another *Ladies' Home Journal* story — this one serialized in June and July 1905 — titled "Two Violins," by Kate W. Patch, continues the inscription of the moral that the good woman lives not for her own glory but for others. In this tale the message to women is very clear: Don't bother to try to achieve recognition on your own; women are lovable only when they nurture the gifts of others in a selfless manner. The story tells of a young musician, who due to a tragic accident realizes that she will not have as brilliant a career as she had hoped. Living vicariously through her fiancé, another violinist, she says she will find her "true" success: "I am restless no longer. Your success, your genius is enough now. All my thwarted ambitions are merged in yours, all my longings are stilled . . . It will be you who give the concerts, . . . but I — what shall I care if I can be there to see, if I can know that the heart of the great violinist rests in mine" (12). In *Ladies' Home Journal* fiction the good woman always gets and keeps her man, even at the expense of her own career.

Even "spitfire" or "saucy" heroines are saved from danger and tamed to domesticity in *Ladies' Home Journal* fiction (Searles 271). Less traditional women are unflatteringly described in this fiction as restless or purposeless. The active and semi-independent woman is taught that her best self and her best interests lie in the domestic sphere. In a curious story called "His Dutch Treat Wife," a young husband tries to be modern and allow his bride to continue her work, which she says she loves. But slowly she comes to realize that she wants to be domesticated. In fact, she believes her husband does not really love her because he does not exert his masculine will to make her quit her job. He must be masculine so she can realize her femininity. She says, "I am so glad to stop work, — I, I don't want to be an individual now" (Tompkins 12). In still another *Journal* story, "The Baby Behind the Curtain," in the October 1905 issue, a young mother who wishes to be on the stage is taught by a successful (but unmarried and lonely) actress that motherhood is the far happier and more enviable position for a woman. In the *Journal's* short fiction, women are shown, over and over again, that happiness exists only for the woman willing to accept love as a substitute for all other aspects of life.

Gilman was not prepared herself to sacrifice life or ambition to others. Her short fiction emphasizes that women can succeed in many roles — as wives, mothers, and career women. Such multiple lives become possible when flexible domestic arrangements and a sound choice of the proper mate prevail. For Gilman, the choice of the right mate is not simply a matter of the heart; it is a matter of politics informed by eugenics as well. In both *Women and Economics* (1898) and *Our Androcentric Culture* (1909–10) Gilman relies heavily upon the theories of Lester Ward, who made the argument that males exist mainly to help females reproduce. Since the female is the primary source of life, of the two sexes, Ward argues, the female is thus the primary sex. The balance of nature had been upset by humans according to Ward's "gynaeocentric theory." So women had to work to regain their original status. In all her writings based upon Ward's theory, Gilman left his essential argument intact because she believed (as Mary Hill humorously avers) that "[d]espite the usual self-righteous justifications for male dominance and power, Ward had proved how transient men really were, how dispensable, how second-rate" (268).

In chapter 9 of *Our Androcentric Culture* (which was serialized throughout the first volume of the *Forerunner* and published as a book in 1911), Gilman argues that women are raised to please men and are brought up in a terrible state of innocence (which is synonymous with ignorance, according to Gilman). She cites a story from the *Ladies' Literary Cabinet* (a magazine with a social agenda similar to that of the *Ladies' Home Journal* but that predated it) called the "Sorrows of Amelia," in which a young girl believes that all men are as good and pure as she is herself. "This fatal credulity was the source of all her misfortunes. It was. It is yet" (*Forerunner* 1: 18). To Gilman, the evolutionary reason for marriage is motherhood, and society owes it to itself, as well as to its young women, to educate them as to what a good marriage partner is. For Gilman, such a partner is loving, kind, and willing to share both life's burdens and pleasures. In the short fiction of the *Forerunner*, Gilman depicts men as having to be taught how to be good marriage partners. It is the women, not the men, in *Forerunner* fiction who have the intelligence and the agency to choose the proper marriage partner. If the man is not quite right to begin with, the woman lovingly changes him so that he becomes what he should be. If that is not possible, the woman in Gilman's stories refuses him.

Gilman refutes the notion that in order to be a proper wife a woman must give up her career and be cheerfully self sacrificing. In contrast to the *Ladies' Home Journal* story, "His Dutch Treat Wife," women in *Forerunner* fiction are encouraged to think for themselves and to choose mates who will love them and encourage them to be creative, contributing members of society. If a mate cannot be both, the message from Gilman is clear: Don't marry. Rather than ever saying "I don't want to be an individual," as the young wife declares in "His Dutch Treat Wife," Gilman's heroines are individuals and are not about to give up that position. To be an individual, for Gilman, means pursuing whatever work or avocation gives meaning and depth to a woman's life outside the familial sphere.

Those of Gilman's stories that are based upon the marriage plot can be divided into three major categories: choosing the right mate; living as a married couple in nontraditional settings, and the dissolving of bad marriages through divorce. Gilman's adaptation of each of these topics suggests a subversion of commonly held perceptions of marriage. In the first case, women choose their mates as opposed to passively waiting to be chosen. In the second group of stories, Gilman demonstrates that one family, in one house, being lovingly nurtured by one self-sacrificing woman is not the only way marriage can succeed. In the third group of stories, Gilman deals with a subject that was taboo during her lifetime, divorce. Divorced and happily remarried herself, Gilman insists upon a woman's right to choose a better mate and a happier future.

An example of a *Forerunner* story in which a woman is asked to choose between her career and marriage is the story "A Cleared Path" (3: 254). In this story Gilman foregrounds the importance of woman's work in the world and strongly rejects the notion that all women wish (either secretly or overtly) to yield to a man's desires. The protagonist, Mary Watterson, owns a diversified business in Los Angeles consisting of a laundry, a sewing service, and a children's clothing shop. Her relations with the workers are honest, just, and kind. Mary falls in love with a man who has recently moved from New England to Montana to begin ranching. His first year at his venture was far from successful, and he is visiting a sister in California. The man, Ransome Woodruff, struggles to deal with his traditional ideas of marriage. He wishes for Mary to give up her business and move to Montana. "He felt so sure of his ground. He had the whole world's judgment on his side; he had reason, right, expediency, law, custom, his own overwhelming demand — and her love!" (253). But Mary, being the wise and modern woman that she is, says to his demand: "A woman may love a man as well as any woman ever did, yet not be willing to give up her work when it is not necessary — if she holds to a higher duty" (254). Since she feels responsible for all the industry in her neighborhood, her sense of duty is real and clear to her. An old friend of Woodruff finally shows him the folly of his attitude. He reminds Woodruff that the ranch is not really his home but merely an investment, and a poorly paying investment at that. Finally, when Mary holds her ground (despite her unhappiness), Woodruff changes his position and decides to move to Los Angeles. To Gilman, Mary's needs are fully as important as Woodruff's, especially since her work is more economically re-munerative and socially significant. Mary is right, then, in refusing to yield to love.

In "Making a Change" (*Forerunner* 2: 331), Gilman teaches how feminine self-effacement often leads to depression and worse consequences. Here, we meet two women who show that motherhood and marriage need not pre-clude interesting and important work for women. Julia Gordin, a young and beautiful musician, is not talented at motherhood. Her mother-in-law, who who lives with the young couple and has just such a talent, offers assistance, but Julia believes that she is doing her wifely duty by suffering and caring for her child without help. One day, thoroughly depressed, Julia attempts sui-cide. Her nimble mother-in-law saves her and declares that hereafter there will be changes. Without conferring with Julia's husband, Frank, who also is tied to traditional values of men at work supporting women at home, his mother begins a "baby-garden," where she cares for her grandchild and for other children as well. Julia returns to teaching music at which she excels and which she loves. The women hire a great housekeeper-cook with their extra incomes, and all live happily together until Frank is told by a colleague that Julia is working. The young husband is furious and confronts his wife. When Julia and his mother point out how happy and well they both are and inform him of the depressive depths to which the previous situation had brought Julia, Frank wisely accepts the women's solution. Later, he confidently boasts of his home life to all who will listen: families are easy to run — when you know how to do it. Gilman's lesson has not fallen short. "Making a Change" expresses more than a young mother's need for individuality and purpose-ful work of her own; the story also shows that traditional views are not nec-essarily the best or the most practical ones for modern marriages. In her October 1911 essay in the *Forerunner*, Gilman states: "A young woman should be allowed to have her career, a happy marriage and children. But "chil-dren are not improved in proportion to their mother's immolation . . . they need Genius" (2: 11).

The plots of "A Cleared Path" and "Making a Change" parallel the cir-cumstances of Gilman's own married life. Such stories may be read as Gil-man's own wish fulfillment or as an attempt to explore other, better choices that she might have made for her own life. At first wed to an artist who be-lieved that she should support his work by keeping his home as a refuge for him, Gilman was made to feel that her own work held little importance. It was only after her separation from Walter Stetson that Gilman was able to assert her own work as of pre-eminent importance to her life. Later, in developing the criteria under which she would marry Houghton Gilman, she made it clear that she would never allow her work to be submerged by the duties of housekeeping. Such self-abnegation, she well understood, treated neither marriage partner fairly; in fact, it must be destructive to individual well-being. Thus in her stories, Gilman uses the circumstances of her own life to locate happier solutions for the fictive women who find themselves in the same predicaments.

Gilman's stories frequently offer solutions for women who wish to maintain a career and a marriage and still keep within the "woman's sphere." The women in her stories, for the most part, are not college educated, professionally oriented "New Women." They are intelligent, capable, middle-class women, and Gilman offers them life-changing careers based upon realistic options within the scope of their lives. Overall, then, the avenues that Gilman opens to her readership (of white, middle-class, American-born, Protestant women) seem realistic enough to suggest that her readers, too, might take a chance on change.

One rather short-lived component of the *Forerunner* was a column called "Personal Problems." It purported to answer readers' queries, but Gilman probably wrote the questions herself since they tie in so precisely with each issue's major theme. (Interestingly, Bok also wrote the personal column, in the *Journal*, under the pseudonym Ruth Ashmore.) Also, the columns appear so early in the history of her publication that it seems unlikely that readers could have submitted them so quickly. The feature is similar to the advice features that appeared in the *Ladies' Home Journal*, with the one difference that Gilman simply eschewed all frivolous topics. In an early entry Gilman answers two questions about a young woman's duty to her ill or elderly parents. The first question, "What is a person's duty to a sick parent?" (2: 280) is answered facetiously. If you are a man, says Gilman, then you must provide them with a home, a doctor, and medicine. If you are a woman, you must give up your calling to serve the patient as a total servant; otherwise you risk the name of "unnatural daughter" (2: 280). Another questioner wonders whether she should marry an older man who will bail her father out of a bad business, even though she does not love him. Gilman replies emphatically that a woman must never give up her life to help her parents, for that constitutes bondage and not mere filial duty.

In that same issue of the *Forerunner*, Gilman fictionalizes her responses to both these queries in the story "Mr. Robert Grey, Sr." It is one of the few stories that follows the marriage plot outline of then contemporary fiction. Gilman, however, has didactically demonstrated the young woman's worth by showing her determination not to be misled by parental or societal pressure into making a poor marriage choice. Gilman is adamant about those men whom women should not marry under any circumstances. In the fiction of the *Forerunner*, women are encouraged to choose the best mate or to choose no mate at all. For example, a woman should not be forced to marry to help elderly parents, as the author emphasizes in "Mr. Robert Grey, Sr." (1.11: 1),[1] nor should she marry for wealth or position, as in "Old Water" (2: 241). And she should most definitely not marry (or remarry) a man who is "An Offender" (1.4: 3), or one who attempts kidnapping and blackmail, as in "A Mischievous Rudiment" (2: 1).

In "Mr. Robert Grey, Sr." we meet a young girl engaged to Jimmy, a sailor who goes to sea. Shortly thereafter, every kind of hardship befalls her parents and their farm. Mr. Robert Grey, an honorable, wealthy member of their church brings them food and gifts. But as his name suggests, Grey is a tired, faded, uninteresting man. His charity maintains the family through hard times. The girl hears that Jimmy's ship is lost at sea, and Mr. Grey begins to court her. She finds him repugnant, but her mother's eyes plead with her to take him. Her father says, "Here is a good kind man who loves you dearly and wants to marry you at once. If you do it you may save your mother's life, — and set me on my feet again for what remains of mine . . . it's plain duty" (1.11: 4). The girl will not marry Mr. Grey. She offers to be his servant or his nurse but not his wife. He marries another. The family survives on what the girl earns from the vegetable garden, and as a nod to the common conventions of such stories, Jimmy is not lost after all but returns to marry his true love. Here, Gilman rewards the girl *not* for being true to one whom she supposed dead but rather for being true to herself. Neither an "unnatural daughter" nor a slave to her parents, the protagonist makes the right marriage choice for herself, and thus Gilman affords her a "happily ever after" conclusion. It is one of the few stories that follows the marriage plot outline of then contemporary fiction. Gilman has, however, didactically shown the young woman's worth by demonstrating her determination not to be misled by parental or societal pressure into making a bad marriage choice.

In "Old Water" and "A Mischievous Rudiment," Gilman creates situations where strong, self-confident young women think quickly, move swiftly, and once again become the heroines of their own lives. Gilman perceived that the control of one's own life was a woman's right and that to exercise that right was her moral and civic duty. In "A Mischievous Rudiment," the antagonist uses the threat of moral ruin as his means of asserting his power, and in "Old Water" the poet would have seen himself and Ellen dead rather than be rejected by her.

In "Old Water," Gilman asserts that when a woman takes her fate into her own hands, she can survive.[2] Ellen Osgood, the protagonist, who is a beautiful and athletic young woman interested in science and math, is wooed by her mother's choice for her, a famous poet, Mr. Pendexter. She cannot stand his lack of athletic prowess or his poems about "dead people and dead times" (2: 255). She lives in the here and now, but for her mother's sake she is polite to the poet. Then, one night, walking along a cliff, he presses his suit. She refuses him and tries to fend off his physical advances. Parodying the sentimental dialogue so often seen in the mass-media periodicals for women, Gilman has Ellen best the effete character of Mr. Pendexter. He grabs Ellen to himself in order to kiss her and pull her to her death saying, "It is your fate! Our Fate! We will die together if we cannot live together" (2: 259). And it was his fate to drown. Ellen, of course, could swim.

A story with a similar theme of a girl saving herself from a bad marriage is "A Mischievous Rudiment." In this story, Ria, a fast-thinking young woman, rescues herself from a bully. Ria is a young lady of property who has assembled her three most interesting suitors for a weekend at her aunt's house. One man, Hugh Wyndham, declares, "A woman — a real woman — needs to be mastered! . . . She loves the man who can make her love him — against her will!" To prove his point and his mastery, one evening, pretending to escort her to a neighboring party, he tells her that instead, he has arranged for them to be married by a justice of the peace. Since it is too late to turn back, she must spend the night with him, and this contrived incident will ruin her reputation. Thinking quickly, Ria announces that she has lost her jewel case from the open car. Returning on the country road they came on, she says she sees the case, and he gets out of the car to retrieve it. Ria slams the car into full throttle, leaving Wyndham on the road. She then returns home and chooses a quiet boy who loves her and who will go out into the world to earn his way so that his income will equal hers. Thus, Gilman insists that it is not enough to be a wealthy man, one must be a worthy man, and worthiness is determined by a desire for equality and a shared sense of purpose in marriage.

Social responsibility achieves supreme significance in all of Gilman's fiction. In her story "An Offender," the morality of the female protagonist keeps her from remarrying her wealthy and handsome ex-husband. The Cortlands have been divorced for two years. They have a young son, Harry, and Mr. Cortland has begun to re-court his wife. But Mr. Cortland owns and operates four streetcar lines with little or no attention to public safety, comfort, or convenience. The settlement house has asked him to make his drivers more aware of the children near the cars. While he is reproposing to his ex-wife, a small child is crushed beneath a streetcar right outside their window. It takes an agonizingly long time to free the small body. Mr. Cortland, moved by the sight, pledges to install a more expensive fender to ward off such accidents. But it is too late. The child has died, and with it, Cortland's last chance. His ex-wife dismisses him, saying that she will never see him again. In this story, a woman who can remarry into luxury, comfort, and position understands that she must not marry a man who is so concerned with his corporation's finances that he condones noise, pollution, and death. Her refusal is at once a personal and a political action with ramifications for women's personal conduct in general. Women need never settle for situations that make them morally uncomfortable or personally unhappy. It is better to remain single than to compromise one's work or sense of self, according to Gilman.

Although "The Offender" most certainly deals with the choices a woman must make about marriage, it is equally concerned with civic responsibility. Such engagement with the larger society's needs is of prime importance to Gilman, and it is foregrounded again and again in both the short fiction and the serialized novels of the *Forerunner*. Gilman often attempts thematic unity around a given issue, such as civic responsibility, within singular issues of her magazine; the January 1910 *Forerunner* is a case in point. In that issue, an essay titled "Private Morality and Public Immorality" suggests that "public evils are what society suffers from most in increasing ratio . . . morality is no longer a mere matter of 'thou shalt' and 'thou shalt not' but a vast complex of mutually interactive conduct in which personal responsibility has some small place" (9). If the streetcar magnate will not improve the safety features of his trollies for the benefit of society, then he must be shown how wrong his actions are. Mrs. Cortland, by refusing to remarry him, demonstrates her free choice and her higher moral sense. Here again, in her short fiction and her essay, the utopian choices Gilman offers women concerning work and marriage adhere to the notion that small, personal changes can create larger, societal improvements.

In "Our Androcentric Culture," Gilman reminds her readers that in order to serve the world all people must realize "not only the sternly, dominant father, and the silently, serviceable other but the real union of all people to sanely and economically manage their affairs" (1.1: 20). Such recognition of women's needs as well as sane and economic home management is shown to be possible in such stories as "In Two Houses" and "Mrs. Elder's Idea." Both these stories demonstrate Gilman's belief that a nontraditional housekeeping setup might make an otherwise untenable situation work. "In Two Houses" (2: 171) is the story of two cousins, heirs to their families' matching and contiguous estates, who take up residence in their respective houses. Diana Blair is a "New Woman," a writer and singer who understands that she can live and work very happily without "[a]ny man's assistance" (171). Her cousin, Marshall Blair, is a doctor and scientific researcher. A thorough misogynist, he exclaims, "Confound all women . . . Feeble, sickly, sentimental, selfish, shallow, idle, luxurious, empty headed, useless trash!" (174). Gilman has him articulate the often heard male remarks about the "New Woman." One summer night, however, while swimming, Marshall develops a cramp and Diana saves him from drowning. On a later occasion, Diana develops food poisoning and Marshall ministers to her in her illness. While she recovers, she enjoys the sound of Marshall's violin playing, which wafts through her open windows. When she is well, she remarks to Marshall that "we are making melodramatic fools of ourselves" (177). They spend time together joining her voice to his violin. Soon they agree to marry. She replies, however, "I am a writer and will never be any man's housekeeper" to his assertion "I am a scientist and no family cares must ever interfere with my work" (177). After their marriage, each lives and works in his and her respective house, and neither is sublimated to the other's career. "In Two Houses" is a story that is utopian in its solution. Gilman had proposed such an arrangement to Stetson during their separation, but he would not adopt it. In this story, as in so many others, Gilman creates a situation where both partners (who value each other's professional accomplishments) are large-spirited humanists who willingly enter into unconventional living arrangements. She shows that, though not many couples can afford to keep two separate domiciles, still it is a solution that some people can elect.[3]

In "Mrs. Elder's Idea" (3: 29), Gilman again teaches that a woman can find joy in her separate space, in her work and in helping others. Her children all grown and her marriage cooling to that "torpid, tepid mutual accommodation which is complacently referred to by the worldly wise as 'settling down,'" (29) Mrs. Elder has little to inspire her. She has a fondness for shopping and does it well. Her husband regards this pleasure as a silly vice. The Elders live in a suburb of Boston, which is a compromise for her love of the city and his passion for farms. One day Mr. Elder announces that he has bought the farm of his dreams and they will be removing to it presently. Heartsick at the prospect of being shut up in a remote country farm, Mrs. Elder finds herself growing depressed. "A dull cloud oppressed her dreams; she woke with a sense of impending calamity, and as the remembrance grew, into awakening pain" (31). Since her husband had not confided his plans to her, she busies herself with silent plans of her own. Contacting two of her unmarried children in Boston, she makes plans to take a large apartment in a boarding house there. Her two children will live with her. There, she supports herself by becoming a professional shopper. When her shocked husband asks, "Where do I come in?" (33) she replies that he may join her in the winter. She remarks that she is going to town next week and that she hopes to see him at Christmas. "When he did come to town, he found an eagerly delighted family and a wife so roguishly young, so attractively dressed, so vivacious and happy and amusing, that the warmth of a sudden Indian Summer fell upon his heart" (33). From that time on, they spent winters in her flat in the city and summers on his farm. "Mr. Elder found that two half homes were really more satisfying than one whole home, and a whole unhappy wife withering in discontent" (33). This utopian answer to the problem of cooled ardor and empty nests works only for those who can afford such a solution. But, in general, Gilman wrote for an audience of women very much like herself: middle-class women whose options were more plentiful than those of working-class women.

Not every marital situation could be improved by domestic revisions, however. For every Mrs. Elder, Gilman understood there were women and men whose lives had come to irreconcilable impasses. She was not averse to presenting fictional characters who, like their author, saw that divorce was the only way to save themselves. Although Gilman's amicable divorce from Stetson was difficult for the public to understand, the situations Gilman presents, in her fiction, as reasons for divorce are rather clear-cut and easy to agree with. In "Mrs. Beazley's Deeds," the husband confiscates all the property that has been left to his wife. In "Turned," the husband has impregnated the housemaid, and in "Being Reasonable," the husband is a bigamist. While it is true that these situations are quite different from those that rent the Stetson marriage, together they make a powerful, unequivocal case that divorce can be a preferable, life-affirming choice.

In all three of these stories, we note again that Gilman's larger answer to the problems of her protagonists is utopian in outlook. Some extant economic situation makes the solution possible but only for middle-class, white women. In the case of Mrs. Beazley, divorce is facilitated by the fact that her husband has not quite sold all the property and the wife's family homestead is still available to her. In "Being Reasonable," the women have recourse to a living in that they are both trained musicians. The heroine in "Turned" can decide to leave her husband because she is a college professor and knows she can get a job. In another utopian element of these stories, the woman who has few resources (because of her class limitations), such as Mrs. Beazley or Gerta Peterson (Mrs. Marroner's maid in "Turned"), finds help from middle-class women who have the knowledge and the resources necessary to effect a rescue. Those women who cannot be their own agents of change find willing female mentors in each of these three stories of the *Forerunner*.

In "Mrs. Beazley's Deeds" (7: 225), for example, we meet a worn-out mother who runs the store of her cruel, selfish, and conniving husband. Church doctrine has taught her to obey her husband and accept her miserable lot. One day Mr. Beazley announces that he is taking in a summer boarder. He introduces a very attractive woman, Miss Lawrence, into his already cramped home. Mrs. Beazley is annoyed at first, but she later begins to like and admire her boarder. In the meantime Mr. Beazley slyly works at selling off the considerable real estate holdings that his wife brought to their marriage. Miss Lawrence gains Mrs. Beazley's confidence and suggests that she does not have to sign the last deed, which will make her propertyless. Mrs. Beazley shrinks, but ultimately she refuses to sign the document. After several other demonstrations of his abuse, Miss Lawrence asks Mrs. Beazley whether she has ever thought of divorcing her husband, but she is told that under New York State law Mrs. Beazley cannot do that. (Adultery was the only reason a divorce was granted in New York at that time.) When Mr. Beazley goes out of town, the women withdraw the entire bank account, sell the store, and move to the old family homestead on a dam where Mrs. Beazley can (conveniently) sell water power for electricity. When Mr. Beazley returns, the judge claims that he has no recourse except to declare that Mrs. Beazley has been deserted. Miss Lawrence turns out to be a well-known New York real estate lawyer who had come to the country for a change of scenery.

The boarder, brought in to spite Mrs. Beazley, proves to be her savior instead. In this story, when the protagonist cannot see how to change her own life, a stronger, more worldly, and more educated single woman must change it for her. But the story shows that even a woman in the most dire circumstances can at least seek help from another woman against the tyranny of an evil man and a bad marriage.

A similar salvation takes place in "Turned." Mrs. Marroner, a middle-aged childless, former college professor discovers that her beloved husband, who is abroad on business, has impregnated their beautiful but dull-witted

Scandinavian maid, Gerta Peterson.[4] Mrs. Marroner's first impulse is to lash out at Gerta, but then she allows reason to rule her emotion and realizes that Gerta is the true victim of this tragedy. She sees that Gerta, who is innocent and trusting, has been lured to her ruin:

> As the older wiser woman forced herself to understand and extenuate the girl's misdeed and foresee her ruined future, a new feeling rose in her heart, strong, clear, and overmastering; a sense of measureless condemnation for the man who had done this thing. He knew. He understood. He could fully foresee and measure the consequence of his act. He appreciated to the full, the ignorance, the grateful affection, the habitual docility, of which he deliberately took advantage. (230)

In "Turned," the woman with agency, Mrs. Marroner, at first adheres to the line seen in the fiction of mass-media magazines.[5] In Catharine Maria Sedgwick's well-known story "Fanny McDermott" (1845), the ruined young woman dies of starvation and exposure, while the man who has destroyed her woos another, wealthier girl. It is a cautionary tale to all innocent young women who would be taken in by well-dressed and seemingly thoughtful men. In "Turned," Mrs. Marroner sees herself, at first, as the woman wronged and she lashes out at the victim. But Gilman creates a new moral paradigm in her fiction in that women are able to determine the true victim and victimizer.

Gilman's flipping of the accepted cultural binary of victim and victimizer was not solely relegated to the participants in a marriage. The responsibilities of parents to children are similarly examined in her story "With a Difference (Not Literature)" (5: 29). The interesting title of this story underscores how certain Gilman was of the difference between *Forerunner* fiction and that of contemporaneous mass-media short stories. This is a tale in which a young girl is wooed, tricked, and ruined by a city roué. Her father is about to turn her out of the house, but her mother stops him. The mother blames herself for not teaching her child about such men. She tells her husband that he cannot force her out, asking him, "[I]sn't it enough that miserable villain has taken advantage of this poor innocent child and brought this shame upon her without you should kick her out to absolute disgrace[?]" (31). She understands that his reaction is just masculine pride at work. He sees the light, and the girl remains at home and educates her siblings about the workings of the world. The reason that this story is "Not Literature" is obvious. In mass-media fiction of that period, such cases are routinely terminated by the father's throwing the unfortunate girl out (usually into a snowy night) as a moral lesson to other girls not to allow themselves to fall into such circumstances. In Theodore Dreiser's novel *Jennie Gerhardt* (1911), the father feels his daughter is a disgrace and he banishes Jennie from his house. Gilman's strongly held belief was that, in real life, parents are morally obligated even to a fallen child. The parents' obligation is to warn their daughters before they get into trouble or to face the consequences of their children's enforced innocence and ignorance. Although Gerta is not her own child, in "Turned" Mrs. Marroner understands that as the employer of a vulnerable young immigrant she is *in loco parentis* and bears a moral responsibility toward the girl. In both "Turned" and "With a Difference," Gilman shifts the responsibility traditionally placed on the ruined girl to put the blame squarely on the man who has ruined her. The indictment becomes a powerful new weapon in an old debate.

Another story that advocates divorce on moral grounds and that shows the power of women working together is "Being Reasonable" (6: 197). In this story, Mr. Cunningham meets a similar united front of women as do Mr. Beazley and Mr. Marroner. Cunningham's lovely musician wife, Mary, married him just after her dearest friend, Betty, disappeared from her life. Betty and she had trained as musicians together, Mary as a pianist and Betty as a vocalist. Mary and her husband live comfortably and well with their little girl. Mary's only sorrow is that her husband works late almost every night and spends little time with her. One evening she goes to the movies and finds her husband with another woman. After a bit of sleuthing, she discovers that the rival woman is none other than her old lost friend. Betty is also married to Cunningham and has an infant son. Mary apprises Betty of their situations. The next night the women surprise him by being together at Mary's home. Both announce they will divorce him. Because Betty has a job and can arrange for Mary to become her accompanist, and because the two women remain financially comfortable, they can make this valiant stand. More important, however, is that the love the two women have for one another is stronger than the love either has for the man.

In her short fiction, Gilman re-visions traditional marriage and demonstrates that women can take initiative to choose a right mate or at least reject the wrong one. Women are shown living in unconventional domestic relationships that make a serious pursuit of their careers possible while they remain autonomous human beings devoted to their married state. Gilman also shows women in untenable circumstances who face the truth about their husbands and marriages and resolve to extricate themselves and begin life afresh.

In every one of the short stories in the *Forerunner*, Gilman questions the absolute truths that were preached from the pulpit and reiterated in the popular media, such as films and magazines like the *Ladies' Home Journal*, and that governed so many women's lives: that good daughters married the men their parents chose; good wives submitted to the wills of their husbands; and good mothers sacrificed their very lives for their children. Although unconventional and even utopian in her solutions to the problems she presents, Charlotte Perkins Gilman uses the periodical to make a strong case for greater female autonomy in ways that were then (as they remain today) persuasive. Gilman understood that when women empower themselves or assist other women in acts of self-empowerment, then and only then does a woman become the heroine of her own story.

NOTES

1 It was only with the beginning of the second volume of the *Forerunner* that Gilman began paginating sequentially. Hence the addition of the "numeral" for all references to stories in the first volume.

2 Another interesting element in this story is its emphasis on adequate physical development for young women. As a girl, Gilman spent some of her happiest hours in a gym in Providence. In her diary she wrote proudly of her growing physical prowess. A book that she kept by her bedside and viewed as almost sacred was *How to Get Strong and Stay That Way* (1879) by William Blaikie. He wrote that "physical fitness is the key to sanity and mental power; to self-respect and high purpose; to sound health and vigorous enduring strength; to genial attractive good nature and sunny welcome cheerfulness" (quoted in Hill 66).

3 Margaret Drabble and Michael Holroyd have chosen just such a domestic situation in their marriage.

4 Gilman was involved with many of the women's organizations that were the bulwark of the Progressive Era. Women such as Jane Addams of Hull House and others who lobbied to improve the working conditions of women and children serve as role models for Gilman's strong-minded change agents such as Miss Lawrence and Mrs. Marroner.

5 For another example of the traditional thinking on "ruined" women, see Lydia Maria Child's story "The Quadroon." Both the Sedgwick and Child story are available in Barbara Solomon, ed., *Rediscoveries: American Short Stories by Women, 1832–1916* (New York: Mentor, 1994).

Craig Monk

ƐMMA GOLDMAN, MOTHER EARTH, & THE LITTLE MAGAZINE IMPULSE IN MODERN AMERICA

Mother Earth, a monthly publication begun in New York City in 1906, was for the anarchist agitator Emma Goldman the realization of a "cherished dream" (*Living My Life* 377). In spite of her acknowledged power of oratory, Goldman believed that the words she spoke from the platform were transitory. She had faith in the power of the written word, and she hoped to employ it for the good of the anarchist cause through the regular appearance of a magazine that would serve as a forum for her ideas and the ideas of her like-minded comrades. She also was aware of the economic sacrifice likely demanded by such a venture. The exclusiveness of commercial magazines had begun to give rise to a new generation of fiercely independent literary publications forced to compete for scarce resources from a relatively small readership.

For the most part, progress toward a Modern aesthetic in the United States can be charted in publications like the *Little Review*, a magazine in which emerging writers were encouraged to shape a new artistic vision. The founding of *Mother Earth*, then, cannot be seen as a major event in the development of the "littles"; instead *Mother Earth* is an important achievement in American letters for it established a precedent for a generation of little magazine editors who operated in the shadow of the commercial publishing industry that Goldman sought to oppose. Although Goldman's publication was conceived as a joining of art and social commentary, she widely acknowledged orthodox literary values and excluded the sort of artistic experiments that defined the "little magazines."

In person, Goldman had a compelling presence. Subsequent assessments of her speaking abilities, like those undertaken by historian Richard Drinnon, have gone so far as to suggest that she remains "perhaps the most accomplished, magnetic speaker in American history" (ii). In Goldman's own time, Margaret Anderson contended that listening to her speak could lead one "to turn anarchist" (*My Thirty Years' War* 54). Anderson observed that the key to Goldman's success was the immediacy of her message and the directness of her delivery: "[S]he says it instead of putting it into books . . . she hurls it from the platform straight into the minds and hearts of the eager, bewildered, or unfriendly people who listen to her" ("The Challenge of Emma Goldman" 6). By the time she decided to begin *Mother Earth*, Goldman was aware of the power she wielded from the platform. In a letter to her colleagues written from the midst of a successful speaking tour, she chided playfully: "After this, I hope you will never again doubt the importance of public meetings and the great and far-reaching influence of my speaking" ("A Letter" 14). But behind this bravado, Goldman began to acknowledge the limits of this itinerant lecturing. Once *Mother Earth* had been launched, she could celebrate the fact that "the spoken word, fleeting at best, was no longer to be my only medium of expression" (*Living My Life* 377). Although she might be putting aside the opportunity to confront her audience in person, she accepted that "the printed thought" was "more lasting in its effect." But Emma Goldman never suggested that she intended to give up the road entirely with the launch of her magazine, although she did later observe happily that "the platform" would no longer be "the only place where I could feel at home" (*Living My Life* 377). Indeed, for all the enthusiasm Goldman expressed at the launch of *Mother Earth*, her touring would soon promote not only her anarchist principles, but also the fledgling magazine on whose pages these principles were articulated. Like many small publications struggling for survival at this time, *Mother Earth* provided Goldman reasonable access to her readership.

By the end of the nineteenth century, the magazine trade was more responsive to the demands of advertisers who discovered that these publications could reach a disparate readership. The material that Emma Goldman wished to publish certainly would not attract the financial backing of powerful interests. Still, in 1906, Goldman was responding to the same desire for creative protest as that which produced the literary insurgence of the Chicago *Chap-Book* (1894–98), the *Green Sheaf* of London (1903–04), and New York's *Papyrus* (1903–12). While a useful distinction on editorial grounds between radical political publications and these more literary magazines defined as "littles" can be made, the issues raised in their daily operations were similar throughout this period.

When *Mother Earth* began, the single copy price was a dime; yearly subscriptions cost one dollar. Unbelievably, that price did not change for the entire twelve-year run of the magazine. There was no profit motive behind the venture. Indeed, the magazine was launched with only the help of a benefit performance in New York by Paul Orleneff's Russian drama troupe. Complications in staging the production forced a change in the bill, and as a result turnouts were much poorer than expected. In her autobiography, Goldman lamented, "The thousand dollars or more we had hoped to realize dwindled down to two hundred and fifty, a sorry capital with which to launch a magazine" (*Living My Life* 378). Goldman's frankness in discussing her finances was a trademark; *Mother Earth* frequently published a detailed account of credits and expenditures at the back of the magazine. This informed readers rather usefully, for example, that it cost $150 a month to print *Mother Earth* during its second year of operation ("Mother Earth Sustaining Fund" 107). With peak circulation of the magazine at five thousand copies, *Mother Earth* exceeded the circulation numbers of its contemporaries (Wexler 122).

Unfortunately, for the magazine to achieve stability and allow Goldman to reach the audience she desired, too few of these sales came from subscribing readers. During the magazine's first year Goldman suggested that more than half of the revenue necessary to print *Mother Earth* was generated by single-copy sales ("To My Readers" 7–8). Without the financial commitment of paid subscribers, she was unable to keep expanding the operation, so securing dedicated new readers became a consuming ambition. This struggle to keep the magazine afloat with paying subscribers may reflect the tension inherent in a Socialist business venture, the strain between making enough money and getting the ideological message across to a wide readership. During the sixth year of publishing, for example, Goldman began to offer free books from among those published or distributed by the anarchists in an attempt to generate greater interest in the cause. The cost of these books would be a small price to pay to enlist long-term supporters. Once an individual had subscribed to *Mother Earth*, however, Goldman was reluctant to remove that person from the mailing list, even if their subscription had lapsed. There were frequent calls for money from "delinquent subscribers" whom she found difficult to abandon but whom she found increasingly difficult to carry without their renewals. *Mother Earth's* dependence on the sale of individual copies left the magazine vulnerable in time of crisis. For example, police raids and seizures could threaten the magazine during any given month.

Dilemmas rooted in editorial decisions also forced Goldman to secure other means for funding the magazine. The *Mother Earth* issue of October 1906 contained material in commemoration of Leon Czolgosz, the Polish emigrant who had assassinated President William McKinley five years earlier and with whose crime the authorities had attempted to connect Goldman. Goldman admitted that while Alexander Berkman and Max Baginski, two of her principal collaborators on the magazine, were enthusiastic about this material, "other comrades" opposed the material "on the ground that anything about Czolgosz would hurt the cause as well as the magazine." Goldman was defiant, determined "never to permit anyone, whether group or individual, to dictate" the editorial policy of Mother Earth to her, even though supporters "threatened to withdraw their material support" ("Living My Life" 386–87). Such setbacks obliged Goldman to concentrate on additional means to secure funds; one of the primary strategies was to expand her speaking engagements by organizing lecture tours. As early as April 1906, Goldman revealed that "friends of Mother Earth in various Western cities have proposed a lecture tour on behalf of the magazine" (Mother Earth 1.2: 6). At this time, she began the Mother Earth Sustaining Fund and by the end of the first year of publishing announced increasingly ambitious tours so that the profits from these engagements could defer printing costs ("Lecture Tour" 18). When speaking of the magazine, Goldman increasingly used a mother-child metaphor when commenting that she was "racing about the country, seeking new friends for her child" (Goldman and Berkman, "Mother Earth" 2).

Her ability to bring out the magazine each month without interruption dwarfs the achievement of the twentieth-century's most important literary publications; just about every "little" of significance experienced some period during which it was forced to publish irregularly. Ever resourceful, Goldman undertook additional fund-raising schemes in New York in this early period. In November 1906 Mother Earth organized a social evening so that "her children" could undertake the "joyous forgetfulness of the troubles of life." Goldman also wished to promote the magazine further and raise funds from the thirty-five cents she charged for admission. But any venture undertaken by the anarchists was looked upon with suspicion by civic leaders, and the police, wise to this well-publicized gathering and in a mood of antianarchist zeal, broke up the party and by doing so contributed to what was described at the time as the magazine's financially "deplorable condition" ("Observations and Comments" 2). In spite of these difficulties, Goldman was proud that Mother Earth was able to continue publishing while "consistently refusing to be gagged by a profitable advertising department" (Goldman and Berkman, "Our Sixth Birthday" 3). Indeed, the magazine struggled on until 1917, when Goldman and Berkman were arrested for opposing the draft and the Post Office refused to handle *Mother Earth* any longer. The two were eventually sentenced and deported, but during this period Goldman arranged to distribute the smaller *Mother Earth Bulletin*, "largely as a means of keeping in touch with our friends and subscribers" ("Freedom of Criticism and Opinion" 1). That publication printed seven issues under very difficult circumstances, ceasing operations after the April 1918 issue. Defiant to the last, Goldman was in jail, and she wrote reluctantly to her supporters that their renegade operation in Greenwich Village should be discontinued, owing to the relentless shadow cast over them by the police. But in light of the chronic financial worries and the pressures from the authorities that eventually caused *Mother Earth* to collapse, it is remarkable that the magazine was able to print 138 consecutive issues during a time in American history marked by zealous suppression of unorthodox political thought. Social and economic discord made Goldman's audiences possible. It is true that the magazine, which usually ran sixty-four pages long, was occasionally compelled to scale back to thirty-two, but Goldman always managed to preserve the focus of *Mother Earth.*

Goldman's tenacity in overseeing financial matters was an extension of the care she took in shaping the editorial direction of the magazine. Originally, *Mother Earth* had been called the *Open Road* in honor of Walt Whitman. While protests from an existing midwestern magazine forced Goldman to change its title at the last minute, the name represented some of the spirit of the quest for freedom she wished to foster through her publication. The first issue of *Mother Earth*, in March 1906, contained an editorial statement, written by Goldman and Baginski, that defined the approach of this "monthly magazine devoted to social science and literature" both for readers and potential contributors:

> *Mother Earth* will endeavor to attract and appeal to all those who oppose encroachment on public and individual life. It will appeal to those who strive for something higher, weary of the commonplace; to those that feel that stagnation is a deadweight on the firm and elastic step of progress; to those who breathe freely only in limited space; to those who long for the tender shade of a new dawn for a humanity free from the dread of want, the dread of starvation in the face of mountains of riches. The Earth free for the free individual! (1)

It is clear from this slogan with the proselytizing tone of "the dread of want" and the "mountains of riches" that Goldman was concerned with reaching out to comrades in the political cause. But this was not intended to be a political call to arms that excluded young writers interested in experimenting with literary form. There was more than a little encouragement in this introduction to daring young writers, precisely the sort of budding literary talents who would animate the century's literary publications. Indeed, writers who were "weary of the commonplace" saw aesthetic experimentation as a means to "strive for something higher." Artistically, it was "stagnation . . . on the firm and elastic step of progress" that was felt at the time by writers like T.S. Eliot, who later commented that through the first decade of the century, there was not "a single living poet, in either England or America, then at the height of his powers, whose work was capable of pointing the way to a young poet conscious of the desire for a new idiom" (58).

What is clear, however, is that *Mother Earth* did not attract the promising new writers that Goldman envisioned for her magazine. By the end of the first year of publishing, she complained that she could not enlist enough "men and women who demand new values from our social, literary and artistic life." Uncovering great numbers of these individuals represented "all too high ideals!" Goldman announced in the magazine: "The publisher did not sufficiently consider the American spirit of commercialism and the lack of interest in any struggle whose practical success is not measurable in dollars and cents" ("A Year's Struggle" 2). Moreover, Goldman refused to hide the literary shortcomings of her existing anarchist brethren. In a short piece titled "Literary Notes" at the back of the first issue of *Mother Earth*, she lamented "that several of the contributions" she received, "while having merits, were not of the form to be used for a magazine" ("Literary Notes" 62). Eventually, Goldman was forced to admit that "the original purpose of gathering brave spirits who could find no expression in other periodicals . . . has not materialized." But while she acknowledged that at least some of "those who are brave cannot write," she seethed at "those who are brave and can write" but who were "compelled to write for money" (Goldman, Berkman, and Reitman 1).

Although Goldman continued to blame the lack of conviction and courage among liberal writers and those she identified as "the New York literati" for the stillborn alliance between art and anarchism in *Mother Earth*, she would later concede that a substantive difference existed between her and the modern writers. While she always resented their lack of support and read it as an abandonment of her venture, she admitted that through the magazine she sought "freedom and abundance in life as the basis for art." Her complaint with many contemporary writers was that they saw art as "an escape from reality," not as a tool for reform (*Living My Life* 395). This acknowledgment indicates that in matters of art Goldman remained concerned primarily with content — of a radical, political nature. The emergence of a modern reconsideration of reality, engaging the existence of that beyond the tangible, was not welcomed by Goldman. Indeed, this suggestion that modern writers were growing too concerned with aesthetic innovation and too neglectful of social and political events was made by activists even as literary magazines, asserting their political allegiances, responded to the events of the late 1920s and 1930s.

There was no such political urgency in 1906, however, and even in the years that followed, radical writers of the liberal persuasion were drawn eventually to Socialism and not to the program outlined in *Mother Earth* (Wexler 124). Not surprisingly, the *Masses*, founded in 1911, thrived during this period, having proven itself more receptive to literary diversity by printing writers like Carl Sandburg and Louis Untermeyer. In his *Demanding the Impossible: A History of Anarchism*, Peter Marshall suggests that Goldman served effectively as a literary doyenne by introducing many American readers to a number of the European writers she admired (398–99). While this is true to some extent — a piece from Russian author Maxim Gorky represented the first creative material published in the magazine — most of these poems and stories were international standards that would have been well known to many of Goldman's subscribers. *Mother Earth* sought to challenge an American suspicion of foreign literature. Literary works tended to illuminate the struggles against injustice that inspired Goldman. Rather than introduce "a new idiom," the literary selections were grounded in the conventions of realism.

The reader of *Mother Earth* fails to get a better sense of Goldman's specific aesthetic principles through the evolution of her literary criticism. Indeed, the unfolding of a critical standard was a central development in the history of most important little magazines. Magazine editors like Margaret Anderson (*Little Review*), Eugene Jolas (*transition*), Alfred Kreymborg (*Glebe, Others*), Harriet Monroe (*Poetry*), and Ernest Walsh (*This Quarter*) defined their publications by issuing critiques, editorials, and manifestos, all to do with art. These little magazines were primarily literary; *Mother Earth* was not. Although Goldman published *The Social Significance of Modern Drama* (1914), she made relatively few specific comments on literature in *Mother Earth*, preferring instead to concentrate on social concerns. Goldman's frequent absences from New York while she was lecturing served to blunt any sharpening of an accumulated aesthetic that might be assembled over a number of issues. When colleagues like Berkman were left to edit the magazine, there was little or no mention of literary matters at all (Solomon 94). Indeed, the issue of Berkman's editorship is a difficult one. Goldman found great personal solace from starting the magazine, a cure from the malaise that had set in following the McKinley assassination and its aftermath. She hoped that *Mother Earth* would similarly reinvigorate her "Sasha" after his release in 1906 from a long prison sentence for attempting to kill industrialist Henry Clay Frick. While they had been comrades and occasional lovers from the time they met in 1889, Goldman and Berkman did not come together over *Mother Earth*, and it proved no panacea for Berkman's ills. The two actually fought over the magazine: they differed on editorial matters, and he charged her with "intellectual aloofness and revolutionary inconsistency" (Goldman, *Living My Life* 393). All of these factors contributed to *Mother Earth's* lack of a coherent literary aesthetic.

While different voices blocked the assembling of a critical aesthetic, Goldman worked hard to keep the magazine from being inconsistent in opinion. She wished to give Berkman and her other allies an opportunity to develop their voice in the magazine, but as its publisher she oversaw the overall approach taken in *Mother Earth*. For example, in *Mother Earth* of October 1908, Hippolyte Havel published a series of reviews titled "Literature: Its Influence Upon Social Life." In the piece, Havel reaffirmed the role of the artist in revolution. "Important changes in the life of a people find their most decisive expression in contemporary art," he maintained. "The work of the artist, the composer, the painter, the sculptor, or the writer mirrors the reflex of the various struggles, hopes, and aspirations of our social life" (329). Certainly, there is nothing here that could be read as out of step with Goldman's personal beliefs, or that even the skeptical Berkman would have failed to welcome. Unfortunately, contributions like Havel's stopped short of providing practical criticism, and in lieu of a precisely defined set of aesthetic values framing the magazine, readers could only look for guidance to the nineteenth-century realists Goldman so admired. Hence, for all its declared interest in contemporary writing, *Mother Earth* put forward literary models out of step with the burgeoning modern ethos. The kinds of writers Goldman wished to attract employed literary models that increasingly were questioned and rejected by contemporary Modernist writers. Margaret Anderson later wrote of Goldman's zeal in talks she gave on "Shaw, Ibsen, Strindberg, Hauptmann," but Anderson believed that Goldman expressed anarchist opinions that reveal the limitations of her critical judgment (*My Thirty Years' War* 83). Goldman simply could not apply her socially progressive ideas to contemporary literature. During a discussion involving Anderson, Berkman, Heap, and Goldman, Anderson was shocked to hear that Goldman believed that Oscar Wilde's "The Ballad of Reading Gaol" represented "better art than" did his *Salomé*. According to Anderson, Goldman condemned to her the direction of modern letters by complaining that "the working-man hasn't enough leisure to be interested" in the seemingly opaque art then becoming fashionable. Berkman summarized the approach taken to literature in their anarchist circle by maintaining, "If only a few people understand the art you talk about that's the proof that it's not for humanity" (*My Thirty Years' War* 126–27).

One notable exception to the general preference for realist literature in Goldman's magazine, however, can be found with the appearance of William Zukerman's "Tendencies of Modern Literature" in the October 1910 *Mother Earth*. Zukerman begins rather tentatively, claiming that he intended "merely to point out some of the chief characteristics of modern literature (and art in general)." He asserts: [T]hat "modern literature must necessarily be subjective and individualistic," because it proceeds from "the soul as its basis," seems to anticipate a condemnation of this art that could never be "objective and social" (262). Zukerman concludes, however, that modern art "elevates man, brings him nearer to God, to goodness, and to beauty." While this transcendence "has been the aim of all great literature," Zukerman claims further that "no school, as a school, did ever come so near to the aim as the modern school of writing." Modern literature, in his view, had achieved a "real greatness," allowing it to be "of such great service to humanity" (266). The juxtaposition of Zukerman's rhapsodic tribute to contemporary letters with the usual dour and cynical treatment of modern art in *Mother Earth* provided a welcomed light moment in the history of the magazine. Indeed, Drinnon complains that "*Mother Earth* lacked a sense of humor . . . the reader was weighed down by the deep Russian seriousness of its pages" (iii). Not only did the magazine eschew the conscious development of the aesthetic ideals that defined literary publications of the day, it also lacked any true sense of debate, playful or otherwise, on artistic matters. Goldman appears to have believed that the creative form her struggle should take needed no explanation, and mindful of the opposition her social doctrines elicited, she offered herself no opportunity to expound the value of literary realism while debating writers who held different views.

If *Mother Earth* cannot take its place with the important literary magazines that flourished in the first years of the century, what is its legacy? There are at least two. First, the publication succeeds in setting down Goldman's anarchist ideals, providing a valuable collection of her thought that subsequently appears, in her autobiography, *Living My Life*. Second, *Mother Earth* provides a vehicle for anarchist writers at a time when their material was unpublishable elsewhere. This persistence served as an exemplar for the literary magazines that would follow.

For more than a decade, *Mother Earth* assembled material central to Goldman's view of anarchism. On the page facing the title page of her autobiography, Goldman defines anarchism as "the philosophy of a new social order based on liberty unrestricted by man-made laws." She maintained that "all governments rest on coercion and force," and "they are therefore harmful and unnecessary" (*Living My Life* ii). Goldman spent years expanding on these ideas in the magazine, applying anarchist principles to such important questions of the day as birth control and prostitution. In "The Tragedy of Woman's Emancipation" in the first issue of *Mother Earth*, for example, she counseled that "true emancipation begins neither at the polls or in courts. It begins in woman's soul" (17). Skeptical of the militancy that characterized many contemporary women's desire to integrate into an existing social and political system that was traditionally defined by men, Goldman warned that "merely external emancipation" had "isolated woman and . . . robbed her of the fountain springs of that happiness which is so essential to her" (10). In the April 1913 *Mother Earth*, Goldman, a notorious atheist, put her case eloquently in "The Failure of Christianity." Proceeding from the assertion of Friedrich Nietzsche and Max Sterner that Christianity served to suppress the individual, Goldman finished her disavowal of the teachings of "the ethical and social Christ" with the heightened tones of slogans equally appropriate to the speaking platform:

> Never can Christianity, under whatever mask it may appear – be it New Liberalism, Spiritualism, Christian Science, New Thought, or a thousand and one other forms of hysteria and neurasthenia – bring us relief from the terrible pressure of conditions, the weight of poverty, the horrors of our iniquitous system. Christianity is the conspiracy of ignorance against reason, or darkness against light, of submission and slavery against independence and freedom; of the denial of strength and beauty, against the affirmation of the joy and glory of life. (48)

Articles by Goldman and those she published show that she is both sharply analytical and obligingly communicative. In her own time, Goldman believed that her ideas were being more widely disseminated and better understood because of the efforts of the magazine. After five years of publishing, Goldman maintained that "many an edition of our better-class dailies has found in *Mother Earth* a source of information and inspiration . . . and have used our magazine for copy on numerous occasions." Although her later arrest suggests she may have been overly optimistic, she claimed in the years before World War I that she detected a "decided change in the tone of the press towards Anarchism and Anarchists" (Goldman and Berkman, "Our Sixth Birthday" 3). Certainly, increased public interest in *Mother Earth*, the continued success of her lectures, and the appearance of her writings in book form during the 1920s afforded the anarchist movement perhaps its greatest prominence in the United States. Like other radical programs, however, anarchism was pushed aside in a flourishing American prowar frenzy, a frenzy that would lead to Goldman's deportation.

Unlike the other literary magazines of this period that were buoyed by women, the more radical magazines contained a dearth of material written by women. Readers of a magazine like the *Masses*, for example, may have been certain that women supported the causes discussed on its pages, yet women almost never participated in the discussions. *Mother Earth* also underrepresented women on its pages, although Goldman's constant editorial involvement helped give the anarchist movement "a feminist dimension" (Marshall 396). *Mother Earth* gave space, however, to other marginalized female figures, like Voltairine De Cleyre. An activist and comrade who had known Goldman since at least the early 1890s, De Cleyre frequently disagreed with Goldman and cannot be seen as part of the *Mother Earth* circle. Alice Wexler holds that De Cleyre is the "contributor of greatest intellectual power and originality . . . apart from Goldman and Berkman" (128). The magazine published a great deal of her work, and after she died, much of the July 1912 *Mother Earth* was devoted to remembrances of her. The editors of the magazine even began an appeal for funds to publish the *Selected Works of Voltairine De Cleyre*, edited by Berkman and Havel.

Ironically, the individual touched most directly by *Mother Earth* also remained just beyond the furthest edge of its circle: Margaret Anderson. Anderson often gave witness to the power of Goldman's speaking presence. In *My Thirty Years' War*, a memoir written in the late 1920s, Anderson spoke of the profound influence of Goldman's ideas:

> I became increasingly anarchist. I began to find people of my own class vicious, people in clean collars uninteresting. I even accepted smells, personal as well as official. Everyone who came to the studio smelled either of machine oil or herring. . . . Anarchism was the ideal expression for my

ideas of freedom and justice. The knowledge that people could be put into prisons and kept there for life had the power to torture me. That humans could be sentenced to death by other human beings was a fact beyond imagination. I decided that I would make my life a crusade against inhumanity. (74)

Anderson's early writings in the *Little Review* show that she was deeply impressed with the persona of Goldman. In "The Challenge of Emma Goldman," published in the *Little Review* (May 1914), Anderson maintains that through seeing Goldman in two lectures, she "came away with a series of impressions, every one of which resolved somehow into a single conviction: that here was a great woman." Anderson offers her readers a thoughtful defense of the anarchist and her ideas. She saw her article as an opportunity for "those who regard Emma Goldman as a public menace, and for those who simply don't know what to make of her . . . to look at her in a new way." Anderson takes aim at the popular belief that anarchists were violent. She states plainly "that dynamite is part of their intellectual, not their physical, equipment." She explains Goldman's intellectual program as "the philosophy of freedom" that sought "radical changes" to be found "not through a patching up of the old order, but through a tearing down and a rebuilding" (5–6).

While Anderson may have admired Goldman, there are clear differences between the two women. Goldman appreciated that the *Little Review* "was alive to new art forms and was free from the mawkish sentimentality of most American publications"; she claimed, however, that the magazine "lacked clarity on social questions" (*Living My Life* 530). Anderson's apparent idealistic conversion to anarchism gave way to the sudden skepticism. Goldman was a profound influence on Anderson precisely because Goldman encountered Anderson as she consciously was refining her own artistic values. Anderson never simply echoed anarchist dogma; instead, she challenged Goldman's ideas and allowed herself to be challenged by them. For example, on Goldman's outright rejection of religion, Anderson incredulously pondered that having "no use for religion" was like having "no use for poetry" ("The Challenge of Emma Goldman" 9).

Little magazine editors like Anderson sought, through this period, to offer their friends, their disciples, and often their heroes an opportunity to circumvent the insular world of commercial publishing. These editors were faced with a dilemma: between a genuine avant-garde impulse to resist an establishment with which they retained only tenuous links and their desire to renew and expand cultural traditions to accommodate remarkable contemporary artistic achievement. It is not hard to see that our view of Modernism, the dominant version of Modern literature recognized today, is a history that was written in the little magazines. The failure of Modern art, and the failure of the little magazine, was the inability of its adherents to effect practical change and to acknowledge Modernism's defining contradictions. Goldman claimed that with *Mother Earth* she hoped "to create a medium through which I might express myself in words more durable than oral language." She also wished "for the clarification of much-be-fogged ideas" ("To My Readers" 7). While the magazine she published for twelve years fell short in its aim to support innovative literary endeavors — hence it is never considered critically with the little magazines that defined a modern aesthetic — *Mother Earth* did preserve its political radicalism and provided durable models of idealism and activism.

Michele L. Mock

"𝒜N ARDOR THAT WAS HUMAN, & A POWER THAT WAS ART": REBECCA HARDING DAVIS & THE ART OF THE PERIODICAL

An entry on Rebecca Harding Davis in the 1898 *National Cyclopedia of American Biography* surprisingly cites the author encapsulating her life in the following manner: "I never belonged to a club nor any kind of society; never made a speech and never wanted to do it" (8: 177). While this activist may never have engaged in group affiliations nor joined the lecture circuit popular to many in the women's rights movement, Davis nonetheless tirelessly devoted her life's work to designing a textualized social activism, one that utilized the public gaze as a positive and reformatory force. Accordingly, to meet her agenda, Davis intentionally employed the periodical, a specular form characterized for its ability to make its reader "look" at herself as she "looks" at the magazine, perusing its contents; in turn, this complex and multifarious text reflects and defines not only the reader but the world around her.[1]

Davis, a prolific writer, composed more than five hundred works — the majority of which appeared first in periodical form. Drawing society's averted eyes to critical issues, Davis textually conjoins her artistry and activism in a theoretical and pragmatic practice she consistently referred to as the doctrine of the "good Samaritan" (*Bits* 148). This author's philosophies and critiques of art, manifest in her first short story, "Life in the Iron-Mills" (1861), argue that a criteria for art should include a categorization of literature according to its animus of social reform and its efficacy in promoting societal change.[2] A textual activist, Davis perceived art not as an elusive and elitist form but rather as a participative and dialogic expression of social activism. She denounced dominant theories held by bourgeois "art-critics," who could not foresee a communicative and melioristic artistry: "The world is full of these vulgar souls that palter with the eternal Nature and the eternal Arts, blind to the Word who dwells among us" ("Blind Tom" 583). The nineteenth-century American periodical, then, was the ideal forum for Davis to enact her philosophies of art as an immediate, accessible, and ameliorating force, one that satisfied her need "for writing of *today*," rather than the lofty, insular, and transcendent art with its accompanying forms that she so frequently denounced.[3]

Davis firmly believed that writing for the popular culture did not disqualify the work as art, nor did it necessarily entail the creation of an inferior product. One of Davis's rubrics of art mandated that in order for art's animus and efficacy to be realized, the lines between "high" culture and popular culture, demarcations as strict as those between genders, must be abolished. In agreement, Elizabeth Stuart Phelps claimed a "personal indebtedness" to Davis for her textual activism, one written, as Phelps wrote, with "an ardor that was human and a power that was art" (119, 120).[4] Davis's complex philosophies of art and activism, further complicated by the "ephemeral" form of the periodical in which they are housed, to use Margaret Beetham's term, testify that Davis perhaps understood that her most effective feminist methodology embraced the periodical and the pen.[5]

This concentration of art and reform is best exemplified in an exposé Davis published in 1870 to awaken public sentiment to unethical practices implemented in insane asylums, to challenge unjust laws regarding incarceration of those deemed mentally ill, and, ultimately, to incite her audience to action. *Put Out of the Way*, serialized in the widely popular and long-running *Peterson's Ladies' National Magazine* (1842–98), is but one example of Davis's attempt to promulgate her philosophies of an efficacious art. The oscillating masculine and feminine tropes of this narrative not only rupture configurations of "woman," "monsters," and "madness" that attempt to imprison women within their bodies, but more important, her gendered economies challenge inequitable legislation informed by these very configurations that made institutional incarceration an actuality for a number of women. In short, Davis's unstable tropes indict the stability of a legal system predicated upon the pathologizing of women's bodies.

Accordingly, Davis's choice of *Peterson's* was deliberate, and she used her power as a writer to solicit social change. Beetham reminds us that writers for the periodical press vied for power in a delicate balance with editors, publishers, advertisers, and readers and, consequently, needed to exercise their power in order to "make their meanings stick" ("Towards a Theory of the Periodical" 20). Serialization in particular, as Susan Belasco Smith tells us, "offers a special form of communication for a writer, involving a complex negotiation by which a writer acts on as well as reacts to a particular and evolving publishing environment" (76). I suggest that Davis was fully cognizant of the inherent power of the periodical and its concomitant mode of novel serialization. *Put Out of the Way* serves as a significant example of Davis's understanding of art, activism, power, and the periodical. Like many nineteenth-century women writers, Davis was cognizant of the extensive audience she could reach through popular women's magazines.[6] As Sharon M. Harris asserts in "Redefining the Feminine," Davis deliberately selected Charles J. Peterson's magazine to publish *Put Out of the Way* in order to expose the abuses of mental health institutions (118). To be sure, Davis's ability to reach a large audience with her writing satisfied her philosophies regarding the animus and efficacy of art; her individual activism embraced the pen rather than the podium as a call for awareness and reform.

Although Davis had already published sixteen works in the *Atlantic* by 1868, it was her husband's essay on the need for mental health reform, "A Modern Lettre de Cachet" that appeared there, two years prior to the publication of her own serial novel in *Peterson's*. In his work, L. Clarke Davis, a Philadelphia attorney, cites several questionable cases of incarceration in Philadelphia institutions, including the prestigious Pennsylvania Hospital for the Insane; he concludes his essay with a call for "official notice and reform" (602). Notwithstanding, Harris tells us in her study of Davis's canon, *Rebecca Harding Davis and American Realism*, that "Clarke's presentation inevitably suffers in comparison to the fictionalized call for reform that Rebecca presented in [*Put Out of the Way*]" (154).

According to Davis, after publication of her husband's work, a "bitter battle" ensued that delayed publication of *Put Out of the Way*. Minimizing her input in their dialogic advocacy, Davis proudly boasted that her husband had fought this battle "single-handed [sic] through press and legislature" in spite of "virulent opposition" (qtd. in Harris, *American Realism* 154). It is important to note here that as a man in the postbellum era, Clarke Davis possessed a greater number of discursive options than Rebecca Harding Davis; moreover, as an attorney, he was able to propose changes in the public, legislative realm that she could solely enact in print. The courtroom provided the forum necessary for Clarke Davis to address legal ramifications of unjust laws; as a politically appointed member of a commission of inquiry, he could recommend the amelioration of sundry laws to the governor. On the other hand, as a woman in postbellum American culture, Davis was not only legally disenfranchised but was also restricted from a variety of professional opportunities to challenge inequitable legal and social practices. Therefore, Davis's letters and her serial novel, *Put Out of the Way*, testify to more than the Davises' own dialogism. Davis's work is testament to her concern regarding women's issues and serves as an example of her advocacy in a realm that was open-ended, immediate, and receptive to her voice. The periodical was a site that not only encouraged her voice but rapidly circulated it far and wide. In spite of its range in print culture, the periodical nonetheless remained a site of contingency and complex meaning. Notwithstanding, the periodical became and remained Davis's forum; as a diverse site rife with contradictory and situated meanings, it was the ideal locus for Davis to enact her feminist vision. Perhaps because Davis's participation in a public sphere was so severely limited, her theories of "answerability" to her art, to use Bakhtin's term, were so pronounced.[7]

Davis, cognizant that art is predicated upon communication, employed *Peterson's Magazine* as the forum for initiating dialogue through the text, what she called a "message to be given." In an 1891 essay entitled "Women and Literature," Davis wrote, "A few women . . . will write . . . simply because there is in them a message to be given, and they cannot die until they have spoken it" (612). To be sure, much of Davis's canon embodies her philosophies of the "good Samaritan" and her "message to be given," predating Bakhtinian theories of answerability.

In spite of the two-year span between publication of the Davises' works, their project was a dialogic one, each clearly interanimating the other. Emphasizing "situated knowledges" — what Donna Haraway calls the "partial, contradictory, permanently unclosed constructions" of knowledge — the Davises textually met their agendas and enacted reform (157). As a result of Clarke Davis's publication, an act of assembly was passed in 1869 that amended inhumane laws of 1836, one of which declared that only one physician was necessary in order to commit. The new Act 54 of 1869 mandated that an individual could be placed in a hospital for the insane by legal guardians, or by friends or relatives in cases of no surviving guardians, but "never without the certificate of two or more reputable physicians." This revised legislation somewhat lessened the possibility of fraudulent committals. It also prohibited interference with inmates' letters addressed to counsel (P.L. Act No. 54: Section 1 and 2, 1869). Prior to the enactment of this law, patients could literally be "put out of the way," with no judicial recourse and no connection to the outside world. As a result of Rebecca Harding Davis's 1870 publication of *Put Out of the Way* and the Davises' continued advocacy,

Clarke Davis was appointed by the governor in May 1874 to a Pennsylvania state commission for inquiry into the condition of the criminally insane. That very month, another act for protection of the insane was passed. Rebecca Harding Davis's philosophies of an accountable, efficacious art thus became concrete, filtered through a transitory form — the periodical.

Davis enjoyed a long history of publication with *Peterson's* magazine. Initially acquainted with Philadelphia publisher Peterson through correspondence with her future husband, Rebecca Harding began writing for the magazine just several months after "Life in the Iron-Mills" appeared in the *Atlantic*. By 1870 *Peterson's* held the largest circulation of women's magazines in the nation; their readership boasted more than 150,000 subscribers, clearly a large audience by nineteenth-century standards. Initially, *Peterson's* was second in circulation only to *Godey's Lady's Book* (1830–98), also based in Philadelphia.[8] During the Civil War, however, *Peterson's* surpassed *Godey's* in subscribers and by 1870 had become the widest-circulating ladies magazine in the nation, less than two decades after its inception (Mott 320). Like *Godey's*, *Peterson's* targeted a female audience and regularly included the incongruous coupling of colored fashion plates, reifying ideals of "woman," and literary works, which either subverted or reified those ideals.[9]

While Davis may have told *Atlantic* editor James T. Fields in 1862 that "[p]eople do *not* like serial tales," she apparently did not believe it (qtd. in Rose 39). The author's pronouncement was apparently one of subterfuge so that she could more comfortably write serials elsewhere for greater financial remuneration. And write she did.[10] Before *Put Out of the Way* was published, Davis saw seven novels serialized in *Peterson's*; in addition to her serial novels, Davis published thirty-four short stories in the magazine before 1870. Overall, in her more than thirty-years' affiliation with Peterson, Davis published twelve serial novels and eighty-two short stories in *Peterson's*. Given this author's prolific publishing history, even in the context of a thriving nineteenth-century print culture, I am unwilling to state that Davis's astute sense of business conflicted with or negated her artistry. I am suggesting, however, that the relationship Davis shared with her editors was a dynamic one; she refused to be victimized by a publishing world microcosmic of the nineteenth-century's doctrine of separate spheres, which, Susan Coultrap-McQuin has argued, often rendered women writers "invisible" (7).

Traditionally, scholars have alleged that a number of Davis's contributions to *Peterson's*, including *Put Out of the Way*, are "trite" and "melodramatic" fictions. Not surprisingly, these works have met with relative neglect, despite Davis's enduring agenda of women's rights and social melioration, themes that have received critical attention when appearing in more prestigious sites like the *Atlantic*.[11] Such criticism (or lack thereof) reflects in part the "logic of exclusion" that Christine Battersby asserts has historically denied genius and artistry to women. In her study of feminist aesthetics, Battersby argues that the "logic of exclusion," an exclusionary paradigm informed by Greco-Roman tradition, gave priority to works reifying phallocentrism, such as those printed in the elitist *Atlantic*, over intersubjective works produced for mass culture and consumption, such as those published in *Peterson's* (4). Preceding feminist aesthetics and poststructuralist critics, Davis challenges the vision of ethereal art or transcendent existence as an alienation of self and other. Such philosophies, she writes, are "like beautiful bubbles blown from a child's pipe, floating overhead with queer reflections on them of sky and earth and human beings, all in a glow of fairy color and all a little distorted" (*Bits* 36). Rather, Davis stresses what Jean Pfaelzer has identified as "connectedness," the means whereby women writers form "a basis for female sympathy across classes and races" (93). Accordingly, the nature of women's writing reflects an intersubjectivity ideally suited for representation within the context of the periodical, a site Beetham describes as "above all an ephemeral form, produced for a particular day, week, or month. Its claims to truth are always contingent, as is clear from the date which is prominently displayed. . . . This affects its material form as well as its meaning" (*A Magazine of Her Own?* 9). The periodical, then, particularly one targeting the female consumer, is the consummate forum to connect and coalesce women's literary representations, one that can enhance our understanding of the situated nature of women's writing. As Battersby notes, "Since a woman in our culture has to construct her self out of fragments, the work that she produces is likely to seem incoherent unless we fit it together into an overarching unity. This unity will not be seamless or monolithic" (151).

Notwithstanding, popular women's periodicals and the literature appearing therein continue to encounter devaluating assessments. In his study *American Literary Magazines*, Edward E. Chielens refuses to consider *Peterson's* "literary." While he notes that the magazine was widely popular and rivaled *Godey's* in circulation (a periodical that is indeed addressed in *American Literary Magazines*), *Peterson's*, despite its success, lived a long but "undistinguished" life, according to Chielens, and does not merit discussion in his study (app. A). Not surprisingly, contributions to such defamed periodicals have suffered similar stigma. Chielens denounces the contents of *Peterson's* as "sentimental and undistinguished" (461). Traditionally, women writing for women have been leveled with allegations of "hack work" and "potboilers" in reference to their literature. It is not surprising, then, to note that Davis's *Put Out of the Way* has largely met with categorizations equally pejorative, or simply, with silence.[12]

Attempting to break the silence surrounding institutional incarceration and asylum care, Davis utilizes *Put Out of the Way* to solicit reform. The editorial column of the June 1870 issue of *Peterson's*, which also carried part 2 of the serial, delivered a message that Davis insisted be printed: "The author wishes us to say that there is no exaggeration in the story for that every leading incident has substantially happened, as can be proved from the records of various courts." Peterson continued, noting that the author's purpose "is not to assail any particular asylum, but rather to assist in awakening public sentiment to the necessity of a reform in the manner in which patients can be committed to such hospitals" (472). Davis deliberately set her narrative in New York as opposed to Philadelphia in order to avoid maligning any particular institution. Relative anonymity was maintained as usual.[13] It is ironic to note that the gendered economies operating in the serial novel interpolated the magazine, for Peterson referred to Davis in the generic masculine form.[14]

In the year *Peterson's* published Davis's exposé, forty-five thousand persons were being treated in insane asylums throughout the country. The field of psychiatry became firmly entrenched in the public consciousness as an increasingly respectable medical, scientific, and legal institution. Along with a growing movement of organized philanthropy, asylum care during the postbellum period also grew extremely politicized. Economics, too, informed institutionalization. In "Two Methods" (1893), Davis, always sensitive to her philosophies of art, denounced society's emphasis on aesthetics as opposed to action. "We Americans," she wrote, "are apt to spend our money upon the buildings in which a work is to be done instead of the work itself." Davis argued that insane asylums are generally "huge, magnificent edifices" because the public is more concerned with the aesthetics of "marble and mortar" than with the care of its inmates, subject to attendants who are "cheaply hired" and lack the appropriate training (416).

The politicization of philanthropy caused Davis to repeatedly question its agency. Care of the mentally ill, which was perceived as a familial duty and responsibility in the early nineteenth century, grew to be seen as the state's duty and responsibility in the eyes of the urban middle class by the latter half of the nineteenth century. Once politicized, the status of the insane became increasingly conjoined to women's status as the "weaker vessel"; their care became symbolic of patriarchal protection, despite the fact that care of the ill and infirm at home was predominantly the task of women. For example, noted health-care expert C. H. Hughes was not alone in his assertion that "[j]ust as the weakness of woman secures to her that chivalrous protection in society which her own frail arms could not obtain for her," so too, should the state care for infirm and insane individuals (189).

Not surprisingly, during the 1860s and 1870s, gender-specific methods of treatment flourished as a result of what Michel Foucault has identified as the "hysterization of women's bodies," whereby the female body became pathologized (*History of Sexuality* 1: 104). Psychiatric and medical spheres, informed by socio-idealogues, hypothesized insanity in the form of gynecological functioning. Myths regarding menstruation and women's reproductive system virtually endorsed women's embodiment as the weaker sex in both physical and intellectual realms. Although he certainly was not the first, Sigmund Freud published his theories of hysteria that posited a direct and causal connection between women's reproductive organs and insanity.[15] Also during this time, Silas Weir Mitchell perfected his rest cure, a paternalistic behavior modification designed specifically for women. By now we readily recognize Mitchell's presence in Charlotte Perkins Gilman's "The Yellow Wallpaper" (1892), but we are less acquainted with Davis's own, early chronicle of the rest cure, "The Wife's Story" (1864).[16] Historian Ellen Dwyer suggests that the nineteenth-century medical and psychiatric establishment, fearful of the female reproductive system, believed that women's "susceptibility to endometriosis and cervical ulceration increased women's susceptibility to insanity" (95). Digital massage, subfumigation, hydrotherapy, and electromagnetic charges were applied to stabilize the "deranged" uterine system. Of all procedures, clitoral cauterization remained the most extreme, but practiced, measure.

In 1871 the Association of Medical Superintendents of American Institutions for the Insane declared at its twenty-fifth meeting that the vast majority of insane persons required institutional treatment (Geller and Harris 102). Nonetheless, Davis challenged the steadfast assumption that all who are committed to a lunatic asylum are insane; she perceived the nominalization to inhabit a slippery and unstable slope, particularly involving legal, medical, and social spheres. In her essay "Paul" (1884), the author classed the insane as the precariously positioned few "who do not look on life from the stand-point of the great majority" (2). Davis's view predates feminist theorist Phyllis Chesler's work by nearly a century. In *Women and Madness*, Chesler notes that the definition of "woman" in patriarchal society in conjunction with orthodox psychotherapy, is basically a prescription for insanity for women (2).

The Davises' efforts meliorated Pennsylvania's legislation regarding commitment of individuals, but other states were reluctant to follow suit. In addition, the judicial system frequently privileged criminals over patients. Those accused of a crime received due process of the law; those committed to insane asylums were denied their constitutional right of due process. Davis, then, continued to battle for the rights denied those committed to hospitals for the insane and the ease with which male family members could legally commit others there, to literally and legally have another "put out of the way." In *Put Out of the Way*, Davis exposes the following: unjust laws that enable a single physician to issue a certificate that can easily commit any individual to an insane asylum; the despotic position of the asylum's director who is given sole supervision of the institution and answers to no one — yet that same superintendent has no power to discharge an inmate without the consent of those who had placed the patient there; the writ of habeas corpus in which the burden of proof of mental health rests upon the inmate and the incarceration alone of the prisoner, which is regarded as prima facie evidence against him or her; cruel and abusive treatment of prisoners; and economic justifications for incarceration and extended commitment of the inmate, in some cases for periods up to thirty years. Given the range of power afforded to male family members in the nineteenth century, it is not surprising to note that many of those inmates were women.

Davis's own experience as a woman writing in the second half of the nineteenth-century print culture would make her acutely aware of what Foucault has termed the "animality of madness" (78). In *Madness and Civilization*, Foucault argues that once equated with monsters, "madmen remained monsters — that is etymologically, beings or things to be shown" (70). Certainly postbellum demarcations of sex, gender, and desire would have given Davis an acute aversion to threats of bestial, monstrous animality by which creative women were metaphorically embodied.[17] From this standpoint, Davis may have been able to equate the shared matrices of those incarcerated unjustly — either the sane, legally "put out of the way," or the mad, "present on the stage of the world," as Foucault has said — with the specularization of women (69). I am suggesting that Davis, doubly circumscribed as a woman artist, consistently utilized a complex, sophisticated form of gendered economies to typify her literature and her reform, as she does in the feminization of protagonist Richard Wortley in *Put Out of the Way*. Davis employed gendered economies as a critical tool to illustrate the debilitating effects of gender construction in a patriarchal culture; in this manner she effectively deployed binary systems of sexuality and gender. Through oscillating and situated gender inversions, Davis frequently feminized male characters and masculinized female characters in order to demystify nineteenth-century essentialized gender demarcations and to call for a reform of institutional practices predicated upon this doctrine of separate spheres that continued to perpetrate injustices upon those disenfranchised and disempowered. Davis's critical exploration of gender exemplified the unstable and reversible nature of gender constructions and the appropriation of women's essential biology for hegemonic production. In this manner, Davis's technique of gendered economies anticipates Foucault's theoretical paradigm of genealogy and contemporary Foucauldian feminists' use of genealogy of gender in order to demonstrate that categorization of sex, gender, and desire is a specific effect of institutional formations of power in order to decenter that power.

Foucault proposes, "Madness is the purest, most total form of *quid pro quo*; it takes the false for the pure, death for life, man for woman" (*Madness and Civilization* 33). Defined as deviant, incarcerated in a private space, the feminized Wortley is powerless to control his destiny; his plight parallels the imprisonment of the subplot's female protagonist, Lotty Hubbard. Integrating the dilemma faced by both characters, Davis incorporates notions of "madness" and "justice" to promulgate her gendered economies, not only to call attention to illicit but legal practices regarding institutionalization, but also to challenge and unmask iniquitous notions of gender that inform these practices. Davis's novel, loosely based upon the case of Morgan Hinchman,[18] integrates Hinchman's experience with factual accounts found in a number of women's asylum narratives. The product of this integration is a character akin to one of Fanny Fern's characters in *Ruth Hall* (1855), the intriguing Mary Leon, who is valued solely as a "necessary appendage to Mr. Leon's establishment" (51). Nonetheless, when he tires of her, Mr. Leon commits his wife to an insane asylum because institutionalization offers an easier solution than divorce. There, incarcerated with countless other women, she dies, "forgotten by the world" (109). Like Davis's work, Fern's fiction is informed by fact. Vacationing in New England in the summer of 1862, Fern visited an insane asylum and was aghast at the disproportionate number of women there; later that year she would theorize why in the *New York Ledger*, citing the vast number of outlets provided for men to release emotional pressure, outlets that she claimed were denied to women (Warren 246).

Davis, however, believed that judicial processes were accountable, and she used the Philadelphia-based *Peterson's* to voice her concerns. An 1852 Pennsylvania state act sanctioned the theft of any married woman's real and personal estate, provided the thief was her husband and his chosen committee of three, one of whom needed to be a practicing physician, could issue a certificate claiming her insanity. Once a woman was pronounced insane and institutionalized, her husband possessed full power to dispose of not only his estate but also hers, as "if his said wife was sane and gave her full consent thereto" (P.L. Act No. 433, Sec. 7, 1852). Not surprisingly, many women spent the remainder of their lives incarcerated in institutions, paid for by the proceeds of their own estates. Some were eventually released and wrote about their unjust incarceration in asylum narratives. For example, Tirzah F. Shedd, an inmate of the Illinois State Hospital for the Insane between 7 July and mid-October 1865, wrote about her horror at discovering the inequities that lurked in American democracy. "It may be a land of freedom for the men," she wrote, "but I am sure it is not for the married women!" (qtd. in Geller and Harris 80). Torn from her three children, Shedd found that her personal liberty was placed entirely in the hands of her husband, who was "fully determined to use this legal power to subject my views to his will and wishes" (80). Legally, in many states, men found it a more expedient procedure to find a committee willing to incarcerate one's wife in a lunatic asylum than to obtain a divorce, a far more complicated judicial process which entailed annulling the marriage contract by a legal act.

Reflective of a number of women's asylum narratives, Davis's novel *Put Out of the Way* follows the incarceration of both Lotty Hubbard and the feminized Wortley. Hubbard is a young woman who finds herself, upon the death of her father, taken into the guardianship of Colonel Ned Leeds until she comes of age to receive her inheritance and, thus, economic independence. Imprisoned in a domestic space, Hubbard symbolizes women's economic dependence and restriction from the public sphere, conditions, Davis stresses, that facilitate the false incarceration of women in asylums. In contrast, Colonel Leeds, symbolic of the patriarchal head, exemplifies the social sanctions that deny women full access to the public sphere, imprisoning them within their bodies and their homes. Like the protagonist of Gilman's "The Yellow Wallpaper," Hubbard eventually grows "sickly and morbid in mind and body from her unwonted confinement" (362); her condition is analogous to the increasing powerlessness experienced by her cousin, Dick Wortley.

Employing reversible gendered economies to better epitomize nineteenth-century women's plight, Davis initially presents a masculine Wortley.

Each scene enacts power relationships that are microcosmic of the era's doctrine of separate spheres; masculinity is equated with either potency or efficacy while femininity is conflated with impotency or inefficacy. Wortley, a "six-foot young fellow, with his hearty voice, yet polished, man-of-the-world address" (359), is highly masculinized; he is the epitome of a "manly man" (360). When Dick discovers Colonel Leeds's plan to marry Lotty to his son in order to gain her inheritance, he confronts both men, who, in turn, become intent on silencing him. Here, Davis reminds her readers of women's continued legal disenfranchisement that has placed them, as Dawn Keetley has noted, as "involuntary subjects within marriage" (347); Davis returns to tropes of gender and silence to illustrate her women readers' status as femes covert. Moreover, Davis also indicts unjust laws that continue to facilitate false imprisonment in asylums while she denounces the infrastructure's capacity for alienation. Leeds assures his son that with the proper economic means, Dick can be silenced: "It is a quiet, safe means, which a gentleman can use with no fear of punishment. There must be secrecy, . . . Only pay enough, and get up your case right, as the lawyers say, you have science and philanthropy both to assist you" (435). Politically astute, Davis recognized that via the matrices of the "law, and science, and philanthropy" (436), one needed only to obtain a certificate from a physician (who need not see the victim) to certify that individual insane and, thus, literally imprison one "for life" (436).

In this manner, Davis also challenges the judicial system. If Wortley had committed a crime, he would have the privilege of counsel and a trial before his peers prior to incarceration for the crime; his trial (and he) also would be scrutinized by the public gaze. Here Davis inverts notions that equate madness with the gaze; Foucault suggests that, historically, madness has been associated with "pure spectacle" (69). As a woman writer exposed to the public gaze, however, and as an activist cognizant of the art of the periodical, Davis believed the gaze could also be utilized as a positive force, a lifting of the veil in order to alter unjust practices through awareness. The same public gaze that guaranteed criminals the right to trial by jury was averted for the insane who were confined to institutions, sometimes for life, "without judge or jury, or a chance to escape" (437). Because the practice escaped public scrutiny, Davis argued, it remained perfectly legal — and perfectly immoral.[19]

Davis possessed a vast body of knowledge regarding nineteenth-century jurisprudence; her canon consistently displays her shrewd grasp of legal machinations. In *Put Out of the Way*, she indicates that statutory law does not technically require the certificate, but rather common law or custom demands it (441). To be sure, patients were not subjected to examination or tests to prove insanity; the institution solely relied upon the physician's certification to define madness as prima facie evidence. As Foucault has suggested, once objectified as mad, all behavior of the "madman" is perceived as insane. Through Wortley's character, Davis shows us that societal conventions of "civilized" discourse and practice do not apply in the insane asylum.

Indeed, a number of asylum narratives substantiate Davis's claims of asylum abuse. One leading expert on jurisprudence of insanity in the mid-nineteenth century wrote, "Many of the depots for the captivity of intellectual invalids may be regarded only as nurseries for and manufactories of madness,— magazines or reservoirs of lunacy, from which is issued, from time to time, a sufficient supply for perpetuating and extending this formidable disease" (qtd. in "A Modern Lettre de Cachet" 598). Or as Adeline T. P. Lunt, an inmate of a facility in New England, wrote upon her release, "INSANE ASYLUM. A place where insanity is made" (12). Before Foucault postulated that the nineteenth century's animality of madness could not be ministered to or rectified through medicine or correction, but only "mastered" by "discipline and brutalizing" (75), Davis addressed the bestial, insane-making treatment patients endured in asylums.

Chthonic detail supports the narrative to better depict the "netherworld-liness" of the asylum as a forgotten underworld of society. Wortley remembers reading that "letters from the patients of insane asylums were generally suppressed," and he slowly comes to the realization that he is indeed "buried alive" (443), when the asylum's superintendent, an inhumane, mechanical man ironically named Dr. Harte intercepts Dick's letters to family and counsel calling for help. Again, Davis returns to issues of voice, signifying that the oppressor can find power only in the silencing of the subaltern.

Davis depicts other power relations through one of the hospital's "keepers," a man whose barbarous treatment of the incarcerated exemplifies the image of animality that Foucault suggests "haunted" the asylums of that period (72). Davis inscribes the scene with predatory and violent terms: "[The keeper's] great carcass of muscle was cool and slow. When the time seemed to him to be ripe, he gave a sniff, and leveled Dick with a foul blow, jumping on his chest with his knees. Dick remained quite quiet there. It did not need any blows, the weight was enough" (158). Thus the beast becomes the "keeper" of the man like Wortley, once described as the "manliest of men" (360). Davis's message to her readers is explicitly clear: this man's use of brute force to subjugate another parallels a patriarchal legal system that strong-arms women to silence. The madness of this system, Davis reminds her audience, not only silences the victim, it dehumanizes the oppressor. Indeed, madness embodies the reversible world. "Madness," to quote Foucault again, "takes the false for the true, death for life, man for woman" (33). Davis utilizes the reversible spirit of gendered economies — the feminization of Dick Wortley — not only to unmask false legal claims, nor solely to illustrate the countless women in the nineteenth century who were subject to institutionalization (a number of them her readers), but also, as the narrative's subplot attests, to draw her readers' attention to society's sanction of women imprisoned in the domestic sphere, economically dependent and powerless. In this instance, however, Davis's protagonist is not contained within a domestic abode but in a cell. These cells are precisely the same, she tells us, as the cells convicts inhabit on death row, except that in the asylum the superintendent is "judge, and executioner, and public" (34). Again, Davis enacts the public gaze as a positive force; her details are accurate and hauntingly factual. In a direct address to her readers intended to secure their attention, Davis graphically depicts the inhumanities perpetrated upon inmates: they are frequently left in a state of nudity; their "cells" are infested by vermin; and they are forced to lie in the "dark and heat, surrounded with creeping, nauseous things, whose shapes [you] could guess at, with the air about [you] filled with fiendish yells and forlorn sobbings from the maniacs in the near cells" (37).

At this point in the narrative, Dick's feminization occurs precisely at the same time his body becomes the site for the breaking of his mind. The appropriation of his body by physical violence is Davis's method of conjoining pressing issues of domestic abuse and the torturous methods asylums employed to "cure" women and the mentally ill. Her descriptions are graphic, far removed from sentimental rhetoric. After another beating as a method of sedation, "Dick Wortley's head dropped to one side, grew sickly and livid as when he was a jaundiced baby: then the blood slowly rose to his mouth, and dripped, dripped on the floor" (35). Davis then reveals haunting details about treatments used for both male and female patients, methods such as the "saddle," the shower-bath, and the "hose" (114), a wooden machine in which victims were strapped on their backs with their head, legs, and arms hanging down in order for the blood to be driven to the brain. Often the procedure lasted until the patient passed out. She also painstakingly details the shower-bath to which Dick is subjected, a tortuous practice in which one slow drop of water after another falls upon a singular spot on the forehead (presumably in order to better reach the brain), "until from the frenzied eyes, and unconscious moans of agony, it seemed as though the tortured soul within was seeking, at eyes and mouth, some means of escape" (85). The only quality attributable to the shower, Foucault notes, is its "violence"; its curative power derived from "destroying even the smallest traces of the extravagant ideas of the insane, which can be done only by obliterating, so to speak, these ideas in a state close to that of death" (172). In other words, the nineteenth century's violent legal methods of "curing" those deemed insane privileged death to difference.[20]

In the femininization of her protagonist, Davis also interpolates recurrent issues of voice and rebellion for her readers. Dick "had learned reticence; he asked no questions, made no comments" (85). Silenced, his feminization is nearly complete; he can no longer rely upon the physical strength he once possessed as a free man; now he looks with "loathing" upon his "trembling hands and legs" (86). He fears that his mind will succumb to the influence of his surroundings, "an insane world, where there was nothing reliable or tangible to grasp by, he began to reason insanely" (37). It is here that Davis finds the scandal of Dick's incarceration. For as Foucault asserts, "The scandal lies only in the fact that the madmen are the brutal truth of confinement, the passive instrument of all that is worst about it. Is this not symbolized by the fact . . . that a sojourn in a house of correction necessarily leads to madness? Having to live in this delirious world, amid the triumph of unreason, how may one avoid joining, by the fatality of the site and the event, the very men who are its living symbol?" (225). Davis's awareness was participatory and political rather than removed and philanthropic, and through Dick's feminization he becomes a tool and object of the patriarchy, a system that was indeed a site of madness. One year prior to the publication of *Put Out of the Way*, Davis wrote, "It is not *women* who have first tainted society and literature; it is not weak, starving, ill-paid women who are to blame for this Gehenna of prostitution that underlies our social fabric" ("Men's Rights" 216).

Returning to the narrative, Dick's feminization is complete; yet his escape is certain, a "hot and cold shiver shot through him as though he had been a woman" (109). Disempowered though he may be, he seeks escape, noting, "I am as weak as an hysteric girl! . . . They've scaled my manhood from me pretty thoroughly"(110). Wortley does escape but unfortunately is captured again on the asylum's grounds. Significantly, once completely feminized, he cannot leave the sanitarium through his own efforts; he can only escape through the active intervention of another. It is crucial to note here that his writing and the *dialogic, volitional act of another* saves him. Davis fuses the climax of the narrative's plot with her philosophies of art's efficacy; her narrative enacts precisely what Davis consistently argues that the art of the periodical should perform. Before his capture on the hospital's grounds, Dick throws a letter across the wall; like Davis's work, her character's epistolary act serves as a call for awareness and a plea for intervention. When Dick is caught and again placed in the hospital among the forgotten souls "who had been kept there for forty, fifty years, whose histories, whose very names, were long ago forgotten," significantly, his letter — his utterance — remains (38). There, it is found by a young girl who symbolizes Davis's interdependent philosophy of the "good Samaritan." A quiet, nondescript girl, Jessy seemingly keeps to herself, yet her act ultimately saves Dick. She quietly pockets the letter, seals it in an envelope, and mails it. In other words, she actively responds to his utterance. The letter reaches the proper channels, and Dick is released. Jessy's private act of charity toward a stranger is the apex of Davis's narrative and the textual embodiment of her philosophies of the active and participatory art of the periodical.

When Dick is released from the asylum, penniless and ill-clothed, Davis attempts to re-"masculinize" him, conjoining freedom with the renewal of his masculinity: "Give me dry clothes . . . and some oysters and I'm a man again" (115). Colonel Leeds and his son continue to worry about Dick's interference with their plans, and even debate the possibilities of murdering Dick, yet they are reminded that until now their immoralities have been sanctioned by law. Davis unequivocally denounces the inanities of an inequitable judicial system by rupturing the narrative with a direct address to her readers: "What a farce" (115).

The novel concludes with Dick and Lotty's marriage, where they live happily in "the Indian Summer of [their] lives." Despite the sentimental rhetoric concluding the story, in which the narrator tells us that the "sun is warm, and God is good" (118), Davis's narrative resists closure: the judicial system remains unchanged, the avarice of institutions continues, and public philanthropy persists as a removed and idealized institution that dismantles the possibility of human relationships. Yet Davis's philosophies of art and reform remain explicitly clear. The character of Jessy, so like Davis herself,[21] reminds readers of the importance of maintaining interdependent relations with others, even those of faceless strangers. Through the narrative and the art of the periodical, Davis exemplifies that the "grasp of the hand" can indeed alter circumstances.[22] Accordingly, Davis's novel did more than serve as the means to question prevailing notions of art, her work utilized a popular women's periodical effectively to draw the nation's averted gaze to this crucial issue in order to reform inequitable legislation. Her choice of *Peterson's* enabled Davis to exemplify doubly her philosophies regarding the animus and efficacy of art in nineteenth-century culture; through a popular women's periodical, she simultaneously enacted her theories of art and activism in both form and content. Representing the art of the periodical, *Put Out of the Way* employs gendered economies to rupture androcentric discourse, thereby unmasking the seemingly stable nature of gender constructs as a highly unstable fortress in which to imprison a sex.

Ten years prior to the formation of the National Association for the Protection of the Insane and the Prevention of Insanity, an association established in 1880 to monitor and reform mental asylums, Davis — a woman who had never joined a committee, association, club, or group — challenged *and altered* inequitable legislation predicated upon an alienation that could render individuals powerless. Legally disenfranchised, this author grasped the dialogic power of the periodical to cast her voice far and wide. This "power," as contemporary Elizabeth Stuart Phelps noted, was "art . . . concentrated upon the passion of humanity and governed thereby in every line she wrote" (119, 120). To be sure, Rebecca Harding Davis recognized that her individual power as an activist required more than passion, it demanded the pen — and the periodical.

NOTES

I would like to thank Mary Critchfield, Patty S. Derrick, James R. DiFrancesco, Susan Alves, and Aleta Feinsod Cane for their invaluable suggestions on earlier drafts of this essay.

1   In *A Magazine of Her Own?*, Margaret Beetham links Victorian women's periodicals with the bourgeois commodity culture and resulting definitions of femininity. Beetham suggests that the woman consumer "was defined both by the activity of looking — whether through plate-glass windows or at newspaper advertisements — and by how she looked herself" (8). Beetham notes that there was indeed a dynamic relationship between the re-visioning and redefining of femininity and the material basis of magazines. Ellen Gruber Garvey also stresses the interrelated web of advertisements, fiction, essays, and editorial material as a coalescing context for nineteenth-century American women consumers. See Garvey, *The Adman in the Parlor: Magazines and the Gendering of Consumer Culture, 1880s to 1910s* (New York: Oxford UP, 1996).

2   My study is informed by Andrew Scheiber, whose work also focuses on the poststructuralist impulses in Davis's fiction that simultaneously engage and subvert. In

"An Unknown Infrastructure," Scheiber suggests that Davis's "Life in the Iron-Mills" is a work dedicated "not to the creation of aesthetic values, but to the interrogation and demolition of them" (102).

3 In a letter accompanying the draft of "John Lamar," Davis urgently wrote *Atlantic* editor James T. Fields, "[W]on't you publish John Lamar as soon as you can? I have a fancy for writing of *today* you see" (qtd. in Harris 73). Notwithstanding, Davis's philosophies regarding the power of the periodical involved immediacy as well as immanence. For example, in "Doctor Pajot," published in *Appletons' Journal* in 1877, Davis implements the Pegasus myth as a metaphor to delineate these philosophies and, thus, dismantle paradigms of "high" culture and elitist art. Her protagonist, Mrs. Pajot, a writer, notes that "Pegasus can show the stuff that's in him by pulling a cart as well as in any other way" (553).

4 In her examination of periodical fiction, "Stories That Stay" (1910), Phelps insisted that "the writer of a short story must know how to tell it; but it is more important that [s]he should have something to tell" (123).

5 See Beetham, *A Magazine of Their Own?* 9. Tania Modleski's work illustrates that the very qualities of magazines — their sense of fragmentation and openness — lend credence to theories that the forum is inherently subversive to masculine cultural norms. See Tania Modleski, *Loving With a Vengeance: Mass-Produced Fantasies for Women* (New York: Methuen, 1982). Accordingly, Davis deliberately conjoins gendered economies with discussions of art throughout her periodical fiction not only to question the animus and efficacy of art but also to subvert traditional engendering of art as "male," hence my use of the term "feminist" to describe Davis's methodology.

6 Sharon M. Harris illustrates that while Davis was unable (or unwilling) to join public demonstrations for women's rights, she privately endeavored to help extend women's rights, particularly in terms of helping needy friends find self-reliance through careers (*American Realism* 121–22). I would add that Davis also utilized her writing as a feminist methodology. Despite his unfortunate choice of words, I cite Davis's eldest son, Richard Harding Davis, who praised his mother for her cultural work: "[Y]ou were always year after year making the ways straighter, lifting up people, making them happier and better. No shrieking suffragette will ever understand the influence you wielded, greater than hundreds of thousands of women's votes" (qtd. in Rose, *Rebecca Harding Davis* 165).

7 Mikhail Bakhtin explained for himself in the following way: "I have to answer with my own life for what I have experienced and understood in art" ("Art" xx). In *Toward a Philosophy of the Act*, Bakhtin would refer to the philosophy Davis called the "good Samaritan" as the artistic process of "answerability," the "moral

philosophy" by which the artist lives and accounts for her art (56). This account-
ability is twofold, he explains, "both from within its product and from the stand-
point of the author as answerable participant" (54).

8 *Peterson's*, however, sold for two dollars a year — one dollar less than its competi-
tor, thus making the magazine more accessible to a greater number (Mott 320).

9 Beetham suggests that the definition of female beauty proved to be a highly
difficult concept to erase. Throughout the century, the "discourse of dress," particularly in the illustrations presented in middle-class women's magazines, continued to define ideals of femininity (*A Magazine of Her Own?* 7). Clearly, the combination of fashion plates and literature that could either subvert or reify the ideals
of feminine beauty depicted in the illustrations makes for a fascinating study of the
complexities inherent in the periodical press as a genre.

10 Davis was an artist with an astute sense of business and learned by trial and error to
navigate through the complex maze of the nineteenth-century publishing world.
Harris tells us that *Peterson's* was known to pay Davis as much as a thousand dollars
for a serialized novel as early as the 1860s (*American Realism* 73). Clearly this amount
was more than she could receive from the *Atlantic*, and the author apparently had
no qualms about making this fact known to Fields: "You know I would like to write
only for you, partly because we are friends, and partly because I am *in earnest* when
I write and I find the audience I like in Atlantic readers. But I'm going to be perfectly
honest now. If I wrote stories suitable for other magazines I could make more." Explaining, "as times are, I am not justified in refusing the higher price," she craftily
urged Fields to "give as much for future articles as you can legitimately afford so that
I can write solely for the A[tlantic] M[onthly]." Davis, however, continued to write
for both periodicals, authoring nine works for *Peterson's* to the *Atlantic's* three that
year, despite her promise to Fields to write "for the Atlantic exclusively for this year
[1862]" (qtd. in Rose 38). See Jane Atteridge Rose, "A Bibliography of Fiction and
Non-Fiction by Rebecca Harding Davis" in *American Literary Realism* 22.3: 67–86.

11 In addition to Davis's *Put Out of the Way*, the stories "The Story of Christine"
(1866), "At Bay" (1867), "In the Market" (1868), and "Clement Moore's Vocation"
(1870), all published in *Peterson's*, are merely a few examples of intriguing works
that continue to receive scant critical attention but exemplify the active women-
centered agenda of Davis's canon. Notwithstanding Harris's critical attention to
"In the Market," one can only assume that an integral aspect of their relative neglect derives in part from their periodical placement.

12 Certainly, my statement precludes Davis scholars Sharon M. Harris and Jane Atteridge Rose, who have both addressed *Put Out of the Way* in their perspective
studies of Davis and her works, *Rebecca Harding Davis and American Realism*
(1991) and *Rebecca Harding Davis* (1993). Clearly, Harris's examination of Davis's

novel has greatly informed my own; it was her critical examination of Davis's novel as an exposé that led me to a greater understanding of Davis as an activist. See Harris, *Rebecca Harding Davis and American Realism* 154–60. In addition, Jane Atteridge Rose's exploration of Davis's novel also notes Davis's work as a well-researched and documented exposé. See Rose, *Rebecca Harding Davis* 75–76. Although another leading Davis scholar, Jean Pfaelzer, does not discuss *Put Out of the Way* in great depth, her *Rebecca Harding Davis Reader* (Pittsburgh: U of Pittsburgh P, 1995) and her examination of Davis's social activism in *Parlor Radical: Rebecca Harding Davis and the Origins of American Social Realism* (Pittsburgh: U of Pittsburgh P, 1996) have greatly enhanced my understanding of Davis as a writer. The scholarly work of Harris, Pfaelzer, and Rose has, in true dialogic fashion, incited and informed my own.

13 After 1865 *Peterson's* generally published Davis's work under the pseudonyms that associated her with *Margret Howth* and *A Second Life*. In *Put Out of the Way*, Davis is identified as the author of *A Second Life*.

14 I intentionally refer to Louis Althusser's theoretical term in which one's positioning may be described as ideological, as in an inserting or "interpellating" of individuals and/or their works into constructed social identities that enable the individual to make sense of the world. See Althusser, "Ideology and Ideological State Apparatuses (Notes towards an Investigation)," and "A Letter on Art in Reply to Andre Daspré" in *Lenin and Philosophy and Other Essays*, trans. Ben Brewster (London: New Left, 1971). 121–73, 203–08.

15 See Rachel P. Maines, *The Technology of Orgasm: "Hysteria," the Vibrator, and Women's Sexual Satisfaction* (Baltimore: Johns Hopkins UP, 1999).

16 Although we have no extant documentation in which she specifically names the Philadelphia neurospecialist, in all probability, Mitchell, a friend of the Davis family, prescribed Davis's rest cure. See Davis, "The Wife's Story," *Atlantic* 14 (1864): 1–19.

17 Dominant gender demarcations in postbellum American society doubly configured the woman artist. Defined by their biology and denied the unencumbered existence integral to the male artist, women were denied artistry at the expense of biology. Women who refused to accept a "natural" existence due to biological essence, choosing artistry instead, were perceived as "unnatural" and, at times, monstrously deviant. In "Resisting the Gaze of Embodiment," Sidonie Smith examines the "metaphysical" male self and the female, embodied "self of essences" (75). Also see Mary Kelley, *Private Woman, Public Stage: Literary Domesticity in Nineteenth-Century America* (New York: Oxford UP, 1984).

18 Morgan Hinchman, a Pennsylvania Quaker, was falsely committed to the Frankford Lunatic Asylum by his wife's family following a disagreement with family

members regarding finances. The physician who had provided the certificate necessary to commit the young Quaker was not his personal physician, nor had he seen the man for four months prior to its issue. After six months of incarceration, Hinchman escaped the asylum and pressed a civil suit for damages against his in-laws (592–5). This case served a pivotal role in Clarke Davis's "A Modern Lettre de Cachet"; Rebecca Harding Davis's inclusion of the case in her novel substantiates the dialogics occurring between wife and husband. In like fashion, Clarke Davis's descriptions of the legal injustices perpetrated against women in his essay's con-clusion point to Rebecca Harding Davis's influence and, ultimately, exemplify the dialogic activity between the Davises.

19 The theme of legal and moral laws is repeated throughout Davis's canon. For a no-table example, see *A Law Unto Herself*, serialized in *Lippincott's Magazine* 2 (1877): 39–49, 167–82, 291–308, 464–78, 614–28, 719–31.

20 Davis's active empathy for victims of debilitating "cures" was rooted in experience. In July of 1863, after nearly four months of marriage, Davis suffered brain fever and was forced to endure the rest cure. "The Wife's Story," written shortly after her treatment, is the product of her "cure"; it too details a psychological break-down and recovery. However, in Davis's depiction of Dick Wortley's recovery, we glimpse a less domestic but equally enclosed image of hell: "It was late in June be-fore he was himself enough to know that the claw-like fingers, picking at the sheet, were his own" (35).

21 Davis saw herself as an unassuming and unattractive figure. Jean Pfaelzer suggests that because Davis envisioned herself as such, she "identified with a series of [her] homely but artistic characters whose creative and sexual passions are stymied by their bodies — as female, plain, or deformed" (49–50).

22 In *Rebecca Harding Davis and American Realism*, Harris reminds us that Davis's "grasp of the hand" image captures one of her "most prevalent metaphors for per-sonal activism" (23). The artist's complex metaphor adopts additional layers of meaning when we examine Roman law regarding marriage ceremonies and the most sacred type of marriage ceremony; this rite placed a woman in manus: to mean literally "in the hand of" her husband. As wives in manus, women were un-der the authority of their husbands and their husbands' families who had power over virtually every aspect of these women's lives (Battersby 55). Davis's legal acu-men and knowledge of legal discourse are manifest in *Put Out of the Way*, and, in all probability, she was quite familiar with the etiology of in manus and deliber-ately employed the metaphor to better serve her feminist agenda.

REFASHIONING
THE PERIODICAL

Susan Alves

LOWELL'S FEMALE FACTORY WORKERS, POETIC VOICE, & THE PERIODICAL

In 1840 Harriet Farley and coeditor Harriott Curtis penned the first editorial for a new publication *The Lowell Offering*. They posed three key objectives of the publication: "to encourage the cultivation of talent; to preserve such articles as are deemed most worthy of preservation; and to correct an erroneous idea which generally prevails in relation to the intelligence of persons employed in the Mills" (1). While all three goals were met during the run of this literary magazine, twentieth-century critical reception has tended to focus only on the third purpose, the ways in which the publication showcases the intellectual activity of working women. The issues of creative talent and of aesthetics continue either to be ignored or questioned. Neither twentieth- nor nineteenth-century critical attention has brought together an analysis of the literary values of these texts with an examination of the historical significance of the literary production of these factory operatives.

Most historical studies of the writings of nineteenth-century New England female factory workers necessarily have focused on the social and cultural significance of contributions to the *Lowell Offering* to the exclusion of any consideration of stylistics. Hannah Josephson insists that "[t]he poetry in the *Offering* was almost completely undistinguished" (189). Philip Foner and Benita Eisler argue that the literary quality of writings by these New England daughters of freemen is a secondary concern to the actual presence of the operatives' works. Eisler asserts:

> Whatever the overblown claims of patrons or admirers . . . the *Offering* itself is, finally, as modest as its title suggests. It represents the first heady efforts of young women in the process of discovering what they had the power to do. Before leaving the mills, "our bright, breezy wide-awake girls" left the first writings by and about American blue-collar women, along with many still unanswered questions about the relationship of work to class, sex, ethnicity, and aspiration in America. (41)

While most historians and literary critics have found the stylistics and conventions of poetry produced by the operatives to be off-putting, other twentieth-century historians such as David Roediger have presented notable analysis of the social implications of diction and syntax in the writings of antebellum Lowell factory workers. Thomas Dublin avoids discussion of literary submissions to the *Offering* and to other 1840s labor periodicals; instead, he characterizes the whole of the writing in the *Offering* as "stilted and conventional" (84). Even literary historian and Lucy Larcom biographer Shirley Marchalonis minimizes the quality of poetic presentations in the *Offering* by Lucy Larcom, characterizing it and the poetry of other female factory operatives as derivative (35).

The problem of twentieth-century critical dismissal of poetry by nineteenth-century American women writers, except Emily Dickinson, is not unique to working-class white women.[1] Joan R. Sherman suggests that both black men and women poets have gone unnoticed because "the poets' books and pamphlets are out of print and their uncollected verse languishes in scattered, inaccessible periodicals" (xv). That these works are unavailable to a twentieth-century and a twenty-first-century readership exacerbates the obscurity of many other popular nineteenth-century women poets and inhibits critical considerations of the aesthetic quality of these works. Yet Cheryl Walker contends that popular poetry by black and white, poor, working-class, and middle-class women of the nineteenth century participates in a shared heterogeneous discourse unified by gender. Responding to Sherman's argument, Walker insists that this "shared discourse" provides a context for evaluating common patterns in the poetry.[2] But many twentieth-century critical appraisals of this poetry have condemned the popular literature by women as imitative precisely because of the stylistic repetition of poetic conventions of their age.

More than their upper-class sisters whose works have begun to be recovered and studied, nineteenth-century working-class women poets have remained in a critical void. By exploring patterns of subjects and literary conventions in the poetry of American white, working-class women writing in Lowell, Massachusetts, at mid-century, this essay will show that these poets employ the periodical to produce a complex, often racialized as well as gendered and class-sensitive, subjectivity. The construction of a multifaceted poetic voice allows these women both to participate in and to stand outside the social and literary traditions of their day.

As nineteenth-century women, many factory operatives attempt to em-

brace the dominant middle-class Cult of True Womanhood by constructing a poetic voice that is pious, pure, submissive, and concerned with the
domestic sphere (Welter 21).[3] This tendency toward True Womanhood is
found most pointedly in the *Lowell Offering's* editorials, short fiction, and
verse. Former New Hampshire and Vermont farmers' daughters — now factory laborers — write as if their current status in the mills is temporary, and
for many women this was true. Poems such as "Home" by A. M. S. and L. L.'s
"Sabbath Bells" suggest that these poets focus their attention on an idealized
time in the past and in the future, a time in which they more fully participate
in upholding such pillars of the American Republic as individual liberty and
freedom of religion. The editorials, short stories, personal narratives, and
poetry of the *Lowell Offering*, like those of many middle-class women's magazines and annuals of the time "sought to convince woman that she had the
best of both worlds — power and virtue — and that a stable order of society
depended upon her maintaining her traditional place in it. To that end she
was identified with everything that was beautiful and holy" (Welter 41). An
example of this ideology of womanhood is in the last stanza of H. S. L.'s
poem, "The Trees and Rill":

'Tis beautiful! I fain would have a home
Upon the banks of such a rill, and share
With nature's children all her luxuries;
And grateful as that silent rivulet,
So cheerfully devote myself to all. (39 – 43)

In this way, Lowell's working-class white women shroud their temporal reality, transforming and defining the meaning of their lives in the factories by
espousing the behaviors and customs of True Womanhood in their poetry.
Such a redefining focus suggests the poet's denial of her daily working conditions and/or her ability to concentrate on a better future.

As female laborers in industrial complexes, these writers exchange their
time and labor for capital, while many embrace the identification of "wage
slave."[4] Such an identification, put forward by labor activists like George
Henry Evans and Orestes A. Brownson in the 1830s and 1840s, does not
simply suggest a willingness on the part of some of these Anglo-American
women to align themselves with the bound slaves of African descent; rather
the semantic operation of the word "slave" points to an anxiety of association by Northern female factory workers with those laboring against their
will in the South. By employing "slave" comparatively as part of the rhetoric

of the labor movement, women workers position their argument for a shorter workday and a stable rate of pay by posing the impossibility of an imbedded racial comparison of whites and blacks:

Oh! isn't it a pity, such a pretty girl as I —
Should be sent to the factory to pine away and die?
>   Oh! I cannot be a slave,
>   I will not be a slave,
>   For I'm so fond of liberty
>   That I cannot be a slave. (Robinson 51)

By exercising a term like "slave" in this context, the poet is not acting in solidarity with black slaves, but calling attention to the "inappropriate oppression of whites" (Roediger 68).

As Northerners, the female factory poets often adopt an impersonal tone in their poetic presentation of black men and women. This tone might suggest the geographical, or territorial, distance between most white operatives and blacks, but a small thriving African American community of several hundred people lived and worked in the mill city. No evidence that free blacks labored in the Lowell factories has been found. Still, because antebellum Lowell was not a segregated city, it is very likely that white female factory workers had regular contact with black women and men who were merchants or worked in such occupations as barbering. Many African American men were in key positions in Lowell's commercial and civic community; some African American women worked in such service professions as housekeeping; many African American families were part of the city's growing middle-class population.[5] Among the meanings suggested by the observational tone regarding blacks in some poems by white female laborers are the possible racist canceling out of Lowell's black community and/or an inability on the part of these white working-class women to comprehend middle-class and merchant-class African Americans within the same populace as blacks in slavery. The objectified representation of black men and women as slaves by these Northern, white, working-class poets in poems such as "The Slave's Revenge" and "The Slave Mother" implies a key difference of perception of economic class in their black figures.

If poems on the issue of slavery reveal a perspective that is relatively constant, those on the subject of work illuminate distinctions between the poetic subjectivities found in the *Lowell Offering*, the *New England Offering* and the *Voice of Industry*. While few such poems appear in the *Lowell Offering* under Harriet Farley's editorship, many can be found in the pages of the

Voice of Industry. Published in 1841, "Fancy," by Harriet Farley as the pseudonymous Fiducia,[6] is one of the few poems on industrial work in the *Lowell Offering.* The tonal force of the poem is energetic, lively, and suggestive of a positive perspective toward life and work:

> O swiftly flies the shuttle now,
> Swift as an arrow from the bow;
> But swifter than the thread is wrought,
> Is soon the flight of busy thought;
> For Fancy leaves the mill behind
> And seeks some novel scenes to find.(1–6)

Recalling the elite work of a poet in Frances Osgood's "A Flight of Fancy," the personification of Fancy in the figure of the mill girl furthers the notion that nineteenth-century women inhabit a sphere of life separate from the real world of business and commerce, while also suggesting that even as they tend their machines, mill girls have dreams of another life beyond the factories.

Represented in a pastoral romantic dream, Fiducia's mill girl figure suggests the poet's racial position as a white woman.[7] The poet's whiteness marks the linguistic configurations and contents of the text, producing her whiteness as an unwritten norm transcribed on the poem as she constructs an innocent festive time imprinted with an assumption of whiteness and occurring outside of the type of class distinctions brought on by industrialism. For example, the figures of the "manly youths, and maidens, too" (Fiducia l. 24) are reminiscent of Wordsworthian or Keatsian figures, white European figures, in festal cavort. While the positive force of the poem seems to travel on the steady rhythm of heroic couplets, the effect of industrialism on "Fancy's festal day" (l. 30) lies buried in the fifth stanza:

> But, hark! what sound salutes mine ear?
> A distant rumbling now I hear.
> Ah, Fancy! 'tis no groundless fear,
> The rushing whirlwind draweth near! (53–56)

Unlike what is found in other *Lowell Offering* poems, in "Fancy" the anesthetizing effects of labor on the female operatives are posited in these last stanzas. Just as the cotton mills were famous for their deadening, deafening noise, so does the poet employ an audibly suggestive image of "rumbling" to hasten the dreamed figure's "early grave."

Moreover, in contrast to the optimistic first stanza that represents a subjectivity allied with middle-class True Womanhood, the pseudonymous

Fiducia brings the poem to closure in a constricted female working-class space:

> For visions such as thine are vain,
> And bring but discontent and pain.
> Remember, in thy giddy whirl,
> That *I* am but a factory girl;
> And be content at home to dwell,
> Though governed by a "factory bell." (69–74)

Farley reworks the bell metaphor of the last stanza of Keat's "Ode to a Nightingale" into the common tolling of a factory bell. Unlike Keat's male speaker who loiters in the pain of alienated human consciousness, this working-class female speaker is called back to her pragmatic life. Such an ending may soothe mill-owning readers' fears about labor unrest among the women and may serve to instruct female factory workers in appropriate behavior. The figure of Fancy, like that of the nightingale, is the apostrophe on which the poem turns. "Fancy" is both exemplary of the optimistic attitude emphasized by Farley and the middle-class supporters of her publication and distinctive in the presentation of the negative narrowing of white female working-class life.

During the entire run of the *Voice of Industry*, edited by William F. Young and Sarah G. Bagley, many poems on labor reform were published in the first column of page one. Among these are poems with titles such as "The Factory Girls' Last Day," "The Toiler's Lament," and "To the Laborer for Humanity." This type of poetry was often reprinted in partisan presses like the *Voice of Industry* and the *National Era*, thus saving these works from complete obscurity then and now. While many female factory operatives in the *Lowell Offering* and in the *Voice of Industry* wrote under a pseudonym as a convention of True Womanhood, the women who took on the provocative subjects of their own city or factory employed a pseudonym for different reasons. Because they necessarily feared blacklisting by mill owners, many activist poets protected themselves by not signing their work.[8]

Much debate by historians has been concerned with the identity of the radical writer Amelia. Former Merrimack Valley Textile Museum archivist Helena Wright argues against associating Sarah Bagley with this poet. By October 1845, Wright claims, Bagley had left the mills and "[t]here was no reason for her not to sign her work." Instead, Wright maintains that "Amelia was far more likely Amelia Sargent, who reported on the Sarah Bagley–Harriet Farley controversy over editorial responsibility and circulation of

the *Lowell Offering* in the *Voice* issue of 25 September 1845, and who also suffered a rebuff from Farley" (n.p.). Appearing originally in the Lowell Female
Labor Reform Association (FLRA) pamphlet *Factory Tracts*, "The Summons" by the pseudonymous author Amelia is a typical example of activist
poetry. Amelia elaborates on a variety of injustices heaped upon the poor
and working class by foreign and domestic tyrants. Written in twelve quat-
rains, this poetic clarion constructs the audience as participants in a tradition of personal freedom and revolution:

> Ye children of New England!
>> The summons is to you!
> Come from the work-shop and the field,
>> With steadfast hearts and true.
>
> Come, fling your banner to the breeze,
>> For liberty and light;
> Come, like the rolling of the seas —
>> The tempest in its might. (1–8)

The title, the exclamatory opening lines, and the alliteration of stanza 2 recall the biblical tradition of Hebrew Scripture and reproduce a bardic tradition in which poets issued calls to action. In this militant poem, too, an assumption of whiteness operates in the representation of a power struggle
between authority and the worker. Naming only the Caucasian-dominated
nations of Spain, Galia, and England in a poetic parallel construction with
"our own boasted clime," the poet effectively racializes and limits the range
of tyrannical power. By leaving the "famished children" and other oppressed
figures as racially neutral, Amelia participates in a repertoire of whiteness
that assumes the whiteness of any racially unmarked figure, as she herself assumes a "New England" and an "American" persona.

    Also frequently found among the poems of the Lowell poets is the blend-
ing of historical, political, or newsworthy subjects with metaphors drawn
from dominant social codes of behavior and seemingly standard images
from nature. Like those of their middle-class counterparts, poems with such
titles as "The Heroine of Columbia," "A Lesson from the Wind," "Liberty
Bells," and "The Mexican War" appear in prominent locations in issues of
Lowell labor periodicals. Of this type of poem, "Factory Blossoms for Queen
Victoria" by *Offering* editor Harriet Farley is an example of the poet's incor-
poration of political and social issues into the traditional poetic forms of the
apostrophe. Both the poet's initialed pseudonym (H. F.) and the poetic voice

of this work claim a subjectivity that functions within the bounds of True Womanhood, thereby stretching those boundaries to include private moral instruction on the seemingly public and political matters of British expansionism, poverty in England, and civil law (see Finch). "Factory Blossoms for Queen Victoria" appears during a period of trade expansion in China and India and Poor Law reform in England. Farley, who in an earlier editorial claimed that factory girls had no place commenting on issues of political concern, employs the poetic form of an apostrophe and takes on a poetic persona to comment on contemporary matters of human justice in Great Britain. With her initials as a pseudonym, Farley may have hoped that she could maintain the appearance of anonymity in spite of her clear shift into the public domain.[9] Farley's construction of poetic subjectivity creates a space from which the white, female, laboring-class poet can address a British queen:

> Lady, accept the humble flowers
>> Which now I tender thee;
> They bloomed not in Parnassian bowers,
>> Nor on some classic tree.
>
> .   .   .   .
>
> But deem me not, when meets your sight,
>> Wanting in courtesy —
> This stubborn Yankee pen wont write,
>> YOUR GRACIOUS MAJESTY. (1– 4, 13 –16)

By representing the speaker as a "Yankee," Farley claims a subjectivity that is American, but an American descended from British, not Irish or African, ancestry. Such positionality asserts a white racial lineage, thus allowing the poetic speaker to share ethnic, racial, and gender affinities with Victoria.

Grounded in this alliance of factory girl and queen, Farley's speaker advises a young Victoria of her profound duty as a True Woman and as the Queen of England to the disadvantaged of her land:

> And, lady, never, since that hour,
>> Could I forget that queen;
> But, ah, in all of regal power,
>> The woman's seldom seen.
>
> I read of wars, so vast and proud —
>> Say, are they always just?

And those whose necks thy warriors bowed,
    Those who *should* kiss the dust.

I read of those by wrongs oppressed
    Beneath a woman's sway:
Lady, could not thy kind behest
    Change their sad lot? Oh, say!

Methinks thou art not ruler there;
    I see the statesman's guile;
In all that speaks of regal care,
    There's diplomatic wile. (49–68)

Harriet Farley's Yankee-factory-girl speaker is problematically positioned in her chastisement of Queen Victoria for wrongs against the poor and the colonized. On the one hand, as Queen, Victoria is her better in power, class standing, education, and family background. But instead of finding the locus of oppression in Victoria as queen, Farley's poetic persona elides Victoria's responsibility by focusing on her role as woman, as wife, as mother. By so doing, the poet renders the queen powerless in the sphere of male politics, thus foregrounding the ambivalent authority position of this nineteenth-century female queen. In her True Womanhood is Victoria's frailty and her potency:

There's better far than pomp or state
    To claim a sovereign's care —
Goodness should always make her great,
    And kindness makes her fair.
Let oft thy words repeated be —
    Traced once in lines of light —
"Speak to me not of policy,
    But tell me, is it right?"

. . . .

Mother, look on *thy* babes, and think,
    If *they* should cry for bread.
Oh, use for *these* thy sceptre well,
    For these let laws be made . . . (109–16, 127–30)

In the address of a factory girl to a queen, the poet posits a parallel relationship of gender, True Womanhood, ethnicity, and race shared by the female factory girl readers of the *Lowell Offering* and the reigning queen of England.

By instructing a young Victoria in her profound duty as a True Woman who happens to be the Queen of England, the poet suggests that her readers, too, are True Women who happen to be factory workers.

Beyond explicitly political works, many regional poems, which Lawrence Buell identifies as "New England's topographically oriented poetry," appear in the *Lowell and New England Offering* (289). For example, "The Rivulet" by Cynthia, "The Trees and the Rill" by H. S. L., and "Winter's Dawn" by Sara of Glen Viola each explore a connection between New England topography and human traits. One of the best examples of a topographical poem is "The River" by a young Lucy Larcom (writing as L. L.). Larcom correlates the river to the socially defined appropriate interior and exterior life of a True Woman. The poet balances the relationship of nature to human fulfillment by constructing three parallel stanzas each of a length divisible by the same number, following a typical pattern of development for New England nineteenth-century regional poetry. In the first and longest stanza of thirty-six lines, she describes a river meandering to the sea:

> Gently flowed a river bright
> On its path of liquid light.
> Not like some rude torrent's course,
> Onward with impetuous force
> O'er its rocky pavement speeding —
> Passing beauties never heeding —
> But its noiseless way pursued . . .
>
> . . . .
>
> Cheering with its presence mild,
> Cultured fields and woodlands wild. (1–7, 11–12)

By focusing on the river, L. L. intensifies the familiar and employs a well-established nature metaphor. Juxtaposing a description of a True Woman's pattern of behavior and relationships in the sixteen-line middle stanza, Larcom represents a female figure as an abstract and racially unmarked refraction of the river:

> Is not such a pure one's life?
> Ever shunning pride and strife —
> Never babbling her own praise —
> Passing happy, peaceful days,
> Noiselessly along she goes,
> Known by kindly deeds she does —

Often wandering far to bless,
And do others kindnesses.
Though *herself* is seldom seen,
Yet we know where she has been (37–46)

By presenting womanly fulfillment within the category of the white, middle-class construction of True Womanhood, L. L. normalizes this particular type of womanhood and thereby participates in a repertoire of whiteness that reproduces "normativity rather than marginality, privilege rather than disadvantage" (Frankenberg 237). As a factory laborer, Larcom would have spent an average of twelve hours a day, six days a week, in the hot and noisy mills with other white working-class women. By embracing the middle-class cultural standard of True Womanhood, she not only erases the role of work in the lives of working women but limits the aspects of working-class women's lives that qualify for this popular definition of womanhood.

The poet extends this topical poem, as well as the assumption of womanly whiteness, into the eschatology in the last, and shortest, stanza:

Thus, by her own virtues shaded,
And by glory's presence aided,
While pure thoughts, like starbeams, lie
Mirrored in her heart and eye,
She, content to be unknown,
All serenely moveth on,
Till, released from time's commotion,
Self is lost in love's wide ocean. (53–60)

While Lawrence Buell asserts that "[t]he correlation of last things — natural, human, eschatological — is, of course, hardly peculiar to the New England muse" (291), this Lowell female factory operative notably participates in formal and traditional poetic models that have been most often associated with upper-class American and British Romantic poets. But while the poet performs a conventional womanly subjectivity, she transcends those limitations to appropriate for herself (and indirectly, for her peers) an elite aesthetic tradition articulated by an empowered and individuated self (see Finch).

A very practical common ground between women poets and readers of different races, classes, generations, and nations is the poetic performance of death. In this category of poetry, intensification of banal objects, emotions, images, and metaphors is acute. Cheryl Walker aptly points out that death was a significant presence in the lives of people in the nineteenth century. "It was common to lose at least a parent, a sibling, a husband, or a child before one was thirty" (xxxi). Such poets as Emma Embury (1806–63), Helen Hunt Jackson (1830–85), Frances Ellen Watkins Harper (1825–1911), Ina Coolbrith (1841–1928), and of course, Lydia Sigourney (1791–1865) published poems with such titles as "The Consumptive," "The Prince is Dead," "The Dying Fugitive," "When the Grass Shall Cover Me," and "Death of a Young Lady at the Retreat for the Insane." Although numerous and heterogeneous, these poems about death written by nineteenth-century women share a conventional intensification of emotion. The white working-class women poets of Lowell contribute widely to this poetics of illness, dying, and death. Their contributions include long lyrics and elegies such as "The Death of Emma," short contemplations such as "The Mother's Prayer," and untitled expressions of sympathy such as a poem found in the correspondence column of the *Voice of Industry*, which ends with this last stanza:

Hope on, fond mother, though you mourn,
   He knows no grief or pain;
He'll rise, when dawns that promised morn,
   And you *will meet again*.

The location of this poetic fragment offers an example of how the domestic sphere extends into the public domain. Even in the early twenty-first century, such fragments expressing grief and offering comfort still can be found on the obituary pages of many newspapers across the United States.

Among these poems on death by nineteenth-century Lowell women is Cordelia A. Priest's "The Dying Girl's Dream." A rather lengthy lyric of seventy-two lines, broken down into twelve six-line stanzas, Priest's poem romanticizes the innocence of an agrarian past while highlighting the effect of urban life and intemperance. The temperance subtext of "The Dying Girl's Dream" participates in a social, literary, and historical reform movement led by women. Approximately contemporary to Priest's poem is "Drinking Song" by the well-known Sigourney, an antidrinking drinking song published in 1848. When Priest engages the subject of death and the theme of temperance, she positions herself, through her female persona, within a wider social community. Employing the nineteenth-century sentimental convention of the persona of a dying girl, the poet shapes her subject in personal terms:

And I saw my sweet mother hov'ring near,
   And she bade me weep no more.

> She looked not sad, my dear papa,
>   As when in this wretched home,
> You left her to die on that long, dreary night (11–15)

The poetic voice functions within the strictures of True Womanhood: the speaker is pure, pious, submissive to a greater will, and concerned with the domestic sphere of home and family. Because few records exist documenting the lives of particular factory operatives, and of female factory workers in particular, it is impossible to know whether or not Cordelia A. Priest is a given name or pseudonym. Although the poem obviously participates in social conventions such as True Womanhood, it also queries the ideology of class embedded in that social code. In the last stanza, the figure of the dying girl embraces the matriarchal lineage of True Womanhood by giving her father a last moral imperative:

> For a moment I mourned, my dear papa,
>   Till I thought of your misery here;
> Then I left that beautiful shore,
>   To warn you to drink, Oh, drink no more,
> If you would meet when your life is o'er,
>   Your child and her mother dear. (67–72)

Due to the significant presence of death in the daily lives of people during this time, death verse not only links poets of different genders, races, and economic classes but also provides a means of comparison among the works of nineteenth-century poets. Yet the conspicuous absence of poems about deaths associated with factory working conditions suggests the erasure of the factory's dangers from not only this collection of poems but from the psyches of American female factory workers as well.

The absence of poetry about work-related illnesses and death certainly suggests the tension out of which many factory operatives wrote. As Daughters of Freemen,[10] as True Women, these poets attempt to write within the social and literary traditions of their day. As the publication of the *Lowell Offering* drew to a close in the fall of 1845, Farley wrote: "The Offering has done its work. It has accomplished all that it ever proposed" (Oct. 1845: 240). And to those who criticized the *Lowell Offering* for its lack of social awareness, Farley wrote:

> There were, sometimes, in its tales, essays, and poems, allusions to trials, griefs, deprivations, and discomforts. The wearisome hours, the monotonous toil, the separation from friends, and the seclusion from the

accustomed healthful and buoyant influences of nature, were spoken of in terms — it might be of regret and sadness, but not of captious discontent. And we are rejoiced at this. We thank them that they have presented themselves to their readers with cheerfulness and self-respect. They have thus done honor to their heads and their hearts. They have shown that their first and absorbing thought was not for an advance of wages or a reduction of labor hours. (Nov. 1845: 263)

As editor of the *Lowell Offering*, she articulates this tension between operatives writing as female factory laborers and genteel True Women. But by noting "allusions to trials" rather than the trials themselves, "sadness" rather than "captious discontent," and the writers' concerns with self-improvement rather than "an advance of wages or a reduction of labor hours," Farley inadvertently sketches out the disjunction between twentieth-century readerly assumptions fueled by historical narratives about the working conditions in the Lowell mills and the actual poems many readers encounter in the *Lowell Offering* and the more militant *Voice of Industry*. As readers, if we are to gain any insight into the literary production of Lowell's female factory workers — literary work that both participates in and stands outside of the aesthetic and social traditions of their day — we must train ourselves to recognize the writerly tensions, including the many transformations of subjectivity, in the seemingly simple and imitative texts.

NOTES

1 A number of critics have addressed this omission, recovering literary works and including these works by nineteenth-century American women writers in their analyses and in their classrooms. Notable among these critics are Nina Baym, Joanne Dobson, Cheryl Walker, Karen Kilcup, Paula Bennett, and Annie Finch.

2 Cheryl Walker, *American Women Poets of the Nineteenth Century*, New Brunswick, NJ: Rutgers UP, 1992. Paula Bennett similarly argues this point in "'The Descent of the Angel': Interrogating Domestic Ideology in American Women's Poetry, 1858–1890" *American Literary History* 7.4 (1995): 591–610.

3 While much has been written about the Cult of True Womanhood, two critical essays best define the social construct. Please see Barbara Welter's "The Cult of True Womanhood, 1820–1860" in *Dimity Convictions: The American Woman in the Nineteenth Century* and Annie Finch's "The Sentimental Poetess in the World: Metaphor and Subjectivity in Lydia Sigourney's Nature Poetry," *Legacy*, 5 (1988): 3–15.

4 David R. Roediger, in *The Wages of Whiteness*, presents an extensive discussion on the use and the function of such terms as "wage slavery," "white slavery," and the

"slavery of wages" in the rhetoric of U.S. labor-management struggles during the 1830s and 1840s; see pages 65–92.

5 Archivist Martha Mayo of the Mogan Center for Labor History in Lowell, Massachusetts, detailed the lives of this mostly middle-class community in a 1994–1995 museum exhibit. I am particularly grateful to Martha Mayo for her time and generous availability in answering my numerous questions about the African American community in Lowell before the Civil War. Brad Parker's book, *Black and Antislavery History of Early Lowell*, also traces the history of African Americans in antebellum Lowell.

6 *Lowell Offering* editor Harriet Farley's choice of Fiducia as a pseudonym allows her to bring the domestic and the public spheres together indirectly. The name comes from the Latin word for *trust*. Connotations of the characteristics of a True Woman and a reliable source, particularly associated with money, are easily drawn.

7 Toni Morrison, in *Playing in the Dark*, outlines a critical project that stresses the "embedded assumptions of racial (not racist) language." She insists that American writers historically have constructed black figures as reflexive, as "an extraordinary meditation on the self; a powerful exploration of fears and desires that reside in the writerly conscious." She argues that an assumption of whiteness has continued to operate on the part of both the writers and the readers of American literature. Morrison asserts that when this assumption remains unwritten and unexamined, the critical gaze is averted from the subject to the object, thus eliding any query into the effect of whiteness on the text.

In her reading of twentieth-century North American white women's life histories, Ruth Frankenberg (*White Women, Race Matters*) systematically examines the construction and function of whiteness. Her study considers the effect of social encoding of whiteness on the subjects' lives. Frankenberg maintains:

> "Whiteness changes over time and space and is in no way a transhistorical essence. Rather . . . it is a complexly constructed product of local, regional, national, and global relations, past and present. . . . And if whiteness varies spatially and temporally, it is also a relational category, one that is constructed with a range of other racial and cultural categories, with class and with gender." (236–37)

Embedded in the invisibility of whiteness in the life histories of Frankenberg's subjects and in the diction, semantics, and poetics of nineteenth-century white female factory workers' poetry is a complex repertoire of relationships, ideology, and culture.

8 Some women wrote under a pseudonym because it was the custom of the time. Pseudonyms allowed women writers a way to retain their private world while participating in the genteel public domain of the literary magazine. For others, the

pseudonym protected the identity of the female factory worker who criticized labor practices. Mill workers, male and female, could be fired from their jobs and find themselves unemployable simply for offering such criticism in public. In *Women at Work*, Thomas Dublin explains:

> As early as 1829 three firms — the Hamilton, Appleton, and the Merrimack companies — agreed not to hire operatives who had left the others' employment without receiving an honorable discharge. In this early intercompany agreement we see the origins of a system of blacklisting aimed at controlling and disciplining members of the mill work force. (59)

In this same text, see also p. 265, n.3 for further discussion.

9 Farley's well-publicized conflict with *Voice of Industry* editor Sarah Bagley over the contents of the *Lowell Offering* indicates that Farley was very concerned with the public perception of her writers as True Women who, although they worked in factories, did not stray into the public sphere. Farley's use of initials allows her work to be recognizable to the working-class writers and readers, as well as to regular readers of the magazine, but may have shielded her identity from a wider audience who might encounter Farley's work reproduced in other periodicals.

10 See D. Roediger's *Wages of Whiteness* and T. Dublin's *Women at Work* for further discussion of this important and complex term. As Daughters of Freemen, many New England women saw themselves as both inheritors of and arbiters of national liberties. Unfortunately, such standings often did not offer economic stability. Many of the women who identified themselves in this way came from destitute northern New England farm families, hence their employment in the Lowell factories.

Amy Doherty

REDEFINING THE BORDERS OF LOCAL COLOR FICTION: MARÍA CRISTINA MENA'S SHORT STORIES IN THE CENTURY MAGAZINE

In the early twentieth century, editors of "genteel" periodicals such as the *Century* magazine turned their ever shifting interests to Mexico, a country that possessed a foreign allure at a comfortable distance from the predominantly Anglo-American northeast. Images such as the photo-essay "Unfamiliar Mexico," which appeared in the September 1915 issue of the *Century*, illustrate a distanced and condescending perspective of the country south of the border. The stark black-and-white photographs in this series include a woman kneeling to wash laundry in a river, a man standing by a hand pump carrying water in a large jug on his back, and a woman walking alone, shrouded in mystery. In each of these images, the Mexican subject is either surprised by or hidden from the viewer. Such images suggest the contemporary view of Mexico as a comparatively undeveloped, tradition-bound, and exotic country.

Writing for the magazine that promoted this perspective of Mexico, María Cristina Mena (1893–1965), an immigrant from Mexico City who lived in New York City in the early twentieth century, presented an "insider" perspective of her country of origin in a series of short stories published in *Century* between 1913 and 1916.[1] Mena wrote these stories during a time of political and social upheaval, when the escalation of the Mexican Revolution and the corresponding shifts in the social structure and economy caused hundreds of thousands of immigrants to flee to the north (Acuña 127). While most of these immigrants settled in the southwestern United States, Mena, who left Mexico at the age of fourteen, settled with family friends in New York City and began publishing at the age of twenty. Having moved from Mexico City at a young age, and having been a part of the upper class in Mexico, Mena held a perspective that in some ways reflected that of her *Century* audience. The daughter of "a Spanish mother and a Yucatecan father of European blood" (Simmen 39), well educated, and fluent in Spanish, English,

French, and Italian (Hoehn 118–19), she wrote from an urbane, bicultural background that defied contemporary views of Mexicans as rural and "uncivilized." Writing of Mexico for an Anglo-American audience, she used the local color tradition of presenting a "native" view of a region far from her urban readership to make the "unfamiliar" familiar to this audience and subtly transformed this tradition by commenting on American imperialism in Mexico.

Although Mena's work has been included in anthologies of regionalist writing, notably Elizabeth Ammons and Valerie Rohy's *United States Local Color Writers: 1880–1920: An Anthology* (1997) and Karen L. Kilcup's *Nineteenth-Century American Women Writers: An Anthology* (1997), critics have not yet analyzed her work within this genre. One of the first mentions of Mena's work as "local color fiction" was in *Chicano Literature* in 1982, when Charles Tatum placed her fiction under the heading "Chicano Local-Color Writers" and stated that her work, along with fiction by Nino Otero, Josefina Escajeda, and Jovita González, belonged to the category of "those who emphasize the folkloric aspect of the Spanish-speaking experience" rather than "those who begin to strive for greater psychological depth and artistic completeness in their works."[2] Tatum's dismissal of Mena's work represents the preference for overtly politically engaged work during the initial recovery of Chicano/a writers. Because her fiction, along with texts by other racially marginalized women writers, was more subtle in its dialogue with Anglo-America, it did not receive further critical consideration until recent revisionist studies of this fiction.[3] For example, Tiffany Ana López's "María Cristina Mena: Turn-of-the-Century La Malinche and Other Tales of Cultural (Re)Construction" recuperates key figures from Mexican tradition such as La Llorona and La Malinche to demonstrate Mena's own tricksterism as a writer for *Century*. Such critical work illustrates the importance of continually revising entrenched readings of gender and genre. To these significant studies, I would like to add an examination of how Mena uses the periodical to redefine the borders of class, race, and nation in her representation of Mexico in local color fiction.

Although early critical studies of local color fiction emphasized its sentimental depictions of rural regions, recent studies argue that it also represented Anglo-American superiority at home and abroad. Race plays a central role in regional fiction, which, as Richard Brodhead writes, "requires a setting outside the world of modern development, a zone of backwardness where locally variant folkways still prevail. Its characters are ethnologically colorful, personifications of the different humanity produced in such non-modern cultural settings" (115–16). On one level, this fiction is similar to a travel narrative, placing its readers in an area far from Boston or New York; often, however, it also aligns the perspective of the narrator with a white urban audience, ultimately representing the region, and the people in it, as backward and inferior to this audience.[4] For example, Thomas Nelson Page's *In Ole Virginia* (1887), serialized in the *Century*, places its readers in the rural American South, and by using local color conventions to contrast the white protagonists (and readers) with African American characters, subtly confirms Anglo-American racial superiority in the years following the Civil War.[5]

In the early twentieth century, as World War I and increased immigration threatened national and racial identities, the purview of regionalism expanded west of the Mississippi and beyond national borders. The guise of travel masks imperialism in the stories that appear in *Century* at the time that Mena published her short stories. Narrating the visit of a white tourist to the Philippines, Jamaica, and California, respectively, stories such as "Race" (Aug. 1914), "Creole Beauties and Some Passionate Pilgrims" (Feb. 1914), and "The Transformation of Angelita López" (Aug. 1914) reveal a merging of foreign and domestic "regions." Such narratives emphasize the racial distinctions between the protagonist/narrator and the "locals," connecting the Anglo-American readers with the "civilized" white, urban narrators, who tell the tales through their relationship with the "natives." In her fiction, Mena not only draws on the travel aspect of local color fiction by showing a glimpse of Mexican life; she also represents the tension between the domestic and the foreign during a period of increased conflict over national borders.

Century maintained an important separation between its targeted readership and "foreigners," both "the foreigner within" and those outside national borders, and the publication's depictions of Mexico and Mexicans at the time that Mena wrote reveal this conflict. Mexico presented a threat to national borders for several reasons. Not only did Mexicans live in the Southwest before that region became part of the United States, but immigration from Mexico increased exponentially during the early twentieth century (Acuña 127). Furthermore, the Mexican Revolution threatened the economic and political ties between the United States and Mexico. In the January 1914 issue of *Century*, an editorial regarding the Mexican Revolution, "The Mexican Menace," conveys this tension. In this essay, W. Morgan Shuster addresses the issue of U.S. intervention in Mexico following the assassination of President Francisco I. Madero by officers under Victoriano Huerta's command (Camin and Meyer 35) and presents the complexities of U.S. involvement in terms that demonstrate a racist perspective of Mexico in the early twentieth century. Referring to the "thousands of ignorant and blameless peons, Indians, and other Mexican citizens who would be found bearing a gun in Huerta's or other ranks" (599), he argues that "the American nation may yet convince Huerta and the Mexican people that his and their failure to heed the civilized world's just admonition will result in the prompt and complete exercise of that international police power which in the end must reside in the leading civilized nations of the earth" (602). The sense of Mexico's dependence on American "civilization" in this essay suggests that the U.S.–Mexican border divides civilized and uncivilized people,[6] a view that persists in *Century*'s own "local color" presentation of Mexican immigrants in the United States.

For example, in "The Transformation of Angelita López" (Aug. 1914), a local color story by Anglo-American writer Gertrude B. Millard, the narrative voice is aligned with Miss Jane Crother, a "Puritan, common-sense ex–New Englander" (547) who resettles in California. Providing the "imperial eye" of local color fiction,[7] Miss Jane is the outsider in the Southwest but acts as a paternalistic landowner, managing the relationship between her Mexican servant, Angelita, and Angelita's shiftless husband, Antonio. Angelita is subservient, docile, and given to passionate impulse, which Miss Crother justifies by saying that "Mexican blood runs differently" (547). Meanwhile, Antonio shifts between jobs, such as railroad construction and farmwork, that serve the wealthy southwestern Anglo-Americans. Intimating the Mexicans' ineffectiveness and dependence on those who benefit from their work, Antonio's boss fires him from his job as a railroad worker, saying "Can't have no blame', low-down greaser shirkin' where I'm boss" (553). Miss Crother, seeking to rectify the situation, speculates that "there was somewhere at least a beet-grower who needed an extra hand" (554). While the need for foreign labor confirms the growth of the nation, which, as June Howard argues, is an important aspect of local color fiction (368), the story maintains distinctions between Anglo-Americans and Mexican-Americans by emphasizing Antonio's failure to adapt to U.S. capitalism. Angelita's final return to Miss Crother's house ('Si 'Tonio mio come no for as' me, I stay een thees 'ouse teel I die" [557]) signifies Mexican dependence on the Anglo-Americans who have usurped their homeland and confirms Anglo-American dominance in the American Southwest.

In comparison with local color writers who create a border between American and "foreign" through the urban narrator and rural subject, Mena merges the urban and rural, Mexican and American, to recreate her home in her short stories. Her upper-class perspective allows her to write in dialogue with *Century*'s portrayals of Mexicans, to negotiate with her editors about the subjects of her stories, and to engage her audience's interest. At the same time, Mena shifts the borders of the local color genre by presenting her own vision of Mexico, skillfully employing her "borderland" position to foreground the political and economic concerns of her native country.[8] Publishing her fiction in issues that also included "Unfamiliar Mexico" and "The Mexican Menace," she draws attention to the racially marginalized characters in "John of God, the Water-Carrier," exposes American imperialism in "The Education of Popo," and counters the stereotypical views of Mexicans in both by revealing Mexican cultural traditions and portraying a sense of community outside U.S. influence. Writing for a magazine that presented Mexico as a site of tourism and imperialism, Mena uses the local color genre to confront her Anglo-American readers with their own presumptions.

To represent Mexico in *Century*, Mena employs both regionalist and local color conventions. In her reading of regionalist writing by racially marginalized women authors, Marjorie Pryse draws a distinction between "regionalism, which features an empathic approach to regional characters that enfranchises their stories and cultural perceptions, and 'local color,' which represents regional life and regional characters as objects to be viewed from the perspective of the nonregional, often urban Eastern reader, and frequently offered for that reader's entertainment" (48). Pryse focuses on women regionalist writers of the late nineteenth century, such as Zitkala-Sä, Alice Dunbar-Nelson, and Sui Sin Far, noting their negotiation of the "rhetorical space 'within' those excluding discourses" (50). While Pryse uses the term "regionalist" to distinguish these authors from "local color writers," it is also important to consider the ways in which racially marginalized writers draw on the more canonical element of this tradition to become published. In the context of *Century*, Mena's fiction was a site of enfranchisement, but it also meant satisfying the interest of the Anglo-American readers who sought escape from their frenetic urban lives and their desire to visit places unknown and exotic through reading. She uses narrative strategies that are common to the local color genre, providing concrete details of Mexican life and dialect that "place" her U.S. reader in Mexico, but also challenges the perception of Mexico as knowable through the regionalist genre itself.

In her first short story, "John of God, the Water-Carrier," Mena sets the stage for her entrance into the *Century* magazine by using local color conventions to detail life in Mexico while subtly criticizing the influence of

American capitalism. This story, which later appeared in the *Monthly Crite-rion* (1927), edited by T.S. Eliot, and was included in *The Best Short Stories of 1928*, evidently appealed to an Anglo audience in the early twentieth century. To interest this audience, Mena writes from an upper-class, urban perspective about Mexican Indians, a marginalized race in Mexico. In this story, Juan de Dios, an *aguador* for the pueblo, decides to go to Mexico City to seek his fortune in order to marry Delores, a young girl whom he saves when her mother dies in an earthquake. In Mexico City, Dios travels from house to house, forgoing the use of the "American force-pumps" (20) to deliver water to the city dwellers in the traditional, and more communal, manner. Then Dios's success as a water carrier changes when his more ostentatious brother Tiburcio shows up with Delores, whom he has married in Juan's absence, and gains his brother's customers by using modern plumbing instead of carrying water. The brothers' pilgrimage to the shrine of the Virgin of Guadalupe resolves the conflict between tradition and modernization. Juan repents for cursing his brother, whose "paralysis"[9] is miraculously healed at the shrine and decides to live out his days as a water carrier to the pilgrims. The elements of local color fiction in this novel — the sense of place, the urban perspective, the use of marginalized characters, and Mena's reference to traditional Mexican figures — reflect and subtly transform the local color tradition.

Writing from her own urban, upper-class perspective, Mena reflects the "ethnologically colorful" element of local color fiction (Brodhead 115) to present Juan de Dios and Tiburcio and their migration from the rural pueblo to Mexico City. While her knowledge of the different sectors of Mexican society demonstrates her "insider" view of Mexico, her presentation of the Indians' perspective of Mexico City establishes her distance from her story's protagonists. For example, when Juan de Dios announces to Delores that he will leave for Mexico City, Mena writes that Delores "looked at him with mingled terror and admiration, for in the imagination of the Indian of the pueblos the City of Mexico is enveloped in formidable and sinister mystery."[10] In her description of Mexico City, Mena shifts from the local color convention of writing about the details of life in a rural area to describing the city's etiquette, with which she is familiar and to which Dios must adjust. She writes:

> The capital, as sensitive of its reputation as an elegant woman, has a code of manners for Inditos, and enforces it in times of peace, peremptorily though kindly. Juan de Dios learned that in the City of Mexico one may

no longer enjoy the comfort of going barefoot, and dutifully he taught his feet to endure the encumbrance of leather sandals. He learned that the city aguador may not blow his whistle to halt the traffic while he gravely crosses the street, but must wait for the passing of many vehicles, some with horses and some outlandishly without. (18)

In this description, Mena alludes to Mexico's modernization, which contrasts with the *Century*'s representations of an undeveloped Mexico in "Unfamiliar Mexico" and the "The Mexican Menace" and shows that she, unlike Dios, is part of this modern world. To further differentiate her class status from that of her subject, Mena contrasts Dios's formal, clipped English, which suggests his awkwardness with English, with her narrator's linguistic fluency. She also places herself outside this community by calling the Mexican Indians "Inditos," a diminutive for "Indian," which implies her own racial superiority. Furthermore, her description of the "mixed rabble of barefooted infancy" at Dios's home (15) and her comparison of Juan de Dios and his brother Tiburcio to "a pair of friendly ants" (20) reveal her upper-class status in a racially stratified society. Mena's position as a Mexican of European descent influenced her perspective of the Mexican Indians and provided a window for her similarly privileged *Century* audience.

Yet, despite its upper-class perspective, Mena's narrative draws attention to the treatment of the Mexican Indians and subtly comments on the influence of American capitalism in Mexico. In her letters to *Century*, she represents her role as a translator for the dispossessed Mexican Indian:

I expect to write more stories of Inditos than of any other class in Mexico. They form the majority; the issue of their rights and wrongs, their aspirations and possibilities, is at the root of the present situation in my unhappy country, and will become more and more prominent when the immense work of national regeneration shall have fairly begun.[11]

This letter refers to the injustices experienced by the Mexican Indians, which led to their fighting in the Mexican Revolution.[12] Prior to the revolution, President Porfirio Díaz's plan for "modernization" included providing "preferential treatment" to foreign, particularly U.S., investors, which allowed the United States to gain control over Mexican capital and ultimately left the Mexicans dispossessed of their land (Acuña 126–27). In the United States at the time that Mena wrote, contemporary studies such as John Kenneth Turner's *Barbarous Mexico* (1910) condemn the dire situation that displaced Mexicans, particularly Indians, faced. Turner investigates the Díaz regime's dispossession of the Indians' land, the enslavement of the Yaqui and Maya Indians, and asserts U.S. complicity in this slavery because of American corporate investment in Mexico and governmental support of Díaz (219). Likewise, Mena alludes to the influence of American capitalism in her mention of the "highly painted and patented American force-pumps" (19–20) that Tiburcio uses for Juan de Dios's customers in Mexico City. By showing how the residents of Mexico City work Tiburcio to the point of exhaustion to have the convenience of modern plumbing, she indirectly criticizes the influence of American capitalism and subtly foregrounds a dispossessed sector of the Mexican population.

Mena's upper-class perspective may seem stereotypical to today's readers; when one considers this work, however, within the context of *Century* in 1913, she portrays a diversity among the Mexican people otherwise absent in the publication. Indeed, she had to argue with her editors for the central role of Juan de Dios, and for maintaining the integrity of her story: "I felt as if I had foisted a white elephant upon an amiable friend, who now begged my permission to make the creature more conformable by amputating its legs, trunk and tail — not forgetting its ears." She accuses the editors of wanting to alter her story because of its focus on a Mexican Indian. "Could it be that the water carrier's lowly station in life made him a literary undesirable? Then what of Maupassant's Norman peasants, Kipling's soldiers and low-caste Hindoos, Myra Kelly's tenement children, and many other social nobodies of successful fiction?" Mena's statement calls attention to a racialized literary hierarchy, which includes a corresponding caste system of "literary undesirables." Although she forcefully argues for keeping her detailed story, she softens her argument by revealing her own upper-class bias:

> and I believe that American readers, with their intense interest in Mexico, are ripe for a true picture of a people so near to them, so intrinsically picturesque, so misrepresented in current fiction, and so well worthy of being known and loved, in all their ignorance.[13]

Here she plays to the desires of her *Century* readers, with "their intense interest in Mexico," and in mentioning the Mexican Indians' "intrinsically picturesque" quality, she presents her argument in local color terms.[14] In order to communicate with her *Century* editors, Mena emphasizes her class superiority even as she criticizes the oppression of the Mexican Indians.

At the end of the story, the transcendent presence of the Virgin of Guadalupe symbolizes the continuation of Mexican tradition in the face of social upheaval. She plays several important roles related to maintaining community: she unites Juan de Dios and Tiburcio, she gives Juan de Dios a way of redemption, and she displaces the influence of U.S. capitalism. As the "first dark Mestiza virgin," the Virgin of Guadalupe "represents the merging of European and Indian culture since she is, in some senses, a transformation or 'rebirth' of the native goddesses" (Rebolledo 50). She is also a significant figure for Mena's own cultural border-crossing as she published her first short story in the *Century*. To present this story to an Anglo-American audience, she had to explain details that would be unfamiliar; for example, her negotiations with her editors reveal that she had argued to keep the details of the pilgrimage to Guadalupe:

> Another passage marked for cutting out was the one telling of the pilgrims eating blessed earth and drinking blessed water and buying blessed tortillas with chile sauce, and tortillas of the Virgin, which are small and sweet and dyed in many colors — a passage that I would almost defend with my life!" [15]

Although Mena's retort may sound "picturesque," she argues to save the signs of her culture; she will not let these important details be lost in translation. Mexican folklore plays an important role in Mena's version of the local color story and provides an important link to her Mexican heritage. As Gloria Velásquez Treviño notes, "John of God" is "based on a religious folktale" (29), and in writing her first short story in the *Century* magazine, Mena translates this folktale for an American audience, ending her fiction with the telling phrase, "And thus Juan de Dios, became veritably, John of God." Although her letters to her editors show that her stories challenged their notion of "local color," the final version of her text includes those elements that she deemed central to her representation of Mexico.

Although she presents this tale in English for an Anglo-American audience, it is important to note that in addition to the North American regionalist tradition, Mena's translation reflects the Latin American genre of "costumbrismo," which is characterized by "irony, good humour, observation of human nature, caricatures of native types, social criticism, and a deeply felt national reality." [16] Treviño's study of costumbrismo, or local color sketches, focuses on those writers who describe "border life" in the southwestern United States, but Mena is also a border writer in the sense that she writes of her Mexican culture for an Anglo-American audience. Developed in a different geographical context, "costumbrismo," like U.S. regionalism, allowed Latin American writers to build a sense of literary and national traditions by portraying regional customs, and along with its romantic strain, this genre includes a strong element of social criticism. While local color fiction in the United States often reflects the perspective of a white, urban narrator who visits a rural place with "exotic" inhabitants, Latin American costumbristas address both country and city life, and often use costumbrismo to comment on such social injustices as the treatment of slaves and political corruption.[17] Mena not only draws on the convention of "local color" familiar to her white, urban audience but also informs her portrayal of her "region" with this more liberating and socially conscious tradition.

While her depictions of Mexican Indians in "John of God" and her correspondence with her *Century* editors prior to this story's publication indicate that she experienced the limitations of the local color tradition, this genre also provided the starting point for more pointed social critique in her later works. After introducing her audience to Mexican culture in "John of God, the Water-Carrier," Mena shifts positions in "The Education of Popo" by presenting the visit of an American family to a Mexican family for "business" purposes, thus challenging the conventional Anglo-American perspective of "the foreign" by presenting the Americans as foreigners in Mexico. While the Arriolas entertain the Cherrys during their visit to Mexico, Alicia Cherry, the recently divorced daughter of the wealthy American family, pursues the fourteen-year-old Popo Arriola, who is enchanted with the attentions of his blond-haired, blue-eyed visitor. Alicia plays along with this relationship, enjoying the attentions of the young Mexican, until her ex-husband, Edward Winterbottom, shows up and her superficial motives become suddenly apparent to the disappointed, but suddenly matured, Popo. Contrasting with "John of God, the Water-Carrier" both in its satire and in its depiction of an upper-class Mexican family, this story of a sexually exploitative relationship symbolizes American imperialism south of the border at the same time that it satirizes the genres of romance and local color, both of which were popular in magazines of the period. This overtly critical portrayal of U.S–Mexican relations reflects the increasingly political stance of women's periodical writing in the early twentieth century.

In the Cherrys' visit to the Arriolas, Mena alludes to the corporate investment of the United States in Mexico and perhaps to her experience as a child, when her own father was a business partner with several Americans during Porfirio Díaz's rule (Simmen 39). The Cherrys have a purely capitalist interest in their Mexican hosts: "Señor Montague Cherry of the United States . . . was manipulating the extension of certain important concessions in the State of which Don Fernando was governor, and with whose operations his Excellency found his own private interests to be pleasantly involved" (47). Mena exposes America's imperialistic relationship with Mexico in this business visit and the demands of the capitalistic American family. As the Arriolas gather "ready-to-serve cereals, ready-to-drink cocktails, a great variety of pickles, and much other cheer of American manufacture" (47) for their American guests, Mena reveals the availability of American consumer goods in Mexico, and in the development of her story she demonstrates that the Mexican people are also targets for this "culture of consumption." [18] Even as she contributes to the consumer culture of the periodical, Mena challenges its imperialistic biases.

Alicia Cherry's pursuit of Popo represents the ultimate consumption of Mexican culture. In her descriptions of Popo's and Alicia's views of each other, Mena presents the racial stereotypes of dominant Americans and subservient Mexicans that the mainstream press perpetuated in advertisements and photographs such as those appearing in *Century*.[19] Confirming Americanized ideals of beauty, Popo is enchanted with Alicia's stereotypically American looks, her "hair like daffodils, eyes like violets, and a complexion of coral and porcelain" (49), and Alicia responds to this admiration by revealing the equally foreign allure of Mexico, noting that the "inhabitants have a deluded idea that blue eyes are intensely spiritual, [and] they get exactly the same Adam-and-Eve palpitations from them that we do from the lustrous black orbs of the languishing tropics" (59–60). Alicia, "a confirmed matinée girl" (56), manifests the Anglo-American view of Mexicans as exotic, just as Popo's image of Alicia reifies the American ideal of blond-haired, blue-eyed beauty. Although Alicia's looks imply delicate femininity, she is the sexual aggressor in this relationship and, at the same time, counters the stereotype of Mexican machismo in her seduction of Popo. Attracted to the appealing image of their pairing, as well as its transgressive nature, Alicia pursues Popo for the pleasure of foreign conquest.

As a social commentary on U.S. exploitation of Mexico, the affair between Alicia and Popo breaks the standards of both the romance and local color genre. When Popo takes Alicia to a "cave behind a waterfall" where he goes "to meditate," saying, "I have loved the cañoncito in a particular way" (658), Mena plays on the details of locale in local color fiction: The place that has spiritual connotations for Popo becomes the site of his seduction. In Mena's description, Alicia seems both ridiculous and sordid: "[S]he suddenly dropped her posings and her parasol, and forgot her complexion and her whalebones, and huddled down beside him in the bracken . . . finding a strange, wild comfort in mothering him recklessly, straight from the soul" (57). Despite her seeming attraction to him, Alicia uses Popo, and then abandons him when her ex-husband Edward is sufficiently jealous. To her surprise, Popo condemns her "with a burst of denunciation in which he called me by a name which ought not to be applied to any lady in any language" (61). In the resolution to this story, the reader sees Alicia through her Mexican hosts' eyes, and Popo's final rejection of Alicia seems apt. Alicia represents the Americans' "consume and dispose" attitude toward Mexico, and Mena succeeds in shifting the sympathies of her American audience through humor, irony, and a deft handling of character beyond caricature.

In her descriptions of Alicia and Edward, Mena satirizes the American view of Mexico as a site for American tourism and imperialism. She illustrates the difference Alicia perceives between "America — beg pardon, the United States" (50) and Mexico through her relationship with Popo and her recounting of this relationship to Edward: "'One thing I've demonstrated,' she continued fretfully, 'and that is that the summer flirtation of our happy land simply cannot be acclimated south of the Rio Grande'" (59). Edward, pleased with Popo for returning Alicia to him, presents him with his highest compliment: "That young fellow . . . is worthy of being an American" (62). Like Alicia, Edward embodies a complacent sense of national and racial superiority as "one of those fortunate persons who seem to prefigure the ideal toward which their race is striving," a "particular type [portrayed] in various romantic capacities, as those of foot-ball hero, triumphant engineer, 'well-known clubman,' and pleased patron of the latest collar, cigarette, sauce, or mineral water" (58). Alicia and Edward are literally products of American capitalism, "ugly American tourists" who expect to be served, see every object as "picturesque," and use the Mexicans for their own pleasure. Countering the Cherrys', and the *Century's*, "knowing" view of Mexico, Mena proves that it is the Arriolas who possess the educated perspective in "The Education of Popo."

In her local color fiction in the *Century*, Mena joins a tradition of writers of color who employ the periodical to comment on Anglo-American racial prejudices. Although she writes from a different vantage point than Zitkala-Sä, for example, she faces related issues of cultural border-crossing in speaking to a white audience in terms they will understand about a culture different from, but part of, her own. Writing from "the double insider/outsider positioning regionalist writing unavoidably generates" (Loriggio 11), Mena negotiates her marginalized position to entertain and inform her audience. While using the genre of local color fiction to present her country of origin, she also expands this genre in her depiction of modern Mexico. Her stories provide further evidence that within the periodical, local color fiction not only allowed readers to view faraway places and people, but also provided a medium for political commentary. Mena's work offers a new perspective on American influence by presenting the intertwining interests of Mexico and the United States from a Mexican point of view. As Pryse notes, "[R]egionalism denotes a particular *view* of American culture, a view from the perspective of marginalized persons, as well as a consciousness of difference" (48). As the borders of American literary studies expand, the study of local color fiction must include the work of María Cristina Mena in its consideration of national and racial borders in the twentieth century.

NOTES

I would like to thank the Recovering the U.S. Hispanic Literary Heritage Project at or of the University of Houston for their grant-in-aid to research Mena's works. This project led to my critical introduction to *The Collected Stories of María Cristina Mena* (Houston: Arte Público, 1997) and provided the foundation for this article. I would also like to express my gratitude to Elizabeth Ammons, my dissertation advisor at Tufts University; and Janice Koistinen and Joe Mohr, who offered helpful comments on drafts of this essay.

1 For a critical edition of Mena's work, please see *The Collected Stories of María Cristina Mena*, ed. Amy Doherty (Houston: Arte Público, 1997). The introduction, which includes biographical information, historical background, and brief analyses of Mena's short stories, provided the primary research for this essay and led to my interest in examining Mena's fiction within a regionalist context.

2 Tatum 33. Also see Paredes 49–50.

3 See also Tey Diana Rebolledo's *Women Singing in the Snow* and Elizabeth Ammons's *Conflicting Stories*.

4 See Brodhead 132–3, 195–210; and Kaplan, "Nation, Region, and Empire," 251–55.

5 Brodhead 122; Kaplan 244.

6 Frederick Jackson Turner's memorable description of the frontier as "the outer edge of the wave — the meeting point between savagery and civilization" (3) is also representative of *Century*'s portrayal of Mexico.

7 In addition to recent discussions of racial marginalization in local color fiction noted above, my reading is also informed by Mary Louise Pratt's *Imperial Eyes: Travel Writing and Transculturation*.

8 Brodhead discusses the opportunities that nineteenth-century regionalism provided in extending access "to groups traditionally distanced from literary lives" (116), a trend that also included Mena in the early twentieth century.

9 Gloria Velasquez Treviño comments on this aspect of Mena's text as indicative of Mena's upper-class perspective: "By indicating that it is only the narrator and

reader who know that Tiburcio's infliction is caused by the pumping, something which the two brothers can't comprehend, the narrator reveals her superior attitude about the lower class of Mexican society" (36).

10 Doherty, *The Collected Stories of María Cristina Mena* (17). Subsequent references will be included in the text.

11 Letter to Robert Sterling Yard [Mar. 1913], Century Company Records. All letters to *Century* editors are included with permission from Century Company Records, Rare Books and Manuscript Division, New York Public Library, Astor, Lenox, and Tilden Foundations.

12 Camín and Meyer note that "the Yaqui resistance to the occupation remained alive, irreducible, and uninterrupted during the whole period of the Porfiriato and the Revolution, part of which was fought with Yaqui troops and part in Sonora against Yaqui insurgents" (5).

13 Mena, letter to Robert Sterling Yard, [Mar. 1913], Century Company Records.

14 For example, Mena specifically mentions the use of local color in a letter to editor Douglas Zabriske Doty, in her comments on his suggested changes to "The Son of His Master," a story of the Mexican Revolution that was not accepted for publication in *Century*. She writes that she "cut out many of the Spanish words — but I must make a special plea for the few that remain, all of them having a definite value of humor, irony, local color, or what not." [Nov./Dec. 1914], Century Company Records.

15 Mena, letter to Robert Underwood Johnson, 4 Apr. 1913, Century Company Records.

16 Kessel Schwartz, *A New History of Spanish American Fiction* (Coral Gables: U of Miami P, 1972) vol. 1, 25 (qtd. in Treviño 68).

17 See Schwartz's discussion of costumbrismo, 25–32.

18 This term,"the culture of consumption," derives from Fox and Lears, *The Culture of Consumption* and is relevant to *Century's* representations of Mexico as a site to be consumed by its Anglo-American audience.

19 López notes the stereotypes presented in *Century's* advertising, particularly the portrayal of Mexicans as serving the leisure class in an advertisement for the Santa Fe Railway (27) and the connection between whiteness and beauty in an advertisement for Pond's Vanishing Cream (32). Both ads appear in the Nov. 1912 issue of *Century*.

Charles Hannon

ZITKALA-SÄ & THE
COMMERCIAL MAGAZINE
APPARATUS

In the winter 1919 issue of the *American Indian Magazine*, Zitkala-Sä began an editorial on behalf of Indian citizenship by recalling a question posed to her by a stranger aboard a train. She was en route to a meeting of the Society of American Indians (SAI), and the stranger, noticing her service pin, asked whether she had a relative in the war. Zitkala-Sä explained that many of her cousins and nephews were then in France and that her pin was for her husband, "a member of the great Sioux Nation, who is a volunteer in Uncle Sam's Army." At that, she writes, "A light spread over the countenance of the pale-faced stranger. "Oh! Yes! You are an Indian! Well, I knew when I first saw you that you must be a foreigner" ("America" 165). Such scenes have become a trope of multiculturalism, rehearsed, as in Ronald Takaki's introduction to *A Different Mirror*, to expose the racial and ethnic categories that white Americans habitually use to evaluate someone else's "Americanness." For Takaki, this seems primarily a matter of identity; he can establish his credentials as an American by explaining to the cab driver who has complimented him on his English that his family has lived in America for over a hundred years. But Zitkala-Sä experienced such confrontations as a matter of both identity and citizenship.

In 1919 Native Americans were not considered American citizens; they were "foreigners," regardless of how long they and their ancestors had lived in America. Under the Dawes Act, Native Americans could only earn American citizenship by giving up their "Indianness" and fully assimilating to Anglo-American culture, a task that was made all but impossible by the Indian Bureau's policy of segregating Indians on reservations and allotments. Indian citizenship was not granted universally until 1924, by an act of Congress that Walter Benn Michaels claims was made possible by changes in America's immigration laws a week earlier. According to Michaels, American legislators passed the Indian Citizenship Act, and thereby included Native Americans in their reformulation of American political identity, as a way of legitimizing their previous effort, in the Johnson Act, to limit European immigration to a percentage of the number of people from each European country already residing in America. "Both Acts," Michaels writes, "participated in a recasting of American citizenship, changing it from a status that could be achieved through one's own actions (immigrating, becoming "civilized," getting "naturalized") to a status that could better be understood as inherited" (32). Thus while Takaki, in the 1990s, can reinforce his Americanness (and also his citizenship status) as a matter of inheritance by pointing to a century of American Takakis, Zitkala-Sä, in her 1919 editorial, was limited to the wartime strategy of asserting the Americanness of American Indians (and thereby promoting the cause of Indian citizenship) by demonstrating the many wartime sacrifices ("actions," in Michaels's terms) of Indians on behalf of America.

Zitkala-Sä's efforts to assert her sense of herself as an American were often countered by discourses of the dominant culture that repressed her assertions and reinscribed Native American identity as something Other. In her editorials in *American Indian Magazine* on behalf of Indian citizenship in 1918–19, Zitkala-Sä was limited by the conventional rhetoric of wartime patriotism, as when she argued in the autumn 1918 issue that if the Indian "is good enough to fight for American ideals he is good enough for American citizenship now" ("Editorial Comment" 114). But her critique of federal Indian policy began long before her tenure as editor of *American Indian Magazine*, primarily in her autobiographical narratives and short stories in *Atlantic Monthly, Everybody's Magazine,* and *Harper's Monthly Magazine.* In these magazines, Zitkala-Sä published scathing indictments of the policies of forced assimilation and acculturation mandated by the Dawes Act, which institutionalized the requirement that Indians "achieve" their citizenship by adopting certain facets of Anglo-American culture. Even in these earlier contexts, however, her exposing of the false morality that presumed to make "Americans" out of American Indians was countered by the ubiquitous discourse of Anglo-Saxon nativism, which asserted, often in the same magazines, the English origins of American political identity. Any examination of Zitkala-Sä's efforts to use the pages of literary and commercial magazines to assert her sense of herself as both a Sioux and an American citizen, therefore, must also include an examination of the discourses of racial nativism that contradicted such efforts.

The pages of the magazines in which Zitkala-Sä published her stories, autobiographical narratives, and editorials are useful sites for such an examination, for several reasons. First, the commercial magazine is an "ap-

paratus" in the Althusserian sense of a location for the production and reproduction of subjects of the state.[1] Although not explicitly an organ of the
state, these magazines nevertheless produced official narratives of American identity that made it possible for readers to recognize themselves as
subjects and to privilege some forms of subjectivity over others. In the context of late nineteenth-century America, the official narrative of American
identity reproduced within the pages of commercial magazines was derived
from the history of the English in America — especially during the colonial
and Revolutionary periods. However, as an "ideological" apparatus, the
commercial magazine is less repressive than other state organs such as the
military, the police, or the public school. The magazine maintains "relative
autonomy" from the state; still determined by the economic "in the last instance" and therefore subject to the prevailing ideological forces of the social formation, subjects working within the magazine apparatus — such as
writers, art designers, and advertisers — nevertheless are relatively autonomous from the state and therefore can assume some agency over the
narratives they produce.[2] In the 1890s, as many magazines began to look to
commercial advertising rather than to subscriptions for operating revenue,
the artwork, advertisements, and editorial pages of commercial magazines
became more overtly the site of state propaganda regarding such issues as
American imperialism, national policy on immigration from Europe and
from Asia, and even the proper labor and gender roles (and sexual identities)
of men and women in American society. As a group, however, writers of
magazine fiction were able to maintain the relative autonomy afforded them
by the ideological nature of the medium. Consequently, as we will see in the
example of Zitkala-Sä, it is often possible to observe an ideological tension
between the narratives of American identity that were produced by "autonomous" writers, and the competing, "official" narratives of Americanness constructed in the editorials, artwork, advertisements, and historical
narratives that appeared on the same pages.

The ideological environment of the early 1900s, when Zitkala-Sä published in *Atlantic, Harper's,* and *Everybody's,* was significantly different from
that of both wartime and postwar America, when she wrote most of her editorials for *American Indian Magazine.* The pages of the 1900 and 1901 issues
of *Harper's* are rife with the discourse of Anglo-Saxon nativism, which had,
since the 1880s, produced a narrative of American identity based, on a political level, upon English democratic institutions, and on an individual level,
upon a heritage of English "blood." As John Higham observes, Anglo-Saxon
nativists experienced a crisis in the 1890s as immigration patterns changed

and the majority of new immigrants stemmed from southeastern, rather than northwestern, Europe. In response, nativists revised their thinking to include northern Europeans, who could be understood as deriving from the same racial stock as the English, that is, among those easily assimilable into American concepts of self-government. But these same nativists drew a hard line against southern Europeans such as Greeks and Italians, whom they saw as inassimilable threats to America's democratic order. When the stranger in Zitkala-Sä's train car identifies her as a "foreigner," it is likely that he is speaking from the position of a subject produced by this late nineteenth-century strain of Anglo-Saxon nativism, because what he perceived was a strong color difference between Zitkala-Sä and himself. Zitkala-Sä's response to the stranger, however — her 1919 editorial — is a response to the strain of nativism that had developed in the intervening years since the 1890s, in reaction not only to continued massive immigration from southeastern Europe but also to the necessity of expanding official definitions of Americanness during World War I. Faced with the dilemma of having to require recent European immigrants to return to Europe as American soldiers, nativists had had to make "Americanization" (except for Germans and Japanese) an almost automatic result of military service. As a result of this "tendency to play up the common ties of interest and purpose among old and new Americans" (Higham 217), the ideological process of Americanization became distinct from the political process of attaining citizenship at the same time that it came to be understood (by immigrants, noncitizen American Indians, and disenfranchised blacks and other minorities) as a step leading inevitably toward full citizenship. For nativists, this marked the beginning of the end of a long effort to exclude non–Anglo-Saxon residents from "becoming" Americans. For Zitkala-Sä, as her numerous wartime editorials attest, it signaled the beginning of what would become an effective campaign to tie Indian citizenship to the achievements of American Indians in military service. Since Indian citizenship, however, did not become a political reality until several years after the end of World War I, we must consider whether it was these alterations in the discourse of nativism from the 1880s through World War I that ultimately persuaded Congress to pass the Indian Citizenship Act, or whether, as Michaels insists, it was the fact that "the Indian's sun was perceived as setting" and, therefore, Indian citizenship simply no longer threatened the new nativists' understanding of what it meant to "count" as an American.

To many nativists at the end of the nineteenth century, even Native Americans could be considered "foreign" because they were not Anglo-Saxon and because their ancestors had no role in the official narrative of the origins of American history.[3] Woodrow Wilson, a Princeton history professor before he became president of the United States, articulated the nativists' exclusionary narrative of American identity and history on a number of occasions in the pages of the most popular literary magazines. The best known of these is Wilson's lengthy *History of the People of the United States*, which appeared serially in *Harper's* beginning in January 1901. Wilson's narrative signaled its Anglo-Saxon nativism, first, by modeling itself after Richard Green's *Short History of the English People*, and second, by according historical primacy in its running title ("Colonies and Nation") to the English experience of America. As the opening line of Wilson's narrative indicates, his understanding of the history of the people of the United States begins only "[w]hen the history of English settlement in America begins, . . ." (*Harper's*, Jan. 1901, 173). The publication of Wilson's narrative in *Harper's* was an "event" for Anglo-Saxon nativism, allowing the magazine's editor, Henry Mills Alden, to proclaim in a commentary upon Wilson's work that "for a century and a half — its longer period — our history is properly English, as racially and radically it must be to the end" (323). Although nativists like Alden and Wilson asserted that the "original" Americans were English-derived, they were equally insistent that by the nineteenth century America's Anglo-Saxons were irrevocably different from the parent stock. Alden, for example, adds that "the conditions of our growth, and especially our national growth, have been peculiar, and have made for us critical moments quite distinct from those punctuating English history" (323). Saturated with the same "race"-inflected nativism, Wilson's narrative of the early colonists who would become the new Americans emphasizes both their hardy English qualities (they are the same forest clearers, organizers, and civilizers that Green glorifies) and the fierce political independence that would ultimately make them a brand of Anglo-Saxons different from their English ancestors.

Wilson's discussion of Nathaniel Bacon in the March 1901 installment of his *History* is a good example of how nativist assumptions about American identity could permeate the pages of a "literary" magazine. Bacon was a colonist who defied Virginia's colonial governor, William Berkeley, by organizing a militia — against the governor's explicit orders — with which he, in Wilson's words, "well-nigh exterminated the Indian tribe of Susquehannocks" (*Harper's*, Mar. 1901, 550). Wilson's celebration of Bacon's rebellion against colonial rule performs the same two nativist functions found in Alden's editorial comments: it marks the American character, first, as indelibly Anglo-Saxon, and second, as "racially" different from the English, as a consequence of the historical contingencies of life in America. Wilson writes, for instance, that Bacon "was of the hot blood that dares a great independence" (548). In Wilson's telling, Bacon threw off one political allegiance (English) for another (American) but retained his "racial" identity and Anglo-Saxon qualities. In nativist rhetoric, Anglo-Saxonism thus became a prerequisite to proper political subjectivity, leading to the invention of an "American Anglo-Saxon" race identity, which could be used further to iterate a distinction from minorities. Equally important for the Anglo-Saxon nativist, however, Wilson's narrative of Bacon's rebellion performs a third function by representing the Indian presence in colonial America as but one more obstacle, analogous to the forests in Green's *Short History of the English People*, to be surmounted by the new American's superior "blood." Wilson's history thus brackets the Indian within a literary (and, ultimately, an ideological) domain that precedes the narrativization of "true" American subjectivity.

Each of these nativist imperatives is reinforced in the pages *of Harper's* by Howard Pyle's illustration of the Indian "aggressions" against the colonists that motivated Bacon to organize his militia (see fig. 1). Divided on the diagonal, the upper right corner in Pyle's drawing signifies obstacles in the way of civilization in America: thick forests that must be cut away; rocky ground that must be cleared and plowed; and hostile natives who must be overcome. The lower half signifies the progress of all that work: a significant portion of the forest has been opened up for settlement by whites, and for agricultural production; and from this we can infer a system of commerce for settler-farmers to market their crops. Most tellingly, Pyle has drawn the dying colonist in the position of a martyr, crucified upon a plow on one side, upon the land on the other, and looking with rapture to the heavens in the knowledge that his death will bring life to a whole new "race" of Americans. Pyle's illustration resonates with Alden's editorial pronouncements upon the irrevocably Anglo-Saxon roots of American identity and with Wilson's narrative of the exclusively colonial (English) ancestry of the people of the United States. Overall, the representation of the Indian in this issue of *Harper's* underscores the major inconsistency of federal Indian policy under the Dawes Act: Indians were forced to give up their own cultures, assimilate to American society, and thereby "become" Americans, but they were consistently excluded from the American polity by nativist rhetoric, which constructed American identity as something that could be achieved only by descendants of the "original" colonial English.

Zitkala-Sä's story "The Soft-Hearted Sioux," published in the same March

Fig. 1. Howard Pyle's On the Warpath *from the March 1901 Harper's. Courtesy Brown County Library, Green Bay, Wisconsin.*

1901 issue of *Harper's* as this episode of Wilson's "History," addresses these contradictions of the Dawes Act by detailing the destructiveness of assimilation for the story's Sioux narrator, even as it reminds the magazine's readers of the government's starvation policies that forced the Sioux onto the reservations, where they putatively were preparing to "become" Americans. The narrator of "The Soft-Hearted Sioux" is an Indian who has returned as a Christian missionary to his tribe. He has learned to reject his own culture, signified by his expulsion of a traditional medicine man from his ailing father's tepee, and consequently, he is rejected by the tribe when he attempts to preach to them. The tribe eventually moves its camp, leaving the narrator to care for his starving father, but the game he might have hunted to feed his father has been replaced by the cattle of encroaching white farmers. When he kills one of these, he is tracked by the farmer; a fight ensues, and the narrator kills the farmer with a knife. The story is told from a prison cell where the narrator waits to be executed for the murder. As Patricia Okker has written, "Zitkala-Sä portrays the narrator's detachment from his own fate as a sign of cultural displacement, and she does so while demanding the reader's own emotional involvement" (94). Overall, the story is a bleak narrative of the historical consequences of federal Indian policy for the Sioux, and a critique of Dawes era propaganda about the government's assimilation policies.

But if we compare the illustration that accompanied this story to the Pyle drawing from Wilson's *History*, we can see how Zitkala-Sä's effort to demand the "emotional involvement" of *Harper's* mostly white, middle-class readers might have been overcome by the nativist themes operating in other discursive regions of the magazine. Frederic Remington chose to illustrate neither the assimilated narrator's rejection by his tribe nor his father's starvation as a consequence of the encroaching whites' displacement of native food sources, but rather, as in Pyle's painting, the Indian's murder of the white farmer (see fig. 2). Moreover, Remington's compositional elements are identical to Pyle's: the threatening Indian occupies the upper right portion, the martyred white, the bottom left. This similarity forces the narrator of Zitkala-Sä's story into the same pre-American discursive domain as that occupied by Pyle's colonial-era Indians; and it positions the white farmer in an even more overtly "martyred" position (this time, on the fields of western expansion) than that of Pyle's colonist. In both pictures, in other words, the Indian's claim to American identity (and therefore American citizenship) is suppressed by the nativist's construction of an exclusively Anglo-Saxon America in which the Indian is relegated to a separate, pre-American discursive domain. What Zitkala-Sä wrote as a critique of federal Indian policy up to and including the Dawes Act, Remington pictures as the same old story of Indians as an obstacle to the construction of an "authentic" American nation.

Zitkala-Sä did not always use fiction to demonstrate her conflicts with the policies of the Dawes Act. In her autobiographical narratives, too, she focused on policies that separated her from her family and forced her assimilation to white culture. In this sense, her experience with the "apparatuses" of American imperialism began long before she became a pupil at White's Manual Institute. The anecdote to which Zitkala-Sä refers in the

Fig. 2. Frederic Remington's At My Feet a Man's Figure Lay *from the March 1901
Harper's.*

winter 1919 *American Indian Magazine* editorial was not the first occasion
on which Zitkala-Sä's "foreignness" became an issue for her while riding a
train. In "School Days of an Indian Girl," first published in *Atlantic* in January 1900, she writes of her experience as an eight-year-old, when she is
taken from her mother to an Indian boarding school in Indiana. Her narrative emphasizes the insistence of other whites on the train in asserting her

difference from them, even as she is en route, supposedly, to learn to occupy a "white" subject position and thereby assimilate to American society. She writes:

> I sank deep into the corner of my seat, for I resented being watched. Directly in front of me, children who were no larger than I hung themselves upon the backs of their seats, with their bold white faces toward me. Sometimes they took their forefingers out of their mouths and pointed at my moccasined feet. Their mothers, instead of reproving such rude curiosity, looked closely at me, and attracted their children's further notice to my blanket. This embarrassed me, and kept me constantly on the verge of tears.
>
> I sat perfectly still, with my eyes downcast, daring only now and then to shoot long glances around me. (48)

In contrast to the later event, when Zitkala-Sä is able to respond to the rudeness of the white stranger by asserting her claim to American identity, at the age of eight she is unable to voice her resistance to the gaze of other children and their parents.

But the contrast between these two moments would have held a number of other valences for Zitkala-Sä. In the intervening years, the railroad had become a metonym in Zitkala-Sä's writing for America's imperialist drive westward, which was directly responsible for the displacement of the Sioux and which led to Zitkala-Sä's involvement in the Indian school system. In recalling her embarrassment as a child riding the "iron horse," Zitkala-Sä makes a connection between the railroad and the telegraph lines that parallel its course and that she recalls pressing right up against her mother's house on the Yankton reservation: "Very near my mother's dwelling, along the edge of a road thickly bordered with wild sunflowers, some poles like these had been planted by white men. Often I had stopped, on my way down the road, to hold my ear against the pole, and, hearing its low moaning, I used to wonder what the paleface had done to hurt it" (48). By making these connections between the "machinery" of expansion and the moment of her own displacement, Zitkala-Sä's narrative of her assimilation to white society reconstructs a discursive moment analogous to the juxtaposition of "The Soft-Hearted Sioux" with Wilson's *History of the People of the United States.* Just as the apparatus of the commercial magazine ratified the nativist construction of American identity (and also the "American" subjectivity of white audiences) by martyring both the English colonist (in Pyle's drawing) and the western cattleman (in Remington's drawing), the railroad, in these two moments from Zitkala-Sä's life, functions as an apparatus that supports the idea of whiteness as a prerequisite of American identity.[4] And as in the drawings, it does so in binary opposition to a constructed Indian Other (the "Susque-hannocks" in Pyle's drawing, the missionary Sioux in Remington's, and Zitkala-Sä herself in both moments on board the train) who is presumed to occupy a "foreign" (and therefore prediscursive) position in relation to the moment of identity formation for the whites. Indeed, the potentiated resist-ances of Zitkala-Sä's narration of her experience as an eight-year-old girl are doubly silenced: first, because the apparatus of the western railroad has al-ready categorized the Indian as Other for the whites on the train; and sec-ond, because the discourses of nativism that permeate the *Atlantic Monthly* (the site of her retelling of the incident) demand, as a foundational moment in the narrativization of American identity, the erasure of the Indian.

Crucial differences exist, however, between these two discursive mo-ments and Zitkala-Sä's use of her experience with the "stranger" in 1919. While, in the earlier moments, the figure of the Indian is silenced by the "ap-paratuses" of the literary magazine and the western railroad, Zitkala-Sä's agency as editor of *American Indian Magazine* allows her to express her re-sistance to the voice of nativist-imperialist America and to assert, in her ad-vocacy of Indian citizenship, her position as a subject both "of" and "in" American society. The duality of this position was crucial for Zitkala-Sä be-cause it was the only way she could justify her ultimate advocacy of certain assimilationist policies of the federal government. For many members of the Society of American Indians, assimilation was the only practical solution to the devastating effects of Indian segregation on government-run reserva-tions. Zitkala-Sä witnessed these during the fourteen years that separate her publications in *Atlantic, Harper's,* and *Everybody's,* and her later editorial work for the *American Indian Magazine.* From 1902–16 she worked with her husband, Raymond T. Bonnin, on the Uintah and Ouray Reservation in Utah, where she organized classes for women on the reservation, and where she saw firsthand the damage done by the Indian Bureau's segregationist policies. For Zitkala-Sä and others, however, assimilation did not mean simply the continuation of existing policies of acculturation, which, as in her own case, damaged both familial and tribal relations and traditions. Instead, it meant the fair enactment of allotment policies, the equal education of In-dian children in nonsegregated state schools, the recognition of tribal self-government, the honoring of existing treaties, and above all, the abolition of the Indian Bureau, whose governing control over reservations was corrupt and wasteful. In contrast to acculturation, which implies the relinquishing of one set of cultural traditions for another, she reconciled herself into an assimilation to American society that would allow the individual tribes to maintain their discrete identities and traditions, to retain, in other words, a native subjectivity that, "in the last instance," was inassimilable to the dominant narrative of American identity formation. In order to claim such a position, Zitkala-Sä had to resist the trend toward "race" that was developing at a fever pitch in the Progressive Era and instead base her argument for Indian citizenship upon the "cultural" qualifications of America's first inhabitants.

One of Woodrow Wilson's most concise expressions of Anglo-Saxon nativism appears in "The Ideals of America," an address delivered in 1901 on the anniversary of the battle of Trenton, and published in the December 1902 issue of the *Atlantic*. The *Atlantic* was the recognized locus of nativist New England intellectuals. In this address, Wilson uses the familiar stages-of-life trope to locate America's "infancy" at the moment of the American Revolution; this, for Wilson, is where America "gets its sense of identity" (721). "Old Colony days," Wilson writes, "and those sudden days of revolution . . . were our own days, the days of our childhood and our headstrong youth" (720). This metaphor of national youth at the moment of the Revolution performs a number of rhetorical functions throughout the remainder of Wilson's address. First, the metaphor of a national "birth" in the late eighteenth century effectively erases Native Americans from the narrative of American identity formation and, as we have seen, marks them as "foreign" to the "ideals of America." Thus, as Wilson develops his metaphor in narrating the era of western expansion, he can write of a nation whose "weak youth turned to callow manhood, [as] we stretched our hand forth again to the west. . . . There lay a continent to be possessed" (725). The West, in Wilson's narrative, is a mass of "long, unending plains which were the common domain, where no man knew any government but the government of the whole people." The acquisition of these plains by the descendants of the Revolutionary "founders," for Wilson, "was to be the real making of the nation" (725).

But Wilson has other goals in the essay than simply to confirm the exclusion of indigenous people from the popular American imagination. His address is also an occasion to justify American imperialism in the Philippines and in Puerto Rico, where America's "maturity" as a democratic nation was offered as a model for those countries' future developments. As Wilson describes it, "They are children and we are men in these deep matters of government and justice" (731). Anglo-Saxon nativists like Wilson founded their narratives of American identity formation upon a belief in American forms of government, which they believed derived from an innate capacity for self-rule among northern Europeans, especially the English, in colonial America. They celebrated this capacity as a matter of heredity and tradition, but as Higham observes, toward the end of the nineteenth century they became fascinated by developing theories of race that suggested that the capacity for self-government was an effect of racial identity, one that separated Anglo-Saxons from other "races" in a fundamental way. Higham locates this turn toward racial thinking at a moment of high anxiety among nativists over increased immigration from southern and southeastern Europe:

> By making the simple (and in fact traditional) assumption that northern European nationalities shared much of the Anglo-Saxon's inherited traits, a racial nativist could now understand why immigration had just now become a problem. Also, the cultural remoteness of southern and eastern European "races" suggested to him that the foreign danger involved much more than an inherited incapacity for self-government: the new immigration was racially impervious to the whole of American civilization! (140)

While Wilson's "Ideals of America" illustrates a turn toward racial thinking, its publication in the *Atlantic* suggests the cultural dominance of this ideology.

For Native Americans who were committed to the goal of Indian citizenship, this developing nexus in the discourses of nativism and nationalism presented a number of challenges. First, the same doctrine that deferred political independence for the Philippines and Puerto Rico until those countries' populations could demonstrate a capacity for self-government was responsible for the predication in the Dawes Act of Indian citizenship upon the complete assimilation of Native Americans to "American" principles of government. Under this rubric, the Indian Bureau established the system of Indian reservations that segregated Indians from the rest of American society, all but ensuring their continued exclusion from the political process while allegedly preparing them to become Americans. Likewise, both the overseas and domestic examples of American imperialism were justified by a paternalistic rhetoric that figured the subjected populations as wards of the state requiring instruction in the ways of democracy. A telling counterpart to Wilson's pronouncements upon Philippine "immaturity" is Theodore Roosevelt's statement that "it is all wrong to try to force the time when the Indian can stand alone, exactly as it would be all wrong to try to force the boy to make his own way when he was eight or nine years old" (327). As a member of the Society of American Indians, Zitkala-Sä was an advocate of assimilation as the only means toward the abolition of the Indian Bureau, which she saw as the primary obstacle to the improvement of living conditions for Indians. But as the concept of race became more influential in both the direction of American imperialism abroad and in attitudes toward immigration and the question of exactly who ought to "count" as Americans, Zitkala-Sä and other members of the Society of American Indians were left with fewer options for making the case for Indian citizenship and against the bureau.

Some Indian citizenship advocates accepted the nativists' coupling of racial identity with the capacity for self-government. Arthur Parker, the Iroquois editor of the *American Indian Magazine* until Zitkala-Sä took over (as acting editor) in 1918, argued that American Indians were better prepared, racially, to assimilate to Anglo-Saxon America than were the less desirable "immigrants" from southern and eastern Europe. Unlike Zitkala-Sä, Parker accepted the idea of acculturation. He based his position, that the "aims and methods of thought [of the assimilated Indian] are thoroughly American," upon two assumptions: that "the assimilation of the Indian means the blotting out of nearly all that was previously his in lines of culture" (Hertzberg 163); and that "[t]he Americanism of which we surround ourselves and in which we believe is of Anglo-Saxon origin" (Hertzberg 156). Parker was prepared to concede defeat in the culture wars of his era, as long as the spoils of war, citizenship, were conferred upon Indians universally. But clearly, Parker's is a double concession. He concedes to the idea that American culture is inherently Anglo-Saxon in origin. But he also collaborates with the increasing racism of the Progressive years as he distinguishes between Indians on one side and blacks and "foreign" immigrants on the other, and pushes for Indian citizenship on the grounds that "there is not the prejudice against good Indian blood that there is against some foreign bloods because of race" (Hertzberg 162–63). Fully cooperating with the nativists' turn toward "race," Parker conceives of citizenship as a status that can be "achieved" through acculturation, provided one also has the right kind of "blood."

Unlike Parker, Zitkala-Sä did not abandon "culture" for "race" in her efforts on behalf of Indian citizenship. Instead, in her work for the *American Indian Magazine* she articulated a number of correspondences between the traditions of Native American tribes and those of "Anglo-Saxon America." In doing so, she contradicted the racial and cultural essentialism of the time and carved out an argument for Indian citizenship based upon indigenous

American principles. An example of this work is an article she wrote and published in her first official year as the editor of *American Indian Magazine*. The opening sentence of this article, entitled "The Coronation of Chief Powhatan Retold," declares that "Mrs. Woodrow Wilson, wife of the President of the United States, is a lineal descendent of Pocahontas" (179). In direct response to the essentialism of Anglo-Saxon nativists' turn toward "race" early in the twentieth century, Zitkala-Sä exposes, first, the irrationality of essentialist concepts of race in a pluralist nation such as America; and second, the falseness of Wilson's own familial (and national) claim to a pure "blood" descent from English colonists. But her critique of racial essentialism in this article is not directed at Wilson personally. Instead, she moves quickly from the personal to the national and political, noting the ironies implicit in the fact that the tour of England by Pocahontas (aka "Lady Rebecca") in the sixteenth century should be repeated in the twentieth century by her distant cousin Mrs. Wilson. Of Pocahontas's tour, Zitkala-Sä writes, "Springing from the tribal democracies of the new world, Pocahontas was the first emissary of democratic ideas to cast-ridden Europe" (179). Thus, the noting of a "remarkable coincidence" becomes, for Zitkala-Sä, an occasion for the assertion of Native American traditions of democracy that predate the American Revolution and that, in Native American historiography, are considered the model for constitutional government in colonial and Revolutionary America. Furthermore, in her "retelling" of the coronation of Powhatan, she emphasizes the uncompromising nature of the "liberty loving" king, of his refusal to bow to receive the crown sent by King James I, and of his offering, in return, "his old shoes and mantle to Captain Newport for his curtesy" (180).

The contemporary reader might well wonder how such a position allowed Zitkala-Sä to ever publish her own work in the *Atlantic*. Appreciating the literary predominance of that magazine, Zitkala-Sä valued the prestige of that periodical. By publishing her work there, however, she allowed her fiction to be classified as "local color," which automatically feminized and deemphasized its political significance. As an activist, this surely must have rankled, but as a pragmatist, she probably traded off the diminution of the story's political punch with its wide dissemination in a culturally dominant magazine.

Within the context of her own refusal to accept graciously the beads and baubles offered to Native Americans by agents of the Indian Bureau, Zitkala-Sä's juxtaposition of the story of Powhatan and Pocahontas with the evidence of Native American agency at the two most celebrated founding moments of the American Republic (Jamestown and colonial New England) helped to make her larger argument that American democracy was built upon an indigenous concept of pluralism and therefore was strong enough to include Native Americans as fully enfranchised citizens.

Zitkala-Sä pursued the "cultural" argument for Indian citizenship in several ways during her tenure as editor of *American Indian Magazine*. In her summer 1919 "Editorial Comment," she praised Charles Eastman's recent cross-country lecture tour on behalf of Indian citizenship, noting that Eastman had been particularly successful with non-Indian audiences: "The American people still remember how their early ancestors fled from the autocracy of Europe to the open arms of the Red Man a few centuries ago" (63). As with the story about Mrs. Wilson and Pocahontas, she thus emphasized the themes of pluralism at a moment that white audiences would consider the origin of "English" America. In other instances, Zitkala-Sä let other members of the society make this argument for her. In the winter 1919 issue, she published an article by Charles Eastman (then president of the society) entitled, "The Indian's Plea for Freedom," in which Eastman, too, seeks to revise the official narrative of early America. Speaking of the English Separatists' quest for "religious and political self-determination," Eastman writes, "They found it, and in their contact with the simple Indian tribes, whom they counted godless and heathen, they unconsciously and in spite of themselves absorbed enough of the Indians' culture to modify their own" (163– 64). Eastman, in harmony with Zitkala-Sä's claims about Pocahontas as "the first emissary of democratic ideas to cast-ridden Europe," goes on to assert that "practically all the basic principles of the original articles of confederation of the Thirteen States were borrowed, either unconsciously or knowingly, from the league of the Six Nations and the Sioux confederacy" (164). In publishing these arguments, Zitkala-Sä did more than suggest a Native American "influence" upon modern America. She sought to interrupt official narratives of the social formation when they asserted an essentialist, "English" origin for modern American institutions.

As editor of *American Indian Magazine*, Zitkala-Sä presented this cultural argument for Native American rights to both an Indian and non-Indian audience.[5] This was particularly urgent in the context of the end of World War I, when the rights of "self-determination" of oppressed populations were literally on the table in Paris. Neither Zitkala-Sä nor Eastman ever missed an opportunity to mention the wartime service of Indians. In the autumn 1918 issue Zitkala-Sä even pointed to traditional Native American foods as further evidence of the Indians' cultural alliance with the rest of America: "Mr. Hoover clearly points out how we may very materially aid our allies in saving wheat for them by our own usage of more corn and potatoes. For a brief moment thought reverts to the red man who gave us his corn and potato" ("Indian Gifts" 115). At such moments, Zitkala-Sä might appear simply to be reproducing white America's ideological figure of the "red man," the noble savage whose passage was necessary for the development of modern America. But her rhetoric also allowed Zitkala-Sä to construct an American "us" that included herself and the Indian readership of the *American Indian Magazine*, as full, if not fully enfranchised, citizens of America. In this way she acted upon her commitment to what Hazel Hertzberg calls the "ideological common denominator" of the modern pan-Indian movement: "the postulate of a non-vanishing Indian race as a vital element in a democratic and progressive nation" (79). Zitkala-Sä's efforts to convey a cultural argument for Indian rights to both an Indian and non-Indian readership faced a further challenge late in the second decade of the 1900s, however, as the explicitly "ethnological" study of Indian cultures came to dominate the national conversation on Indian issues — not only in popular magazines and journals, but also in the *American Indian Magazine*.

Zitkala-Sä's insistence upon "culture" rather than "race" as the grounds upon which to make the case for Indian citizenship allowed her to reject Parker's strategy of asserting a "racial" affinity between Indians and Anglo-Saxons, and thus interrupt the pattern of (Indian) self-assertion and (Anglo-Saxon) suppression that characterized the policies of the Dawes Act. By stressing cultural affinities instead, Zitkala-Sä made the case that in a pluralist America, essentialist ideas about the "origins" of American identity are illogical and irrational. But her emphasis upon culture also carried certain risks because it coincided with the emergence, from within the discourse of anthropology, of the practice of ethnography and of an "ethnological" perspective upon Native American cultures. As James Clifford and other postmodern critics of the ethnographic method have observed, this modern ethnological perspective was devastating in its representations of other cultures because in its language and narrative conventions it enacted a structure of ethnographic "salvage" in which textualization and narrativization are considered portents of cultural extinction. "It is assumed," Clifford writes, "that the other society is weak and 'needs' to be represented by an outsider (and that what matters in its life is its past, not present or future)" (113). At precisely the same time that Zitkala-Sä was making the "cultural" argument for the political inclusion of Native Americans, these "academic" discourses were ensconcing Native Americans within a prediscursive region of the popular American imagination, representing Indian culture as the prehistory of the narrative of American identity formation. This final turn toward "ethnology" is observable in the pages of the 1920 *American Indian Magazine* (the last issue published), and it is responsible for Zitkala-Sä's abandonment of the commercial magazine as an apparatus for the production of a pluralist American subjectivity and for her decision instead to engage more directly in the political process as a lobbyist for Indian rights organizations in Washington, D.C.

The *American Indian Magazine* underwent a number of editorial changes in 1920, illustrating its ideological harmony with the nation's newest "official" (ethnological) discourses on the Indian. Now edited by Thomas L. Sloan (Omaha), a controversial figure in the Society of American Indians because of his advocacy of the peyote religion (Hertzberg 46–7), the 1920 issue of the magazine was dominated, first, by an ethnological approach to the study of American Indians. Without irony, the statement of editorial policy for the new magazine proclaimed that "the Indian immortalized by James Fenimore Cooper in his *Leather Stocking Tales* and upon the stirring canvases of Frederic Remington is the Indian of a vanishing race." Despite Sloan's avowed concern with contemporary issues that "unless solved speedily, threaten [the Indians'] very extinction as a race," the 1920 issue was comprised entirely of articles by anthropologists and museum curators. Hertzberg notes, "None of the signed articles were [sic] written by Indians. It was not to be, like its predecessor, a magazine of Indian opinion written largely by Indians, but rather a magazine about Indians written mostly by whites, and yet at the same time the official publication of the Society" (190). In addition to the new emphasis on the ethnological interest of the American Indian, the 1920 issue was dominated by a desire to entertain and to exoticize. The editorial policy statement predicates its rationale for the magazine upon the fact that "[m]any are the thrills connected with the tales of the American Indian and his old, free, outdoor existence on the plains of the West." And the solicitation for advertisers at the end of the issue promises that the retooled magazine's illustrations will "represent the most unusual action photographs of Indian life obtainable" ("Advertising" 45). This dual emphasis in the new magazine upon the exoticization of "the Indian" and the narrativizing of "him" as part of America's historic past presented a further challenge to Zitkala-Sä and other reform-minded members of the Society of American

Indians who sought a contemporary political identity for assimilated, but not necessarily acculturated, American Indians.

Zitkala-Sä's departure from the *American Indian Magazine* at the emergence of its new focus on the ethnological study of Indian cultures suggests that she no longer considered it an efficient instrument for the construction of this identity. She had learned the lesson, from her previous engagement with commercial magazines outside of her editorial control, that her gestures of resistance and opposition would be subject once again to overwhelming anti-Indian discourses of the social formation, as the new *American Indian Magazine* promised to represent them. One of the first advertisements to appear in the revised *American Indian Magazine* suggests one manner in which these discourses would pervade the magazine. The 1920 issue carried an advertisement for Stetson hats that declares the West "won" and the Plains Indians part of the "romance" and "tragedy" of the nation's "storied past" (see fig. 3). The illustration accompanying the advertisement depicts a cowboy energetically "busting" a bronco, suggesting that this, rather than the continuing displacement of Plains tribes, comprised the real work of "winning the West." Significantly, the illustration in the Stetson advertisement is a close approximation of James Earle Fraser's famous sculpture, *End of the Trail*, which Fraser first created in 1894 and which won the gold medal for sculpture at the 1915 Panama–Pacific International Exposition in San Francisco (see fig. 4). But whereas in Fraser's sculpture both the position of the horse and the posture of the Indian signify the defeat and near starvation of Plains tribes as a consequence of America's imperialist policies in the West, in the Stetson advertisement the nearly identical positions and postures romanticize these policies as the achievements of "rugged individuals" (provided they wear the proper head attire). The power of the commercial advertisement as a discursive "region" of the magazine reproducing the dominant fictions of the social formation (in this case, reproducing the purely "ethnological" existence of American Indians) is clear from this example. With only a few intertextual references to history and sculpture, and a deft displacement of discursive signifiers, even an advertisement for a hat can be enlisted in the larger projects of silencing ideological opposition and romanticizing oppression, even within the pages of a magazine ostensibly concerned with preventing the "very extinction" of a race.

This is the dilemma of the commercial magazine as an Althusserian apparatus: it provides authors a certain amount of autonomy, yet at some basic

Fig. 3. Advertisement for Stetson® hats in August 1920 American Indian Magazine.

level it is determined by the dominant social, political, and economic forces of society. When she assumed the editorship of the *American Indian Magazine* in 1918, Zitkala-Sä took a hard line on issues that had divided the society's membership, such as the peyote religion and the Indian Bureau (both of which she wanted to eliminate). In this way she was able to use her editorial position to accomplish clear political objectives. In lobbying for Indian citizenship, however, she was limited, at first, to existing immigrationist and civil rights rhetoric. Her development of, and support for, a "cultural" argument for Indian citizenship was a significant addition to this debate, one

Fig. 4. James Earle Fraser, End of the Trail, *1915. Plaster. Cat. No. 68.01.01. National Cowboy Hall of Fame, Oklahoma City.*

that began in her earliest publications for the literary magazines and that she was able to develop even more forcefully in her editorials in the *American Indian Magazine.* Beyond these instances, however, Zitkala-Sä's autonomy as a writer and editor was limited by the discourse of Anglo-Saxon nativism, which determined the editorial policies and decisions of the literary magazines for which she wrote early in her career.

Yet Michaels goes too far in claiming that in the 1920s the ethnological argument simply won the day; and that, when American legislators granted

Indian citizenship in 1924, it was because "the Indian's sun was perceived as setting" (38). Such a reading of the history elides the work of Zitkala-Sä and others who had criticized policies of the Dawes Act since the end of the nineteenth century and who actively lobbied Congress on behalf of Indian Rights, as members of the Society of American Indians and long after that organization ceased effectively to exist (after 1920). In 1922 a number of Indian Rights groups joined forces to defeat the Bursum Bill, which would have compromised Indian claims to more than twenty-two million acres of non-allotted lands. In 1923 these groups organized as the American Indian Defense Association, whose members, although not always in agreement on particular issues, represented a new political force in Washington. The association produced a Committee of One Hundred whose mission was to advise the Secretary of the Interior on specific Indian policies, and this committee included many who were previously associated with the Society of American Indians (Hertzberg 200–02). It is difficult to know what effect the presence in Washington of the Committee of One Hundred had on the final passage of the Indian Citizenship Act of 1924 or what role Zitkala-Sä played in formulating their policy statements and lobbying efforts on individual issues. We do know, however, that she remained in Washington following the passage of the act and formed a new organization, the National Council of American Indians, whose purpose, as stated on the council's letterhead, was to "Help Indians Help Themselves in Protecting Their Rights and Properties" (qtd. in Hertzberg 207). Clearly, Zitkala-Sä did not stop looking for ways to assert her agency on behalf of Indian issues when she abandoned the magazine in 1920 or even when the prize of Indian citizenship was granted four years later.

NOTES

1   For Louis Althusser, "*all ideology hails or interpellates concrete individuals as concrete subjects,* by the functioning of the category of the subject" ("Ideology" 173). Magazines are a portion of the communication–Ideological State Apparatuses (ISAs) that Althusser posits, along with such Repressive State Apparatuses (RSAs) as the military, the prison system, and the police, as the primary machinery of ideological reproduction. Whereas RSAs use physical violence to reproduce the ideological needs of the social formation, communication–ISAs maintain "relative autonomy" with regard to other social structures and operate primarily through ideology. For more on the difference between RSAs and ISAs, see Robert Paul Resch, 213–16.

2 "The class (or class alliance) in power," Althusser writes, "cannot lay down the law in the ISAs as easily as it can in the (repressive) State apparatus" ("Ideology" 147).

3 In Higham's classic definition, nativism is the "intense opposition to an internal minority on the ground of its foreign (i.e., 'un-American') connections" (4).

4 Sidonie Smith has also noted that in "her critique of the mission education of 'Indians,' Zitkala-Sä invokes and ironizes the metaphor of the train as an engine of enlightenment and progress" (132).

5 Although Indians were the primary audience for Society of American Indian publications, the Society targeted non-Indian audiences from the very beginning. The Society created an "Associate" class of membership for non-Indians (Hertzberg 72); and its constitution, approved at the 1912 Society conference, included the following objective: "To present in a just light a true history of the race, to preserve its records, and emulate its distinguishing virtues" (Hertzberg 80).

Michelle Campbell Toohey

"*A DEEPER PURPOSE*" *IN THE SERIALIZED NOVELS OF FRANCES ELLEN WATKINS HARPER*

In 1994 the Schomburg Library of Nineteenth-Century Black Women Writers republished *Minnie's Sacrifice, Sowing and Reaping,* and *Trial and Triumph*, three short novels written by Frances Ellen Watkins Harper for the *Christian Recorder*, a nineteenth-century African American journal. Bringing these novels back into print has not only redefined Harper's oeuvre but has focused attention on the significant political role of the periodical in the Post Reconstruction Era. Three works previously ignored by literary scholarship have been made accessible to new readers. In effect, editor and scholar Frances Smith Foster has helped to reinstate the periodical as both a literary and political source for black readers of the nineteenth century.

Although Harper often addresses a broad cultural spectrum in her speeches and writing, these rediscovered novels are specifically written to the nineteenth-century black community in a periodical dedicated to enhancing their daily life by encouraging concrete problem-solving skills. These novels clarify many of the questions about multivocality that are raised by twentieth-century black feminist critics. Previously, Harper's fiction has been categorized as simplistically didactic, but a review of the current critical theory concerning *Iola Leroy*, Harper's last novel, in relation to her newly republished novels *Minnie's Sacrifice* and *Trial and Triumph* shows that Harper promotes a strong political agenda of vital self-determination for her own race while exposing complicated issues for the dominant white community. Significantly, the periodical provided the space and the audience she needed for a unique communication with readers of her own race.

Hazel Carby, the editor of *Iola Leroy*, notes that this novel was written "for the edification of black youth; a contribution toward their education in the ethical and moral precepts of intellectual leadership" (xvi). Carby's claim is supported by Harper's serialization of her earlier novel, *Minnie's Sacrifice*, in the *Christian Recorder*, a publication unquestionably written for the black audience of the African Methodist Episcopal Church. Significantly, the purpose of the mulatto figure becomes a sermon of injustice and violation to an audience struggling with the effects of slavery and postwar discrimination. Harper consciously uses this genre to engage her white audience in *Iola Leroy*. Harper's character differs dramatically from the mulatto represented in works by white women writers such as Lydia Maria Child. Harper's protagonists occupy problematic social spaces, offering a textual representation of social inequalities well known to black readers.

Only in the periodical press can Harper literately address the complex social and political concerns of the postwar black community with the intimacy of audience required for building a community from the inside. By choosing to publish domestic novels in the *Christian Recorder*, Harper can both model and expose the American values denied to her audience by the dominant culture. In *Domestic Allegories of Political Desire: The Black Heroine's Text at the Turn of the Century*, Claudia Tate reassesses the role of the domestic novel as it applies to African American women writers in the nineteenth century, suggesting that this type of genre critiques the hypocrisy of an American ideology that denies home and hearth to black women while requiring it for white women (108). Tate redefines the authority of the African American woman writer who adapts the extant genre of the domestic allegory to the political necessities of legitimating racial and sexual desire previously denied to a colonized race.

While Harper is manipulating the genre expectations of the domestic novel, she is also using the dialogic nature of novelistic discourse to effect political change. She not only uses her authorial voice to discuss her agenda for the black race, but she creates characters to carry the conversation forward. Mikhail Bakhtin asserts that this "illumination of one language by means of another" creates a kind of double-voicedness in the novel that extends the base of knowledge, creates options, and discovers previously unthought-of solutions (*Dialogic Imagination* 361). Thus, Harper employs a double-voiced discourse in which she creates characters who speak from the intersection of their own historical, political, and social moments. These discourses become primary while the author's voice is refracted through them but is not constitutive. In effect, the author herself is in dialogue with the individual voices of her characters.

Furthermore, this dialogue between Harper and her characters includes the readers of a predominantly black publication. In their day-to-day lives, the readers of a serialized novel read self-contained episodes that reflect their own historical, political, and social moments by means of characters who face the same challenges. In the time between parts of the novel being published, a public dialogue takes place, an "illumination of one language by means of another" during which her readers constitute their own voices in response to Harper's fiction. Harper gives her readers their own space for a multiple-voiced discourse that challenges individual readers to ruminate on solutions that would transform their lives collectively and personally.

Another characteristic of the novel, particularly effective in relation to the cross-sectional audiences of periodical publication, concerns its potential for a diversity of social speech types, including what Bakhtin refers to as *skaz*: the vernacular or everyday oration of characters. Because other genres are often boundaried by stylistic requirements, the flexibility of the novel to connect with all social registers of language creates a multiform equally hospitable to classical rhetoric as it is to oral dialect, each in artistic tension with the other. For Harper, the serialized novel offers a much broader dialogic space to interrogate not only the presentation of her political positions but also the dissenting opinions of dialogic participants, both on the printed page and through oral communication. As was the custom of the nineteenth-century readership, each new chapter of Harper's serialized novels would have been read aloud as it became available, so that the oral nature of such an event became an opportunity for communal discussion and reflection.

This literary approach to a political dialogue is particularly effective for a reading public that already was communicating through varying social registers of language. In speaking of *Iola Leroy*, Linda Koolish claims that it is a subversive text based on the complex language of folk figures, "shrewd manipulators of codes and disguises" (161). She suggests that colonization creates a multilevel discourse familiar to the oppressed group but purposefully miscommunicated to the dominant group. Bakhtin's idea of skaz in novelistic discourse allows the dissenting voices equal status in a political dialogue that typically is controlled by the educated elite of the dominant group. As Janet Gabler-Hover points out in her discussion of the very popular and financially lucrative Civil War series in the postwar *Century*, the African American presence was excluded for the most part in the postwar dialogue. In other instances, she says that the writers in the publication exhibited "a pathological attitude toward the African-American race and its place in America" (240).

With such an oppositional literary presence, Harper's task is to find a publication opportunity open to the postbellum black community so they can communicate on levels appropriate to all participants, whether educated or illiterate. While the white press was trying to erase the horrors of slavery in an attempt at moral catharsis and economic reunification, the black periodical became one of the few vehicles left to continue the discussion of slavery's repercussions. The serialization of the novel gave Harper's readers access to a political dialogue they desperately needed during the backlash of a nation that had turned its attention and passion to other concerns. For the African American community, racial discrimination was not a closed issue.

Bakhtin's third characteristic of novelistic discourse redefines the novel as a continually generative process rather than a closed production, describing the political praxis of the novel's form as "a spring of dialogism that never runs dry — for the internal dialogism of discourse is something that inevitably accompanies the social, contradictory historical becoming of language" (*Dialogic Imagination* 330). By consistent access to their own political process as it develops through Harper's writing and their own reader response, her audience becomes complicitous with this "becoming of language" after every episode. They learn to decenter the dominant discourse through the multiple levels of signification that occur in the development of the language itself to accommodate continually changing historical, political, social, and spiritual events, both on a personal and communal level.

Multiple subjectivity and multilayered discourse become the vehicles of meaning in Harper's use of a strategy that Julia Kristeva suggests has always existed in American politics: "In America, though, it seems to me that opposition to constraint is not unique, isolated and centralized, but is *polyvalent* in a way that undermines the law without attacking it front-on" (274). This observation describes accurately the process that Harper uses to disrupt a discourse still enormously powerful and colonizing, a political conversation that for a time rallied around icons of religious sentimentality in antebellum prose but lost interest in the superficiality of its own idealism during the Post Reconstruction Era. By looking more closely at Harper's newly resurrected novels *Minnie's Sacrifice* and *Trial and Triumph* and their publication in the periodical press, we can see more clearly how Harper's dialogic strategies to undermine the reified oppression of extant laws and the backlash of new Jim Crow laws operated.

Serialized for a black readership intent on moral and social transformation, these three novels show that Harper is highly aware of her audience and the implications of plot structure, characterization, and dramatic style to educate an emerging African American cultural presence. While critics may equivocate as to Harper's subversive intent in *Iola Leroy*, they can substantiate much of their analysis by considering the polyvocality of these serialized novels and how it ruptures the essentialism of a dominant discourse that marginalizes readers who are not white. Naming marginality as a site of transformation for black subjectivity, bell hooks states: "I am moved by that confrontation with difference which takes place on new ground, in that counter-hegemonic marginal space where radical black subjectivity is seen, not overseen by any authoritative Other claiming to know us better than we know ourselves" (*Yearning* 22).

The double-voicedness of author and characters in *Minnie's Sacrifice*, written twenty years before *Iola Leroy*, disrupts black stereotypes as Harper creates characters who are self-reliant, community-oriented, and strong-willed in the midst of a struggle with the colonizing assumptions of the white race. Again, by serializing this novel, she allows her audience the time and space to carefully consider the implications of such stereotyping. Each episode becomes a Sunday sermon designed to destroy the self-limiting cultural assumptions that many of her own race accepted. Through an inversion of genre expectations in the tragic mulatto story, Harper achieves a site of transformation in *Minnie's Sacrifice* clearly defined as that of "radical black subjectivity." While some critics may judge this early novel as lacking in the semantic complexity of her later fiction, the interplay of discursive registers from strictly African American perspectives significantly interrogates viewpoints within the black community in a unique way.

In *Iola Leroy* Harper often resorts to a more diffuse and conciliatory racial discourse, but in *Minnie's Sacrifice* her readers are African Americans with whom she opens a dialogue about racial issues in their own space and time. The *Christian Recorder* is not only part of their political life but, more importantly in terms of racial uplift, a primary vehicle of their spiritual life as well. Harper's characterization of the relationships between black and white, slave and master, man and woman inverts the white essentialism that allows colonization of the African race. Diana Fuss summarizes such a dynamic: "[I]n the hands of a hegemonic group, essentialism can be employed as a powerful tool of ideological domination; in the hands of the subaltern, the use of humanism to mime . . . humanism can represent a powerful displacing repetition" (32). By shifting subject positions from white voices who claim a privileged understanding to African American voices who now claim the same entitlement, Harper is able to "mime" essentialist assumptions so that they support her own political agenda.

In *Minnie's Sacrifice* Harper reverses the white literary tradition that stereotypes black characters, choosing instead to essentialize the white slave mistress Camilla, allowing her audience to place the tenets of humanism now in the voice of the "subaltern." Camilla's superficial altruism is set in tension with the agony of her slave Miriam whose daughter has been raped by Camilla's father, the supposedly humanistic master willing to accommodate his white child's every whim while easily condemning his black child to slavery. The readership of the *Christian Recorder* must have immediately recognized an irony with which many of them struggled in their day-to-day lives.

Another curious disruption of stereotype important to Harper's readership concerns the relationship of race and skin color. In this novel Harper assigns a Latin racial heritage to another white master, saying of Mr. LeCroix that "he did not feel the same pride of race and contempt and repulsion for weaker races which characterizes the proud and imperious Anglo-Saxon" (11). Curiously, Harper feels she must qualify her character's genetic heritage to explain a mind-set willing to pass the mulatto child as white.[1] Apparently, in her mind, Anglo-Saxons are so tainted with racism that they can never relinquish the one-drop-of-Negro-blood rule, no matter how closely the child resembles their own genetic heritage, an essentialist attitude Harper is willing to promote to educate her readers about superficial appearances deriving from the rape and brutalization of African American women.

As Harper's characters recount tales of horror about the genteel slave mistresses and morally corrupt slave masters, the figure of the octoroon or mulatto child becomes a textual representation of Toni Morrison's assertion that "a serious intellectual effort to see what racial ideology does to the mind, imagination, and behavior of masters" (12) is valuable. Harper's portrayal of whites in *Minnie's Sacrifice* shows to her readership that such a racial ideology results in spiritual weakness, isolation, material obsession, overwhelming anxiety, and moral bankruptcy. In the later serialized novel *Trial and Triumph* Harper succinctly defines this effect on the slaveowners in the conversation of Mr. Thomas: "The Negro was not the only one whom slavery subdued to the pliancy of submission. Men fettered the slave and cramped their own souls, denied him knowledge and then darkened their own spiritual insight" (214). If Harper can establish the spiritual victimization of the white race by slavery, she can restore the dignity of her own race through spiritual strength. And what more appropriate place to do this than from the authority of the *Christian Recorder*?

Arguably, this periodical may have had little effect on the opinions of the dominant culture that actively sought to minimize a collective guilt about racial injustice after the Civil War, but, again, Harper dealt with that contingency through her speeches and publications written specifically to the larger culture. The mind-set that she addresses through the *Christian Recorder* concerns the internalization of an inferior identity accepted both consciously and unconsciously by her black readership, who were exposed daily to such indoctrination in the white press. Harper wanted her readers, like her audiences for her speeches, to see and believe not only in their own equality but also to disempower the stereotypes of their victimizers, even if only in the moral sphere.

The religious press of the African Methodist Church affords Harper the space to expose the racial injustice of nineteenth-century religious ideology. Unequivocally, Harper denies the Christian position to the colonizing discourse, redefining religious images experientially rather than dogmatically. The black race is not baptized by water but by the "fire and blood" of slavery and war (73). Kristeva says that mimesis of religious tropes "may appear as an argument complicitous with dogma — we are familiar with religion's use of them — but they may also set in motion what dogma represses" (112). In *Minnie's Sacrifice* the tropes of Moses, motherhood, and divine immanence intersect to expose an American religious dogma willing to repress the rights of an entire race.

The contrast between Camilla and Miriam dramatizes Harper's strategy of disrupting white literary conventions by comparing the moral strength of these two women in the disclosure scene that informs Louis of his true racial identity as a black man. Both women want to dissuade Louis from fighting for the Confederate army, but their approaches differ significantly. Camilla uses the standard patriotic rhetoric of the dominant culture, worrying that Louis "should go against his country and raise his hand against the dear old flag" (58). In much more vital language Miriam sees that Louis may victimize his own people: "Miss Camilla, I can stand it no longer; — that boy is going to lift his hand agin his own people" (57). Determined to tell Louis he is of slave descent, she stands "like some ancient prophetess, her lips pronouncing some fearful doom" (59).

In contrast, Harper describes Camilla as "deadly pale, and trembling like an aspen leaf; but her eyes were dry and tearless," an embodied personification of Morrison's declaration of how slavery has wounded the white masters in this portrait of a blanched and frightened woman. At this point in the novel, Camilla's position as surrogate mother in Louis's life falters as Miriam regains her role of enlightened mother through a reversal of discursive power. Readers become aware that the speech of Miriam, the slave, comes from a spiritual strength much more transformative and powerful than the superficial discourse of colonization that allows Camilla only a confused, weak response to any ethical dilemma.

Louis, who formerly calls the South his mother, must now readjust his loyalties to a race he has formerly judged inferior. Miriam educates Louis experientially by telling him to ask help only from the slaves on his way north as he tries to evade the Southern soldiers looking for him as a deserter. Stylistically, Harper's discourse again ruptures stereotypes through the still "white" eyes of Louis, who finds he can trust his own race even when they perceive him as white: "The very black and homely looking woman . . . so gloomy and sullen in her countenance that he felt repelled" rescues him with "a look of tenderness and concern" as her husband Sam easily dupes his white master into telling him pertinent information that allows Louis to escape (62). Louis learns quickly about the subversive dialogue of his race.

This counterdiscourse of the black savant manipulating white slave owners is characteristic of even Harper's earliest works and settles any questions about the innovative dimensions of Harper's use of dialect. While white authors of the period often misappropriate the African American dialect for questionable political or entertainment purposes, Harper approaches such communication strategies with respect and authenticity. In a culture where the African American voice is trivialized, Harper returns that voice to her readership, using her own discursive brilliance to authenticate the subversive multivocality of a dialect that has allowed her people to survive. Significantly, Harper meets the challenge of not only legitimating such a voice to the dominant culture but also to the diverse audience of the *Christian Recorder*. Nineteenth-century black readers, former slaves in particular, must appreciate the strengths of their survival apart from the symbolism of a humanistic rhetoric that has enslaved them both literally and metaphorically.

While the *Christian Recorder* is a religious periodical, for Harper it becomes a forum not only to educate her readers spiritually but to mobilize them politically. Refusing to leave her readers with any icon of "America the Beautiful" even in the North, Harper makes two subtle observations in *Minnie's Sacrifice* concerning the Abolitionist discourse of Northern humanism as somehow liberating for the slave. First, she says: "Throughout the length and breadth of the land, from the summit of the rainbow-crowned Niagara to the swollen waters of the Mexican Gulf; from the golden gates of the sunrise to the gorgeous portals of departing day, there was not a hill so high, a forest so secluded, a glen so sequestered, nor mountain so steep, that he

[Moses] knew he could not be tracked and hailed in the name of the general government" (39–40). Four years before the publication of *Minnie's Sacrifice*, Harper had used similar rhetoric in her essay "The Colored People of America": "[L]et them [any nation] feel that, from the ceaseless murmur of the Atlantic to the sullen roar of the Pacific, from the thunders of the rainbow-crowned Niagara to the swollen waters of the Mexican gulf, they have no shelter for their bleeding feet, or resting-place for their defenseless heads ..." (*Brighter* 99). This corruption of the natural environment by slavery that extends to the breadth of the entire United States and its territories makes a mockery of the rights of any man, slave and citizen alike. By detailing so vividly the beauties of nature and setting them in tension with the grotesqueness of hunted men and women in this environment, Harper emphasizes the violation not only of the slave's humanity but of the natural law itself.

Harper also suggests that even the character of Quaker Thomas, a white man, must break the law in order to follow his own religious dictates: "Thomas would have gladly given him [Moses] shelter and work, and given him just wages, but he dared not do so. He was an American citizen it is true, but ... he had not the power under the law of the land to give domicile" (39). By this example, readers realize that a significant gap exists between rhetoric and reality of the "law of the land." While the Abolitionists could promise freedom in the North through the Underground Railroad, often they could not deliver such freedom. As long as the official law condoned slavery, the individual conscience remained impotent. For Harper's readers, a justification for civil disobedience can be inferred from Thomas's position. Harper suggests that the failure of the Post Reconstruction institutional promises to the newly freed African Americans might require such resistance. The recovery of the serialized novel *Minnie's Sacrifice* is a significant step in understanding Harper's development as both an artistic and a political voice. Through this novel and its publication in the periodical press, it becomes clear that Harper was far from being an assimilationist; rather, her discursive strategy directly challenges her own race to dialogically re-vision their participative speaking positions.

In Harper's third republished novel, *Trial and Triumph*, the depiction of the complexity of the African American experience in the nineteenth century becomes primary.[2] *Trial and Triumph* (1888), Harper's last known serialized novel, is notable for two reasons: First, the significant characters in the novel are all African American, speaking together in a dialogue about specifically black concerns in the Post Reconstruction Era; and, secondarily, it can be viewed as a kind of morality play with its interplay of vices and virtues struggling over the individual soul.

The dialogue Harper constructs allows a more direct consideration of black voices and their responses to their own responsibilities and problems. Through such a stylistic construction, Harper is able to address her political agenda forcefully and openly to an audience of educated African Americans whom she hopes to engage in racial uplift. Not only through their conversation but also through modeling appropriate behavior, Harper's characters further explicate many of her themes. This multiplication of black alterability provides the readers of the *Christian Recorder* with options in their own lives.

Before *Trial and Triumph*, Harper has used allegory effectively in some of her short stories, including "The Triumph of Freedom — A Dream" (1860) and "The Mission of the Flowers" (1869). In *Trial and Triumph* she builds on her classical education and the model of morality to consider the theme of nature versus nurture in what may be her most autobiographical writing. Young Annette Harcourt, an illegitimate child raised by her grandmother and surrounded by a variety of influences that will either harm her or benefit her, bears a possible resemblance to Harper, although Harper's biographical details still remain somewhat mysterious for such a conclusive comparison. On the nature side of this issue, Annette is at an extreme disadvantage socially and morally because of her genetic heritage and because she no longer has a mother to guide her. If Harper were to succumb to a deterministic view, her heroine would have little chance of success. Harper, however, does not leave Annette solely to her sad "antenatal history" but says that "in that restless, sensitive and impulsive child was the germ of a useful woman with a warm, loving heart" (184–85). Harper further urges her readers to see such children as their responsibility. The entire village, as another African tradition demands, must take care of the many displaced children in the black community after the end of slavery.

Because Harper involves her didacticism in the novelistic form, the monologic prescriptions of vices and virtues become multiplicitously complicated. While some characters speak from strong didactic positions, they are in constant dialogue with lived events that expose personal histories, racial and gender discrimination, and political and spiritual motivations. Harper layers her text with the double-voicedness of characters who speak from their own historical moments, allowing readers not only to hear a moral position but also to understand its genesis and interrelationship with the lived experiences of each character as well. Her readers are challenged to identify their own relationship to this dialogue. Because of the accessibility of the *Christian Recorder* to members of the African Methodist Episcopal Church, a moral discussion of the characters' positions and opinions could easily become an everyday occurrence. In all probability, these characters became figures of great interest to her audience.

The first of three female characters introduced in *Trial and Triumph* is Annette's grandmother, who, according to Harper's assessment of the soul's primary needs, falls more to the side of vice than virtue. The grandmother's inadequacy stems not from any shortage of her obvious love and care of her children but from her inability to educate them in moral strength. While the grandmother will fight to provide material necessities for Annette, "for the hunger of the heart she had neither sympathy nor comprehension" (185). Once, in chastising Annette, the grandmother calls her "the scabby sheep of the flock," damaging her self-respect as "the words struck deeper than blows" (184).

Harper suggests to her audience that such negativism toward children abuses them as much as the physical punishment another "vice" character, the neighbor Mrs. Larkin, advocates for the child. Mrs. Larkin, a woman who gives "all her attention to the forms of religion" but has "missed its warmth and vivifying influence from her life," has little compassion for the child (199). Countering these two women in Annette's life is the virtuous Mrs. Lasette, formerly a teacher and now the embodiment of enlightened motherhood. Her conversations provide Annette the self-respect, love, and moral fortitude needed to overcome an unfortunate environment and heredity. Holding mothers' meetings and counseling young people, Mrs. Lasette is one of the "[w]omen of the better class of their own race, coming among them awakened their self-respect" (198).

Harper uses the forum of the periodical that has historically championed enlightened motherhood to the American culture at large, but she extends such tenets to a readership struggling with family displacement and cultural abuse by the very formulators of an idealized motherhood iconography. One of Harper's strengths as a periodical writer is her ability to connect intimately with the practical needs of her readers. Just as women's magazines have traditionally covered the personal lives of readers and offered pragmatic advice, Harper's fiction compares and contrasts mothering practices of the dominant culture, assessing their value to women of her own race, many of whom deal with illegitimacy and parental absence. If readers empathize with Annette, they now have Mrs. Lasette as the model of an appropriate response to such a child by a black mother.

Conflicting male characters round out the trials and triumphs of Annette, providing more material for discussion by Harper's readers. After deserting her mother, Annette's father Frank Miller becomes a successful saloon keeper not subject to the humiliation and social condemnation reserved for "fallen" women. Living in the same town as his daughter, he ignores his paternal duties, exemplifying one of Harper's most criticized vices, irresponsibility. Representing the opposing virtue to Miller's position of vice, the Reverend Lomax examines those qualities needed both politically and spiritually by African American men to achieve racial uplift. Just as the trope of enlightened motherhood must be refigured for black women, Harper's male readers must redefine themselves as fathers and leaders in the community. The periodical becomes a vehicle not only of mirroring the significant choices to be made but also a forum for building a group consensus through active discussion.

Through the voice of Mr. Thomas, Harper further illuminates issues as they relate to the white race, again complicating the pragmatic choices that the members of the black community will now have to make if they hope to remain in America and thrive. The dialogue between Mr. Thomas and his white friend Mr. Hastings concentrates on the responsibilities of members of each race in the Post Reconstruction Era to understand and recreate reciprocal race relations. With indignant ire, Mr. Thomas chastises the white race:

Yes, you know us as your servants. The law takes cognizance of our crimes. Your charitable institutions of our poverty, but what do any of you know of our best and most thoughtful men and women? When we write how many of you ever read our books and papers or give yourselves any trouble to come near us as friends or help us? Even some of your professed Christians are trying to set us apart as if we were social lepers. (222)

Harper strongly reiterates many of the complaints she has already initiated on the speaker's platform, but unlike in an oral address she is able here to validate an opposing viewpoint.

Harper displays a pragmatic understanding of the honest discussion that must take place between the races, a dialogue not traditionally represented in the literature of the dominant culture. Mr. Hastings listens carefully to Mr. Thomas, accepts his anger as just, but also reminds him that great changes for black men have recently been effected because of white participation and that now it is his race's turn to show self-reliance: "No, Mr. Thomas, while you blame us for our transgressions and shortcomings, do not fail to do all you can to rouse up the latent energies of your young men to do their part worthily as American citizens and to add their quota to the strength and progress of the nation" (221).

Not stopping with a simplistic presentation of two monologic points of view, both of which sustain their own truth, Harper further demonstrates a dialogic openness to process, a trait of a publication medium that encourages speculation between serialization. When Mr. Thomas curtly cuts off Mr. Hastings with the assumption that another white man is making excuses, his friend brings him back to the dialogue, reiterating, "I want to see things from the same standpoint that you do." To Mr. Hastings' remarks that the black race has to be self-reliant, too, Mr. Thomas accedes: "I am conscious of the truth and pertinence of your remarks, but bear with me just a few moments" (223). This discussion continues through diverse racial complaints until the interchange of the speaker's opinions with the reflections of the listener-becoming-respondent results in "a new view of the matter" (225) for each of the men. Significantly, neither man monologically capitulates to the other man's opinion, but each, in turn, leaves the conversation with a new understanding of pertinent racial challenges. Modeling this type of dialogue is invaluable to black readers dealing with the complex social and emotional issues of the Post Reconstruction Era. It is a tribute to Harper that she never succumbs to the sentimental or simple explanation.

The discussions of these strong male characters elucidate numerous questions facing the African American race, from the injustices of institutionalized religion to the discriminatory practices of businessmen. With the female voice of Mrs. Lasette, they form a chorus of advice tempered with their own experiences through which Harper justifies their authority to her audience. While Annette, the orphaned child, listens to all these voices and learns from the dialogue, Harper's readers also are encouraged to broaden their understanding.

Harper's characterization of Annette prefigures the kind of artistic realism found in her later works. While many of her characters seem disembodied virtues or vices, Annette professes a spirit and humor Harper later reserves for her folk characters. For Harper, Annette prefigures what Bakhtin refers to as carnivalization in the novel. "Carnival is a place for working out, in a concretely sensuous, half-real and half-play-acted form, *a new mode of interrelationship between individuals*, counterposed to the all-powerful socio-hierarchical relationships of noncarnival life" (*Problems* 123 — emphasis in original). This notion of carnivalization seems even more pertinent when such discourse is presented through the medium of the periodical and the interrelationship is extended to an audience faced with an intense "non-carnival life." At the bottom of the social scale, Annette has a "discourse freed from the authority of all hierarchical positions" and is free to be "eccentric and inappropriate" as she tests the moral positions around her (*Problems* 123). She has the ability to challenge, disregard, and create a "new mode of interrelationship" culturally denied to the African American race. And the African American readership can participate equally in the "half-real, half-play-acted form" available in the space between Harper episodes. Like Annette, Harper's readers can create their own solutions entirely independent of even the author's control because the time before publication of the next episode belongs to them, for their own "working out." The next episode then becomes a comparison with their own formulations rather than a construction of them. In effect, the structure of the novel serialized in periodical publication encourages them to own their process, in direct challenge to the dominant culture that has denied them that right.

In a sentimental ending, Annette, the illegitimate and impoverished child, marries the "catch" of society, Mr. Luzerne. Annette's discourse loses its former vitality as the heroine fades into sainthood and the vices lose any possibility of victory. While Harper begins and ends with conventional expectations that expose her political praxis, she reminds her readers in her final paragraph: "I have essayed to weave a story which I hope will serve a deeper purpose than the mere amusement of the hour" (284).

The three rediscovered, serialized novels by Frances Ellen Watkins Harper do indeed weave a story for us. The "deeper purpose" of this find for twentieth-first century readers is strikingly similar to the one intimated by Harper. Specifically, through the critical appreciation of these texts, we can further examine the transformative value of the periodical press, reestablishing a vital literary link to political and social energy for Harper's *Christian Recorder* audience as well as for ourselves.

NOTES

1 Harper's attitude toward color and the Anglo-Saxon race, as opposed to the Latin races, raises interesting racial questions for further study of nineteenth-century ethnicity.

2 Because the theme of Harper's second republished novel, *Sowing and Reaping*, is temperance rather than the specifically post-war African American issues of the other two novels, I have chosen to delete it from this study at this time. But the effects of alcohol consumption on the black community in the Post Reconstruction Era certainly bear further study.

WORKS CITED

Acuña, Rodolfo. *Occupied America: A History of Chicanos.* 2nd ed. New York: Harper, 1981.

Adams, John R. *Harriet Beecher Stowe: Updated Edition.* Boston: Twayne Publishers, 1989.

"Advertising in 'The American Indian Magazine' Reaches a 'Selected Reader' Group." *American Indian Magazine* Aug. 1920: 45.

Albertine, Susan. Introduction. *A Living of Words: American Women in Print Culture.* Knoxville, U of Tennessee P, 1995. xi–xxi.

Alden, Henry Mills. "Editor's Study." *Harper's Monthly Magazine* Jan. 1901: 321–24.

Althusser, Louis. "Ideology and Ideological State Apparatuses (Notes Towards an Investigation)." *Lenin and Philosophy and Other Essays.* Trans. Ben Brewster. New York: Monthly Review Press, 1971.

Amelia. "The Summons." *Voice of Industry.* 7 Nov. 1845: 1.

Ammons, Elizabeth, and Valerie Rohy, eds. *United States Local Color Writers: 1880– 1920: An Anthology.* New York: Viking/Penguin, 1997.

Anderson, Benedict. *Imagined Communities.* London: Verso, 1983.

Anderson, Margaret. "The Challenge of Emma Goldman." *Little Review* May 1914: 5–9.

———. *My Thirty Years' War.* New York: Covici, Friede, 1930.

Bakhtin, Mikhail M. "Art and Answerability." *Art and Answerability: Early Philosophical Essays by M. M. Bakhtin.* Eds. Michael Holquist and Vadim Liapunov. Austin: U of Texas P, 1990. 1–3.

———. *The Dialogic Imagination: Four Essays by M.M. Bakhtin.* Ed. Michael Holquist. Trans. Caryl Emerson and Holquist. Austin: U of Texas P, 1992.

———. *Problems of Dostoevsky's Poetics.* Ed. and trans. Caryl Emerson. Intro. Wayne C. Booth. Theory and History of Literature, Vol. 8. Minneapolis: U of Minnesota P, 1984.

———. *Toward a Philosophy of the Act.* Ed. Vadim Liapunov and Michael Holquist. Trans. Liapunov. Austin: U of Texas P, 1993.

Battersby, Christine. *Gender and Genius: Towards a Feminist Aesthetics.* Bloomington: Indiana UP, 1989.

Baym, Nina. *American Women Writers and the Work of History, 1790–1860.* New Brunswick, NJ: Rutgers UP, 1995.

———. *Novels, Readers, and Reviewers: Responses to Fiction in Antebellum America.* Ithaca, NY: Cornell UP, 1984.

———. "Reinventing Lydia Sigourney." *The (Other) American Traditions:*

Nineteenth-Century Women Writers. Ed. Joyce Warren. New Brunswick, NJ: Rutgers UP, 1993. 54–72.

Beetham, Margaret. *A Magazine of Her Own? Domesticity and Desire in the Woman's Magazine 1800–1914.* London: Routledge, 1996.

———. "Towards a Theory of the Periodical as a Publishing Genre." *Investigating Victorian Journalism.* Eds. Laurel Brake, Aled Jones, and Lionel Madden. London: Macmillan, 1990. 19–32.

Benardete, Jane, and Phyllis Moe, eds. *Companions of Our Youth: Stories by Women for Young People's Magazines, 1865–1900.* New York: Unger, 1980.

Bennett, Paula. *"The Descent of the Angel:* Interrogating Domestic Ideology in American Women's Poetry, 1858–1890." *American Literary History* 7 (1995). 591–610.

Berkson, Dorothy. "'Born and Bred in Different Nations': Margaret Fuller and Ralph Waldo Emerson." *Patrons and Protegés: Gender, Friendship, and Writing in Nineteenth-Century America.* Ed. Shirley Marchalonis. New Brunswick, NJ: Rutgers UP, 1988.

Berlant, Lauren. "The Female Woman: Fanny Fern and the Form of Sentiment." *The Culture of Sentiment: Race, Gender, and Sentimentality in Nineteenth-Century America.* Ed. Shirley Samuels. Oxford: Oxford UP, 1992.

Birnbaum, Michele. "'Alien Hands': Kate Chopin and the Colonization of Race." *American Literature* 66.2 (1994): 301–23.

Bok, Edward. "3000 Sensible Girls." *Ladies' Home Journal.* May 1900: 6.

Bonner, Thomas, Jr. "Christianity and Catholicism in the Fiction of Kate Chopin." *Southern Quarterly* 20.2 (1982): 118–25.

Boren, Lynda S., and Sara deSaussure Davis, eds. *Kate Chopin Reconsidered: Beyond the Bayou.* Baton Rouge: Louisiana State UP, 1992.

Brodhead, Richard H. *Cultures of Letters: Scenes of Reading and Writing in Nineteenth-Century America.* Chicago: U of Chicago P, 1993.

———. *The School of Hawthorne.* New York: Oxford U Press, 1986.

———. "Sparing the Rod: Discipline and Fiction in Antebellum America." *The New American Studies: Essays from Representations.* Ed. Philip Fisher. Berkeley: U of California P, 1991. 141–70.

Buell, Lawrence. *New England Literary Culture.* Cambridge: Cambridge UP, 1986.

Camín, Héctor Aguilar, and Lorenzo Meyer. *In the Shadow of the Mexican Revolution: Contemporary Mexican History, 1910–1989.* Trans. Luis Alberto Fierro. Austin: U of Texas P, 1993.

Carby, Hazel V., ed. Introduction. Harper, *Iola Leroy or Shadows Uplifted,* ix–xxx.

Cary, Alice. "About My Visit to Uncle William's." *Ladies' Repository* 1853: 400–403.

———. *Clovernook Sketches and Other Stories.* Ed. Judith Fetterley. The American Women Writers Series. New Brunswick, NJ: Rutgers UP, 1987.

Chesler, Phyllis. *Women and Madness.* New York: Avon, 1972.

Chevigny, Bell Gale. *The Woman and the Myth: Margaret Fuller's Life and Writings.* Boston: Northeastern UP, 1994.

Chielens, Edward E. *American Literary Magazines: The Eighteenth and Nineteenth Centuries.* Vol. 1. Westport, CT: Greenwood, 1992. 2 vols.

Chopin, Kate. Account/Memo Books, 1888–1895 and 1888–1902. Kate Chopin Papers. Missouri Historical Society, St. Louis.

Clifford, James. "On Ethnographic Allegory." *Writing Culture: The Poetics and Politics of Ethnography.* Eds. James Clifford and George E. Marcus. Berkeley: U of California P, 1986. 98–121.

Cooke, Rose Terry. "Ann Potter's Lesson." *Atlantic Monthly* 1858: 419–28.

———. "Dely's Cow." *Atlantic Monthly* 1865: 665–72.

———. "Miss Lucinda." *Atlantic Monthly* 1861: 141–59.

———. "Sally Parson's Duty." *Atlantic Monthly* 1857: 24–33.

Coultrap-McQuin, Susan. *Doing Literary Business: American Women Writers in the Nineteenth Century.* Chapel Hill: U of North Carolina P, 1990.

Cutts, Richard. Introduction. *Index to the Youth's Companion 1871–1929.* Metuchen, NJ: Scarecrow, 1972. Courtesy of the Rare Books and Manuscripts Room, Boston Public Library.

Cyganowski, Carol Klimick. *Magazine Editors and Professional Authors in Nineteenth-Century America: The Genteel Tradition and the American Dream.* New York: Garland, 1988.

Damon-Moore, Helen. *Magazines for the Millions: Gender and Commerce in the Ladies' Home Journal and the Saturday Evening Post, 1880–1910.* Albany: State U of New York P, 1994.

Davis, L. Clarke. "A Modern Lettre de Cachet." *Atlantic Monthly* 1868: 588–602.

Davis, Rebecca Harding. *Bits of Gossip.* Boston: Houghton 1904.

———. "Blind Tom." *Atlantic Monthly* 1862: 580–85.

———. "Doctor Pajot." *Appletons' Journal* ns 2 (1877): 551–56.

———. "Men's Rights." *Putnam's Magazine* ns 3 (1869): 212–24.

———. "Paul." *Independent* 3 Jan. 1884: 2.

———. *Put Out of the Way. Peterson's Magazine* 57 (1870): 355–67, 431–43; 58: 30–41, 109–18.

———. "Two Methods." *Independent* 30 Mar. 1893: 416.

———. "Women in Literature." *Independent* 7 May 1891: 612–13.

Deiss, Joseph Jay. *The Roman Years of Margaret Fuller.* New York: Cromwell, 1969.

Dictionary of American Biography. Eds. Allen Johnson and Dumas Malone. New York: Scribner's, 1930.

Dobson, Joanne. "Sex, Wit, and Sentiment: Frances Osgood and the Poetry of Love." *American Literature* 65 (1993). 631–650.

Douglas, Ann. *The Feminization of American Culture.* New York: Avon, 1977.

Drinnon, Richard. Introduction. *Mother Earth.* New York: Greenwood Reprint, 1968.

Dublin, Thomas. *Women at Work: The Transformation of Work and Community in Lowell, Massachusetts, 1826–1860.* New York: Columbia UP, 1979.

Dwyer, Ellen. "The Weaker Vessel: Legal Versus Social Reality in Mental Commitments in Nineteenth-Century New York." *Women and the Law: A Social Historical Perspective.* Vol. 1. Ed. D. Kelly Wisberg. Cambridge, MA: Schenkman, 1982. 119–32. 3 vols.

Eastman, Charles. "The Indian's Plea for Freedom." *American Indian Magazine* Winter 1919: 162–65.

"Editorial Notes." *National Magazine* 1852: 96.

"Editor's Table." *Peterson's Magazine* 1865: 312.

Edwards, John E. "Novel Reading." *Ladies' Repository and Gatherings of the West: A Monthly Periodical Devoted to Literature and Religion.* 3 (1849): 115–117.

Eisler, Benita, ed. *The Lowell Offering: Writings by New England Mill Women, 1840– 1845.* New York: Lippincott, 1977.

Eliot, T.S. *To Criticize the Critic and Other Writings.* New York: Farrar, 1965.

Emerson, Ralph Waldo. *Selected Prose and Poetry.* New York: Rhinehart, 1954.

Farley, Harriet. [Editorial] *Lowell Offering.* 1845: 240.

———. [Editorial] *Lowell Offering.* 1845: 263.

———. "Factory Blossoms for Queen Victoria." *Lowell Offering.* 1842: 1.

Farley, Harriet, and Harriott H. Curtis. [Editorial] *Lowell Offering.* 1840: 1.

Fern, Fanny [Sara Payson W. E. F. Parton]. *Ruth Hall.* 1855. Ed. Joyce W. Warren. New Brunswick, NJ: Rutgers UP, 1986.

Fetterley, Judith. "Entitled to More Than 'Peculiar Praise': The Extravagance of Alice Cary's *Clovernook.*" *Legacy: A Journal of American Women Writers* 10 (1993): 103–19.

"Fiducia" [Harriet Farley]. "Fancy." *Lowell Offering.* 1841: 117–118.

Finch, Annie. "The Sentimental Poetess in the World: Metaphor and Subjectivity in Lydia Sigourney's Nature Poetry." *Legacy* 5 (1988): 3–15.

Fishkin, Shelley Fisher. "'Making a Change': Strategies of Subversion in Gilman's Journalism and Short Fiction." *Critical Essays on Charlotte Perkins Gilman.* Ed. Joanne B. Karpinski. New York: Hall, 1992. 237.

Foner, Philip. *The Factory Girls.* Urbana: U Illinois P, 1977.

Foster, Frances Smith, ed. Introduction. Harper, *Minnie's Sacrifice*, xi–xxxvi.

Foucault, Michel. *The History of Sexuality: An Introduction.* Vol. 1. Trans. Robert Hurley. New York: Random House, 1990. 3 vols.

———. *Madness and Civilization: A History of Insanity in the Age of Reason.* Trans. Richard Howard. New York: Random House, 1988.

Fox, Richard Wightman, and T. J. Jackson Lears. *The Culture of Consumption: Critical Essays in American History, 1880–1980.* New York: Pantheon, 1983.

Frankenberg, Ruth. *White Women, Race Matters: The Social Construction of Whiteness.* Minneapolis: U Minnesota P, 1993.

Fuller, Margaret. "American Literature; Its Position in the Present Time, and Prospects for the Future." *Papers on Literature and Art, Part II.* New York: Fowler and Wells, 1846. 137–38.

———. *"These Sad But Glorious Days": Dispatches from Europe, 1846–1850.* Eds. Larry J. Reynolds and Susan Belasco Smith. New Haven: Yale UP, 1992.

Fuss, Diana. *Essentially Speaking: Feminism, Nature, and Difference.* New York: Routledge, 1989.

Gabler-Hover, Janet. "The North-South Reconciliation Theme and the "Shadow of the Negro" in *Century Illustrated Magazine.* "*Periodical Literature in Nineteenth-Century America.* Eds. Kenneth M. Price and Susan Belasco Smith. Charlottesville: UP of Virginia, 1995. 239–56.

————. *Truth in American Fiction: The Legacy of Rhetorical Idealism.* Athens: U of Georgia P, 1990.

Gannon, Susan R. "'The Best Magazine for Children of All Ages': Cross-Editing St. Nicholas Magazine (1873–1905)." *Children's Literature* 25 (1997): 153–80.

Garland, Hamlin. "The Light of the Star." *Ladies' Home Journal* 1904 Jan.: 11–12, Feb.: 7–8, Mar.: 11–12, Apr.: 14, May: 4.

Geller, Jeffrey L., and Maxine Harris. "Period II: 1866–1890." *Women of the Asylum: Voices from Behind the Walls, 1840–1945.* New York: Doubleday, 1994. 89–107.

Gibbons, John Cardinal. "The Restless Woman." *Ladies' Home Journal* Jan. 1902: 6.

Gilman, Charlotte Perkins. "Being Reasonable." *Forerunner* 6 (1915) 197–201.

————. "A Cleared Path." *Forerunner* 3 (1912): 253–58.

————. "Happiness." *Forerunner* 2 (1911): 259–61.

————. "In Two Houses." *Forerunner* 2 (1911): 171–77.

————. "Making a Change." *Forerunner* 2 (1911): 311–15.

————. "A Mischievous Rudiment." *Forerunner* 2 (1910): 1–5.

————. "Mr. Robert Grey, Sr." *Forerunner* 1.1: 1–4.

————. "Mrs. Beazley's Deeds." *Forerunner* 7 (1916): 225–32.

————. "Mrs. Elder's Idea." *Forerunner* 3 (1912): 29–33.

————. "An Offender." *Forerunner* 1.3: 1–6.

————. "Old Water." *Forerunner* 2 (1911): 255–59.

————. "Our Androcentric Culture or Our Man Made World" *Forerunner*: 1 (1909–1910): passim.

————. "Personal Problems." *Forerunner* 2 (1910): 280.

————. "Private Morality and Public Immorality." *Forerunner* 1.3: 9–11.

————. "Turned." *Forerunner* 2 (1911): 227–32.

————. "With a Difference (Not Literature)." *Forerunner* 5 (1914): 29–32.

————. *Women and Economics: A Study of the Economic Relation Between Men and Women as a Factor in Social Evolution.* Boston: Small Maynard, 1898. Reprint, edited with Introduction by Carl Degler. New York: Harper, 1966, and Source Book Press, 1970.

Goldman, Emma. "The Failure of Christianity." *Mother Earth* Apr. 1913: 41–48.

————. "Freedom of Criticism and Opinion." *Mother Earth Bulletin* Oct. 1917: 1.

————. "Lecture Tour." *Mother Earth* Jan. 1907: 18.

————. "A Letter." *Mother Earth* June 1906: 13–14.

————. *Living My Life.* Garden City, NY: Garden City Publishing, 1934.

————. "Observations and Comments." *Mother Earth* Apr. 1906: 2–6.

————. "To My Readers." *Mother Earth* Dec. 1906: 7–8.

————. "The Tragedy of Woman's Emancipation." *Mother Earth* Mar. 1906: 9–18.

Goldman, Emma, and Max Baginski. "Mother Earth." *Mother Earth* Mar. 1906: 1–4.

Goldman, Emma, and Alexander Berkman. "Mother Earth." *Mother Earth* Mar. 1908: 1–2.

————. "Our Sixth Birthday." *Mother Earth* Mar. 1911: 2–4.

Goldman, Emma, Alexander Berkman, and Ben L. Reitman. "To Our Friends." *Mother Earth* Mar. 1914: 1–2.

Green, John Richard. *A Short History of the English People*. New York: Harper, 1892–94.

Gunning, Sandra. *Race, Rape, and Lynching: The Red Record of American Literature, 1890–1912*. Oxford: Oxford UP, 1996.

H. S. L. "The Tress and the Rill." *Lowell Offering*. 1842: 94.

Hale, Sarah Josepha. "Editors' Table." *Godey's Lady's Book* Mar. 1850. *Godey's Lady's Book Online*. 1995. U. Rochester. 11 Mar. 1997 <http://www.history.rochester.edu/godeys/03-50/et.htm>

———. "Editors' Table." *Godey's Lady's Book* Apr. 1850. *Godey's Lady's Book Online*. 1995. U. Rochester. 11 Mar. 1997 <http://www.history.rochester.edu/godeys/04-50/et.htm>

———. "Editors' Table." *Godey's Lady's Book* Feb. 1857. *Godey's Lady's Book*. Ed. Hope Greenberg. 1996. U Vermont. 19 June 1997. <http://www.uvm.edu:80/~hag/godey/shtable/>

———. "Female Education." *Ladies' Magazine* Jan. 1828: 21–27.

———. "Female Seminaries." nos. 2 and 3. *Ladies' Magazine* Apr. 1833: 176–79, May 1833: 228–31.

———. "How Ought Women to be Educated?" *Ladies' Magazine* Nov. 1832: 508–515.

Haraway, Donna J. *Simians, Cyborgs, and Women: The Reinvention of Nature*. New York: Routledge, 1991.

Harper, Frances Ellen Watkins. *A Brighter Coming Day: A Frances Ellen Watkins Harper Reader*. Ed. Frances Smith Foster. New York: Feminist P, 1990.

———. *Iola Leroy or Shadows Uplifted*. Ed. Hazel V. Carby. Boston: Beacon, 1987.

———. *Minnie's Sacrifice, Sowing and Reaping, Trial and Triumph: Three Rediscovered Novels by Frances E. W. Harper*. Ed. Frances Smith Foster. Boston: Beacon, 1994.

Harris, Sharon M. *Rebecca Harding Davis and American Realism*. Philadelphia: U of Pennsylvania P, 1991.

———. "Redefining the Feminine: Women and Work in Rebecca Harding Davis's 'In the Market.'" *Legacy* 8 (1991): 118–21.

Havel, Hippolyte. "Literature: Its Influence Upon Social Life." *Mother Earth* Oct. 1908: 329–31.

Hearder, Harry. *Italy during the Age of the Risorgimento, 1790–1870*. New York: Longman, 1983.

Hedrick, Joan D. *Harriet Beecher Stowe: A Life*. New York: Oxford, 1994.

Heininger, Mary Lynn Stevens. *At Home with a Book: Reading in America, 1840–1940*. Rochester: The Strong Museum, 1986.

Hertzberg, Hazel. *The Search for an American Indian Identity: Modern Pan-Indian Movements*. Syracuse, NY: Syracuse UP, 1971.

Higham, John. *Strangers in the Land: Patterns of American Nativism, 1860–1925*. 1955. New York: Atheneum, 1963.

Hill, Mary Armfield. *Charlotte Perkins Gilman: The Making of a Radical Feminist, 1860–1896*. Philadelphia: Temple UP, 1981.

Hoehn, Matthew, ed. *Catholic Authors: Contemporary Biographical Sketches: 1930–1947*. Newark: St. Mary's Abbey, 1948. 118–19.

Hoffman, Frederick J., Charles Allen, and Carolyn F. Ulrich. *The Little Magazine: A History and a Bibliography*. Princeton, NJ: Princeton UP, 1947.

Hoffman, Nicole Tonkovich. "Legacy Profile: Sarah Josepha Hale." *Legacy* 7.2 (Fall 1990): 47–55.

hooks, bell. *Art on My Mind: Visual Politics*. New York: New, 1995.

———. *Yearning: Race, Gender and Cultural Politics*. Boston: South End, 1990.

Howard, June. "Unraveling Regions, Unsettling Periods: Sarah Orne Jewett and American Literary History." *American Literature* 68 (1996): 365–84.

Hughes, C. H. "The Rights of the Insane." *Alienist and Neurologist* 4 (1883): 183–89.

Hunt, Peter, ed. *Children's Literature: An Illustrated History*. Oxford: Oxford UP, 1995.

Hutton, Frankie, and Barbara Straus Reed, eds. *Outsiders in 19th-Century Press History: Multicultural Perspectives*. Bowling Green, OH: Bowling Green State UP, 1995.

Johnson, Hugh. "Race." *Century Magazine* Aug. 1914: 616–23.

Jones, Anne Goodwyn. *Tomorrow Is Another Day: The Woman Writer in the South, 1859–1936*. Baton Rouge: Louisiana State UP, 1981.

Jordan, David, ed. *Regionalism Reconsidered: New Approaches to the Field*. New York: Garland, 1994.

Josephson, Hannah. *The Golden Threads: New England's Mill Girls and Magnates*. New York: Duell, Sloan and Pearce, 1949.

Kaplan, Amy. "Nation, Region, and Empire." *The Columbia History of the American Novel*. Ed. Emory Elliott. New York: Columbia UP, 1991. 240–66.

———. *The Social Construction of American Realism*. Chicago: U of Chicago P, 1988.

Keetley, Dawn. "Victim and Victimizer: Female Fiends and Unease over Marriage in Antebellum Sensational Fiction." *American Quarterly* 51.2 (1999): 344–84.

Kelley, Mary. *Private Woman, Public Stage: Literary Domesticity in Nineteenth-Century America*. New York: Oxford UP, 1984.

Kelly, R. Gordon, ed. *Children's Periodicals of the United States*. Westport, CT: Greenwood, 1984.

———, ed. *Mother Was a Lady: Self and Society in Selected American Children's Periodicals, 1865–1890*. Westport: Greenwood, 1974.

Kennedy, Maravene. "A Thoroughbred Girl." *Ladies' Home Journal* 22 (1905):16.

Kessler, Carole Farley. *Charlotte Perkins Gilman: Her Progress Toward Utopia with Selected Writings*. Syracuse, NY: Syracuse University Press, 1994.

Kilcup, Karen, ed. *Nineteenth-Century American Women Writers: An Anthology*. Cambridge, MA, and Oxford, UK: Blackwell, 1997.

Koolish, Lynda. "Spies in the Enemy's House: Folk Characters as Tricksters in Frances E. W. Harper's *Iola Leroy*." *Tricksterism in the Turn-of-the-Century American Literature: A Multicultural Perspective*. Eds. Elizabeth Ammons and Annette White Parks. Hanover, NH: UP of New England, 1994. 158–85.

Koppelman, Susan. "Short Story." *The Oxford Companion to Women's Writing in the United States*. Eds. Cathy N. Davidson and Linda Wagner-Martin. Oxford: Oxford UP, 1995. 798–803.

Kristeva, Julia. *The Kristeva Reader*. Ed. Toril Moi. New York: Columbia UP, 1986.

Larcom, Lucy. "The River." *Lowell Offering*. 1842-3: 21.

Lehuu, Isabelle. "Sentimental Figures: Reading *Godey's Lady's Book* in Antebellum America." *The Culture of Sentiment: Race, Gender, and Sentimentality in Nineteenth-Century America*. Ed. Shirley Sanuels. New York: Oxford UP, 1992. 73–91.

Lewis, Tess. "Margaret Fuller: The American Mind Writ Large." *The American Scholar* 65:2 (1996): 284–92.

Library of Southern Literature. Vol. II. Atlanta: Martin & Hoyt 1909.

"Literary Notes." *Mother Earth* Mar. 1906: 61–62.

López, Tiffany Ana. "María Cristina Mena: Turn-of-the-Century La Malinche, and Other Tales of Cultural (Re)Construction." *Tricksterism in Turn-of-the-Century American Literature: A Multicultural Perspective*. Ed. Elizabeth Ammons and Annette White-Parks. Hanover, NH: UP of New England, 1994. 21–45.

Loriggio, Francesco. "Regionalism and Theory." Jordan, 3–27.

Lukens, Margaret A. "Columnist of Conscience: Margaret Fuller's New York Years." *Margaret Fuller: Visionary of the New Age*. Ed. Marie Mitchell Olesen Urbanski. Orono, ME: Northern Lights, 1994.

Lunt, Adeline T. P. *Behind Bars*. Boston: Lea and Shepard, 1871.

Marchalonis, Shirley. *The Worlds of Lucy Larcom, 1824–1893*. Athens: U of Georgia P, 1989.

Marshall, Peter. *Demanding the Impossible: A History of Anarchism*. London: Fontana, 1993.

McArthur, F. F. "Unfamiliar Mexico." *Century* Sept. 1915: 729–36.

Mena, María Cristina. *The Collected Stories of María Cristina Mena*. Ed. Amy Doherty. Houston: Arte Público, 1997.

———. "The Education of Popo." *Century* Mar. 1914: 653–62.

———. "John of God, the Water-Carrier." 1913. *The Best Short Stories of 1928 and the Yearbook of the American Short Story*. Ed. Edward J. O'Brien. New York: Dodd, 1928. 77–93.

———. "John of God, the Water-Carrier." *Century* Nov. 1913: 39–48.

———. "John of God, the Water-Carrier." 1913. *Monthly Criterion: A Literary Review* (1927): 312–31.

———. Letter to Robert Underwood Johnson. 4 Apr. 1913. Century Company Records.

———. Letter to Douglas Zabriske Doty. [Nov./Dec. 1914]. Century Company Records.

———. Letter to Robert Sterling Yard. [Mar. 1913]. Century Company Records.

Michaels, Walter Benn. *Our America: Nativism, Modernism, and Pluralism*. Durham, NC: Duke UP, 1995.

Millard, Gertrude B. "The Transformation of Angelita López." *Century* Aug. 1914: 547–57.

Miller, Julius. "Creole Beauties and Some Passionate Pilgrims." *Century* Feb. 1914: 558–65.

Miller, Perry, ed. *Margaret Fuller: American Romantic*. Garden City, NY: Anchor, 1963.

Morrison, Toni. *Playing in the Dark: Whiteness and Literary Imagination*. Cambridge: Harvard UP, 1992.

"Mother Earth Sustaining Fund." *Mother Earth* Apr. 1907: 107.

Mott, Frank Luther. *American Journalism: A History, 1690–1960*. 3rd ed. New York: Macmillan, 1962.

———. *A History of American Magazines*. Cambridge, MA.: Harvard UP, 1938–68. 5 vols.

Nathan, Rhoda B., ed. *Nineteenth-Century Women Writers of the English-Speaking World*. Westport, CT: Greenwood, 1986.

"Observations and Comments." *Mother Earth* Dec. 1906: 1–5.

Okker, Patricia. "Native American Literatures and the Canon: The Case of Zitkala-Sä." *American Realism and the Canon*. Ed. Tom Quirk and Gary Scharnhorst. Newark: U of Delaware P, 1994. 87–101.

———. *Our Sister Editors: Sarah J. Hale and the Tradition of Nineteenth-Century American Women Editors*. Athens: U of Georgia P, 1995.

Olson, Mark, John Judson, and Richard Boudreau. "Felix Pollak: An Interview on Little Magazines." *The Little Magazine in America: A Modern Documentary History*. Ed. Elliott Anderson and Mary Kinzie. New York: Pushcart, 1978.

Osgood, Frances Sargent. "A Flight of Fancy." *Nineteenth-Century American Women Writers: An Anthology*. Ed. Karen Kilcup, Cambridge, MA, and Oxford, UK: Blackwell, 1997: 129–131.

Paredes, Raymond A. "The Evolution of Chicano Literature." *Three American Literatures: Essays in Chicano, Native American, and Asian-American Literature for Teachers of American Literature*. Ed. Houston A. Baker. New York: MLA, 1982. 33–79.

Parker, Brad. *Black and Antislavery History in Early Lowell*. Lowell, MA: B. Parker, 1986.

Patch, Kate. "Two Violins." *Ladies' Home Journal* 1905 June: 5, 50; July: 12.

Patte, Fred Lewis. *A History of American Literature Since 1870*. New York: Century, 1915.

"Periodical Literature." Editorial. *National Magazine*. July 1852: 1.

Pfaelzer, Jean. "Domesticity and the Discourse of Slavery: 'John Lamar' and 'Blind Tom' by Rebecca Harding Davis." *ESQ* 38 (1992): 31–56.

———. "Subjectivity as Feminist Utopia." *Utopian and Science Fiction by Women: Worlds of Difference*. Ed. Jane Donawerth and Carol Kolmerten. Syracuse, NY: Syracuse UP, 1994. 93–106.

Pfister, Joel. *The Production of a Personal Life: Class, Gender, and the Psychological in Hawthorne's Fiction*. Stanford, CA: Stanford UP, 1991.

Phelps, Elizabeth Stuart. "Stories That Stay." *Century* 81 (1910): 118–24.

Pratt, Mary Louise, *Imperial Eyes: Travel Writing and Transculturation*. London and New York: Routledge, 1992.

Price, Kenneth M. and Susan Belasco Smith, ed. *Periodical Literature in Nineteenth-Century America*. Charlottesville: UP of Virginia, 1995.

Priest, Cordelia. "The Dying Girl's Dream." *Voice of Industry.* 25 Sept. 1845: 1.

Pryse, Marjorie. "Reading Regionalism: The 'Difference' It Makes." Jordan, 47–63.

Quinn, Arthur Hobson. *American Fiction: An Historical and Critical Survey.* New York: D. Appleton, 1936.

Rebolledo, Tey Diana. *Women Singing in the Snow: A Cultural Analysis of Chicana Literature.* Tucson: U of Arizona P, 1995.

Resch, Robert Paul. *Althusser and the Renewal of Marxist Social Theory.* Berkeley: U of California P, 1992.

Reunion: Hartford Female Seminary, 9 June 1892. Hartford, CT: Case, Lockwood and Brainard, 1892.

Rideing, William Henry. Letters to William Morris Colles, 1894–1918. Ms.Am.144. Rare Books and Manuscripts Room, Boston Public Library.

Robbins, Sarah. "Gendering the History of the AntiSlavery Narrative: Juxtaposing *Uncle Tom's Cabin* and *Benito Cereno, Beloved* and *Middle Passage.*" *American Quarterly* 49.3 (1997): 531–573.

Robinson, Harriet H. [Untitled] *Loom and Spindle* (1898) reprint Kailua, HI: Press Pacifica, 1976.

Roediger, David R. *The Wages of Whiteness: Race and the Making of the American Working Class.* London: Verso, 1991.

Roosevelt, Theodore. "Indian Citizenship." *American Indian Magazine* 4 (1916): 326–27.

Rose, Jane Atteridge. *Rebecca Harding Davis.* New York: Twayne, 1993.

Ryan, Mary P. *Empire of the Mother: American Writing about Domesticity, 1830–1860.* New York: Institute for Research in History and Haworth, 1982.

Scheiber, Andrew J. "An Unknown Infrastructure: Gender, Production, and Aesthetic Exchange in Rebecca Harding Davis's 'Life in the Iron-Mills.'" *Legacy* 11 (1994): 101–17.

Schwartz, Kessel. *A New History of Spanish American Fiction.* Vol 1. Coral Gables: U of Miami P, 1972.

Searles, Patricia, and Janet Micklish. " 'A Thoroughbred Girl': Images of Female Gender Roles in Turn-of-the-Century Mass Media." *Women's Studies* 10 (1984): 261–81.

Seyersted, Per, ed. *The Complete Works of Kate Chopin.* Baton Rouge: Louisiana St. UP, 1993.

Shaker, Bonnie James. "Coloring Locals: Identity Politics in Kate Chopin's *Youth's Companion* Stories, 1891–1902." Diss. Case Western Reserve U, 1998.

———. " 'Lookin' Jis' like W'ite Folks': Coloring Locals in Kate Chopin's 'A Rude Awakening.'" *Louisiana Literature* 14.2 (Fall 1997): 116–25.

Sherman, Joan R. *Invisible Poets: Afro-Americans of the Nineteenth Century.* Urbana: U of Illinois P, 1989.

Shuster, W. Morgan. "The Mexican Menace." *Century* Jan. 1914: 593–602.

Sigourney, Lydia. "Drinking Song." *Nineteenth-Century American Women Writers: An Anthology.* Ed. Karen Kilcup, Cambridge, MA, and Oxford, UK: Blackwell, 1997. 45–46.

Simmen, Edward, ed. *North of the Rio Grande: The Mexican-American Experience in Short Fiction.* New York: Penguin, 1992. 39–84.

Smith, Sidonie. "Cheesecake, Nymphs, and 'We the People': Un/National Subjects about 1900." *Prose Studies* 17 (1994): 120–40.

———. "Resisting the Gaze of Embodiment." *American Women's Autobiography: Fea(s)ts of Memory.* Ed. and Introd. Margo Culley. Madison: U of Wisconsin P, 1992. 75–110.

Smith, Susan Belasco. "Serialization and the Nature of *Uncle Tom's Cabin.*" *Periodical Literature in Nineteenth-Century America.* Eds. Kenneth M. Price and Susan Belasco Smith. Charlottesville: UP of Virginia, 1995. 69–89.

Smith-Rosenberg, Carroll. *Disorderly Conduct: Visions of Gender in Victorian America.* New York: Oxford UP, 1985.

Solomon, Martha. *Emma Goldman.* Boston: Twayne, 1987.

"Stetson: The Hat Whose Fame Began with the Winning of the West" (Advertisement). *American Indian Magazine* 7 (Aug. 1920): 46.

Stowe, Harriet Beecher. "Can I Write?" *Hearth and Home.* 9 Jan. 1869: 40–41.

———. "The Canal Boat." *The Harriet Beecher Stowe Reader.* Ed. Cynthia Reik. Hartford, CT.: Stowe-Day Foundation, 1993.

———. "The Cheapness of Beauty." *Hearth and Home.* 20 Mar. 1869: 200.

———. "Faults of Inexperienced Writers." *Hearth and Home.* 23 Jan. 1869: 72.

———. "Growing Things." *Hearth and Home.* 6 Mar. 1869: 168.

———. "How May I Know That I Can Make a Writer?" *Hearth and Home.* 30 Jan. 1869: 88.

———. "How Shall I Learn to Write?" *Hearth and Home.* 16 Jan. 1869: 56.

———. *The May Flower and Miscellaneous Writings.* Boston: Phillips, Sampson 1855.

———. *The Pearl of Orr's Island: A Story of the Coast of Maine.* 1862. Boston: Houghton, 1896.

———. *Stories, Sketches, and Studies.* Cambridge: Riverside Press, 1896. [reissuing of sixteen pieces from *The May Flower,* along with essays that originally appeared in the *Atlantic Monthly* and the *Christian Union*]

———. "The Woman Question." *Hearth and Home.* 7 Aug. 1869: 520.

Streitmatter, Rodger. "Josephine St. Pierre Ruffin: Pioneering African-American Newspaper Publisher." *A Living of Words: American Women in Print Culture.* Ed. Susan Albertine. Knoxville, U of Tennessee P, 1995. 49–64.

Takaki, Ronald. *A Different Mirror: A History of Multicultural America.* Boston: Little, 1993.

Tate, Claudia. *Domestic Allegories of Political Desire: The Black Heroine's Text at the Turn of the Century.* New York: Oxford UP, 1992.

Tatum, Charles. *Chicano Literature.* Boston: Twayne, 1982.

Taylor, Helen. *Gender, Race, and Region in the Writings of Grace King, Ruth McEnery Stuart, and Kate Chopin.* Baton Rouge: Louisiana State UP, 1989.

The Making of America. 1996. U of Michigan and Cornell U Libraries. July 1999. <http://www.umdl.umich.edu/moa/index.html>

Thoreau, Henry David. *Walden and Civil Disobedience*. New York: Penguin, 1986.

Thurston, Herbert, and Donald Attwater, eds. *Butler's Lives of the Saints*. New York: Kenedy, 1956.

Tompkins, Jane. *Sensational Designs: The Cultural Work of American Fiction, 1790–1860*. New York: Oxford UP, 1985.

Tompkins, Juliet. "His Dutch Treat Wife." *Ladies' Home Journal* June 1905: 12.

Toth, Emily. *Kate Chopin*. Austin: U of Texas P, 1990.

Treviño, Gloria Louise Velásquez. "Cultural Ambivalence in Early Chicana Prose Fiction." Diss. Stanford U, 1985.

Turner, Frederick Jackson. *The Frontier in American History*. 1920. Rpt. New York: Holt, 1985.

Turner, John Kenneth. *Barbarous Mexico*. Chicago: Kerr, 1910.

Urbanski, Marie. "Margaret Fuller's *Woman in the Nineteenth Century*: The Feminist Manifesto." *Nineteenth-Century Women Writers of the English-Speaking World*. Ed. Rhoda B. Nathan. Westport, CT: Greenwood, 1986.

Vanlandingham, Phyllis. "Kate Chopin and Editors: 'A Singular Class of Men.'" Perspectives on Kate Chopin: Proceedings of the Kate Chopin International Conference, 6, 7, and 8 April, 1989. Chicago: Northwestern UP, 1989.

Von Mehren, Joan. *Minerva and the Muse: A Life of Margaret Fuller*. Amherst: U of Massachusetts P, 1994.

Walker, Alice. "In Search of Our Mothers' Gardens." *In Search of Our Mothers' Gardens*. Ed. Alice Walker. New York: Harcourt, 1983. 241–43.

Walker, Cheryl. *American Women Poets of the Nineteenth Century*. New Brunswick, NJ: Rutgers UP, 1992.

Warren, Joyce W. *Fanny Fern: An Independent Woman*. New Brunswick, NJ: Rutgers UP, 1992.

Warren, Joyce W. "Uncommon Discourse: Fanny Fern and the New York Ledger." *Periodical Literature in Nineteenth-Century America*. Eds. Kenneth M. Price and Susan Belasco Smith. Charlottesville: UP of Virginia, 1995. 51–68.

———. "The Cult of True Womanhood: 1820–1860." *Dimity Convictions: the American Woman in the Nineteenth Century*. Athens: Ohio UP, 1976.

Welter, Barbara. *Dimity Convictions: The American Woman in the Nineteenth Century*. Athens: Ohio University Press, 1976.

Wexler, Alice. *Emma Goldman: An Intimate Life*. New York: Pantheon, 1984.

Wilson, Christopher P. *The Labor of Words: Literary Professionalism in the Progressive Era*. Athens: U of Georgia P, 1985.

Wilson, Woodrow. "Colonies and Nation: A Short History of the People of the United States." *Harper's* Jan.–Mar. 1901.

———. "The Ideals of America." *Atlantic* 1902: 721–34.

Wright, Helena, ed. *Factory Life as It Is: Factory Tracts*. (1845) reprint Lowell, MA: Lowell Publishing, 1982.

"A Year's Struggle." *Mother Earth* Feb. 1907: 2–4.

Zitkala-Sä. "America, Home of the Red Man." *American Indian Magazine* 6 (1918): 165–67.

————. "The Coronation of Chief Powhatan Retold." *American Indian Magazine* 6 (1918): 178–80.

————. "Editorial Comment." *American Indian Magazine* 6 (1918): 113–14.

————. "Editorial Comment." *American Indian Magazine* 7 (1919): 61–63.

————. "Indian Gifts to Civilized Man." *American Indian Magazine* 6 (1918): 115–16.

————. "School Days of an Indian Girl." *American Indian Stories*. 1921. Lincoln: U of Nebraska P, 1985.

————. "The Soft-Hearted Sioux." *Harper's* (Mar. 1901): 505–09.

Zukerman, William. "Tendencies of Modern Literature." *Mother Earth* Oct. 1910: 263–66.

CONTRIBUTORS

Susan Alves currently serves as the curriculum coordinator for the English Department at Rockport (MA) High School. She holds a Ph.D. from Northeastern University where she is now senior lecturer teaching courses on women writers and African American literature. She has published articles on factory poets Ethel Carnie and Lucy Larcom, as well as the poet May Sarton.

Janet Gebhart Auten teaches in the College Writing and the Women's and Gender Studies Programs at American University in Washington, D.C. Her published articles include work on teaching stories by women regionalists and on teaching writing in college. Her research interests center on antebellum women writers and their world.

Aleta Feinsod Cane received her Ph.D. from Northeastern University. She is an independent scholar who has published essays on Charlotte Perkins Gilman, Gerard Manley Hopkins, Anzia Yezerskia , and Sarah Josepha Hale. She is currently working on a book about four radical female editors of the Progressive Era.

Amy Doherty received her Ph.D. from Tufts University. She has edited the *Collected Stories of María Christina Mena* published by the Arte Publico Press, 1997. She is currently a visiting assistant professor of English at the University of Illinois at Urbana-Champaign.

Annamaria Formichella Elsden is an assistant professor of English at Buena Vista University in Storm Lake, Iowa, where she teaches American literature and creative writing. She has published an essay on Harriet Beecher Stowe in *Legacy: A Journal of American Women Writers* and continues to write on issues of gender, travel, and nationalism.

Charles Hannon is an instructional technologist at Gettysburg College. He has published articles on William Faulkner, Richard Wright, and Carson McCullers, and on the use of technology in teaching American literature and culture. His work has appeared in *The Faulkner Journal, Genders* and *College Literature* as well as in a number of online publications.

Michele L. Mock is an assistant professor of English at the University of Pittsburgh at Johnstown. The former managing editor of *Legacy: A Journal of American Women Writers,* Mock is the author of several articles on the works of Rebecca Harding Davis as well as Emily Dickinson. She is currently completing a book-length study of Davis and her periodical prose as well as editing a collection of Davis's correspondence with James and Annie Fields.

Craig Monk is an assistant professor in the Department of English at the University of Lethbridge in Alberta, Canada. His research focuses on the role of the little magazine and the development and transmission of Modernism in Europe and

North America. His work has appeared or is forthcoming in *American Studies International, Canadian Review of American Studies, History of Photography, Journal of Modern Literature, Mosaic*, and the *Oxford Quarterly Review*.

Sarah Robbins is an associate professor in the English Department at Kennesaw State University, where she is the director of northwest Georgia's National Writing Project site and where she has served as principal investigator for numerous grant-funded projects supporting collaborations with area public schools. As a faculty member in the university's professional writing graduate program, she specializes in literacy studies, particularly research on authorship and pedagogy in varying social contexts. She also teaches courses in American studies, women's studies, and English education. *Domesticating Literacy: Nineteenth-Century American Middle-Class Women's Maternal Literary Pedagogy* is her current manuscript-in-progress.

Bonnie James Shaker is an assistant professor of journalism at Youngstown State University, where she is also an affiliate faculty member to the American Studies Program. She has published on Kate Chopin in *Louisiana Literature* and is a contributor to the forthcoming *Defining Print Culture for Youth: The Cultural Work of Children's Literature* (Ohio State UP).

Michelle Campbell Toohey is an assistant professor of English at Westmoreland County Community College and received her Ph.D. from Indiana University of Pennsylvania in English with an emphasis on ecofeminist criticism and dissent literature. She has previously published in *ISLE, Studies in the Humanities*, and *Reading the Lost Borders: A Collection of Essays on Mary Austin* from the University of Nevada Press. Her current research interrogates American women's political discourse in the nineteenth century.

INDEX

Brisbane, Albert, 25
Brodhead, Richard, 65n, 66, 74, 166, 170, 177n
Browning, Robert, 98
Brownson, Orestes, 151
Buell, Lawrence, 158–59
Bunker Hill Monument, 16n
Bursum Bill, 200
Byron, Augusta, 50
Byron, Lady, 15

California, 31, 101, 167–68
Camin, Hector Aguilar and Lorenzo Meyer, 168
Carby, Hazel, 18n, 202
Cary, Alice: "About My Visit to Uncle William," 70; *Clovernook*, 67–69; "Old Christopher," 68
Century, 12, 169, 176
Certosa (Italy), 37
Chap-Book, 83–84, 114
Chesler, Phyllis, 133
Chesnutt, Charles, 2
Chester Museum (Great Britain), 36
Chicana/o writers, 166
Chicano Literature, 166
Chielens, Edward E., 131
China, 156
Chopin, Kate, 6–7, 10, 78–85, 88, 89n–91n: "At the 'Cadian Ball," 83; *The Awakening*, 78, 82, 85; "Caline," 85; "Dr. Chevalier's Lie," 85; "For Marse Chouchoute," 85; "The Kiss," 85; "La Belle Zoraïde," 83, 85; "A Lady of Bayou St. John," 85; "Lilacs," 83–84; "Polly," 85; "A Respectable Woman," 85; "A Rude Awakening," 89n; "A Singular Class of Men," 81, 84; "Three Portraits," 84; "Two Summers and Two Souls," 85, 90n; "The Unexpected," 85; "A Visit to Avoyelles," 85; "The White Eagle," 85; "Wiser than a God," 85; "The Wood-Choppers," 85
Christian Keepsake, 54

Christian missionaries, 185
Christian Recorder, 14, 202–203, 206–209, 211–12, 215
Christian Science, 122
Christianity, 38, 43n, 122
Cincinnati's Semicolon Club, 50
Civil War, 45, 48, 130, 167, 204, 208
Cleveland, Grover, 87
Colles, William Morris: "The Mexican Menace," 167, 169, 171; "Unfamiliar Mexico," 12, 165, 169, 171
Colored American Magazine, 14–15
Committee of One Hundred, 200
Communist Manifesto, The, 40
Confederate Army, 208
Conger-Kaneko, Josephine, 9, 10
Congress, 179, 182, 200
"Consumptive, The," 160
Cooke, Rose Terry: "Ann Potter's Lesson," 70–71; "Dely's Cow," 72; "Miss Lucinda," 72–74; "Sally Parson's Duty," 75
Coolbrith, Ina, 160
Cooper, James Fenimore, 70
Corn Laws (Great Britain), 35
"costumbrismo," 173–74, 178n
Crother, Jane, 168
Cult of Domesticity, 4, 6–7, 13
"Cynthia," 158
Czolgosz, Leon, 9, 115–16

Dall, Caroline, 17n
Davis, L. Clarke, 128, 138, 146n
Davis, Rebecca Harding, 10–11, 126–42, 142n–46n: "At Bay," 144n; "Blind Tom," 127; "Clement Moore's Vacation," 144n; "In the Market," 144n; "John Lamar," 143n; "A Law Unto Herself," 146n; "Life in the Iron Mills," 10, 143n; *Margret Howth*, 145n; "Men's Rights," 140; *Put Out of the Way*, 11, 127–30, 132, 134, 136–37, 140, 142, 144n–46n; *A Second Life*, 145n; "The Story of Christine," 144n; "Two Methods," 132; "The Wife's